The Dressmakers of
Auschwitz

Lucy Adlington is a British dress historian with more than twenty years experience researching social history. Adlington runs History Wardrobe, a company which presents costume-in-context talks across the UK. Her non-fiction publications include *Women's Lives and Clothes in WWII: Ready for Action* and *Stitches in Time – The Story of the Clothes We Wear*. Lucy Adlington lives on a farm in Yorkshire.

LUCY ADLINGTON

The Dressmakers
of Auschwitz

*The True Story of the Women
Who Sewed to Survive*

HODDER

First published in Great Britain in 2021 by Hodder & Stoughton
An Hachette UK company

This paperback edition published in 2022

I

A CIP catalogue record for this title is available from the British Library

Paperback ISBN 9781529311983
eBook ISBN 9781529311990

Typeset in Plantin Light by Palimpsest Book Production Limited,
Falkirk, Stirlingshire

Printed and bound in Great Britain by Clays Ltd, Elcograf S.p.A.

Hodder & Stoughton policy is to use papers that are natural,
renewable and recyclable products and made from wood
grown in sustainable forests. The logging and manufacturing
processes are expected to conform to the environmental
regulations of the country of origin.

Hodder & Stoughton Ltd
Carmelite House
50 Victoria Embankment
London EC4Y 0DZ

www.hodder.co.uk

Dedicated to the dressmakers and their families

Contents

Introduction

'How could you believe it?'

These are some of Mrs Kohút's first words to me, once I have been welcomed into her home and overwhelmed by supportive relatives. Here she is, a small, bright woman dressed in smart slacks, blouse and bead necklace. Her hair is short and white; her lipstick is rose pink. She is the reason I have flown around the world, from the north of England to a modest house in the hills, not far from the great city of San Francisco, California.

We shake hands. At that moment history becomes real life, not just the archives, book stacks, fashion drawings and fluid fabrics that are my usual historical sources for writing and presenting. I am meeting a woman who has survived a time and place now synonymous with horror.

Mrs Kohút sits at a lace-covered table, offering home-made apple strudel. During our meetings she has a backdrop of scholarly books, mingled with flower bouquets, pretty embroideries, family photos and colourful ceramics. We ease into the first interview by browsing the 1940s dressmaking magazines that I brought to show her, then examining a stylish, red wartime dress from my own collection of vintage clothes.

'Good quality work,' she comments, running her fingers over the dress's embellishments. 'Very elegant.'

I marvel at how clothes can connect us across continents and generations. Underlying the shared appreciation of cut, style and skill is a far more significant fact: decades before, Mrs Kohút was handling fabrics and garments in a very different context. She is the last surviving dressmaker from a fashion salon established at Auschwitz concentration camp.

A fashion salon in Auschwitz? The very idea is a hideous anomaly. I was staggered when I first saw mention of the 'Upper Tailoring Studio', as it was called, while reading about links between Hitler's Third Reich and the fashion trade, in preparation for writing a book about global textiles in the war years. It is clear that the Nazis understood the power of clothes as performance, demonstrated by their adoption of iconic uniforms at monumental public rallies. Uniforms are a classic example of using clothing to reinforce group pride and identity. Nazi economic and racial policies aimed to profit from the clothing industry, using the proceeds of plunder to help fund military hostilities.

Elite Nazi women also valued clothing. Magda Goebbels, wife of Hitler's insidious Propaganda Minister, was known for her elegance and she had few qualms about wearing Jewish creations, despite the Nazi obsession with erasing Jews from the fashion trade. Emmy Goering, married to Reichsmarschall Hermann Goering, wore plundered luxury, albeit claiming she had no idea of the provenance of her assets. Eva Braun, Hitler's mistress, adored couture, even having her wedding dress delivered across burning Berlin in the last days before her suicide and Germany's surrender, wearing it with Ferragamo shoes.[1]

And yet, a fashion salon in Auschwitz? Such a workshop encapsulated values at the core of the Third Reich: qualities of privilege and indulgence, bound up with plunder, degradation and mass murder.

The Auschwitz dressmaking workshop was established by none other than Hedwig Höss, the camp commandant's wife. As if this conjunction of fashion salon with extermination complex was not grotesque enough, the identity of the workers themselves makes for the ultimate impact: the majority of the seamstresses in the salon were Jewish, dispossessed and deported by the Nazis, ultimately destined for annihilation as part of the Final Solution. They were joined by non-Jewish communists from Occupied France, who were fated for incarceration and eradication because of their resistance to the Nazis.

This group of resilient, enslaved women designed, cut, stitched and embellished for Frau Höss and other SS wives, creating beautiful garments for the very people who despised them as subversives and subhuman; the wives of men actively committed to destroying all Jews and all political enemies of the Nazi regime. For the dressmakers in the Auschwitz salon, sewing was a defence against gas chambers and ovens.

The seamstresses defied Nazi attempts to dehumanise and degrade them by forming the most incredible bonds of friendship and loyalty. As needles were threaded and sewing machines whirred, they made plans for resistance, and even escape. This book is their history. It is not a novelisation. The intimate scenes and conversations described are based entirely on testimonies, documents, material evidence and memories recounted to family members or to me directly, backed up by extensive reading and archival exploration.

Having once learned that such a fashion salon existed, I began deeper research, with only some basic information and an incomplete list of names – *Irene, Renée, Bracha, Katka, Hunya, Mimi, Manci, Marta, Olga, Alida, Marilou, Lulu, Baba, Boriskha*. I had almost given up hope of finding out more, let alone learning full biographies about the dressmakers, when the Young Adult novel I wrote set in a fictional version of the workshop – titled *The Red Ribbon* – caught the attention of families in Europe, Israel and North America. Then the first emails arrived:

My aunt was a dressmaker in Auschwitz
My mother was a dressmaker in Auschwitz
My grandmother ran the dressmaking workshop in Auschwitz

For the first time I had contacts with the families of the original dressmakers. It was both shocking and inspirational for me to begin discovering stories of their lives and fates.

Remarkably, one of the group of dressmakers is still alive and well and ready to talk – a unique eyewitness to a place that exemplifies the hideous contradictions and cruelties of the Nazi regime. Mrs Kohút, 98 years old at the time of our meeting, spills out stories even before I can ask questions. Her memories range from being showered with nuts and candy as a child during the Jewish Feast of Tabernacles, to watching a school friend in Auschwitz have her neck broken by an SS man with a shovel, simply for speaking while working.

She shows me pictures of herself before the war, as a teenager in a nice, knitted sweater holding a magnolia, then one from several years after the war, wearing a stylish coat modelled along the lines of Christian Dior's famous New Look. To see these photographs, you would never guess the reality of her life during the years in-between.

There are no photos of her harrowing one thousand days in Auschwitz. She tells me that on each of these thousand days she could have died a thousand times. Her words create the images as she moves from one memory to another, fingers now rubbing the seams of her trousers, making the creases sharper and sharper – a small sign of emotions that are otherwise held in check. English is her fifth language, honed during long years in the USA. She switches easily from one language to another, and I do my best to keep up. I have a pen and paper ready for scribbled shorthand and a long list of questions. Mrs Kohút pokes me as I fumble to set up my phone video.

'You listen!' she commands.

I listen.

I

One of the Few Who Survived

After two years I came to the Auschwitz headquarters building,
where I worked as a seamstress in the sewing room for SS
families. I worked 10–12 hours a day. I am one of the few
who survived the hell of Auschwitz. — Olga Kovácz[1]

A day like any other.

By the light of two windows, a group of women in white headscarves sat sewing at long wooden tables, heads bent over garments, needles in, needles out. It was a basement room. The sky beyond the windows did not represent freedom. This was their refuge.

They were surrounded by all the paraphernalia of a thriving fashion salon; all the tools of their trade. On the tables, coiling tape measures, scissors and bobbins of thread. Stacked nearby, bolts of every kind of fabric. Scattered around, fashion magazines and the crisp tissue of dressmaking patterns. Next to the main workshop was a private fitting room for clients, all under the aegis of clever, capable Marta, who not long since had run her own successful salon in Bratislava. Supporting Marta was Borishka.

The seamstresses did not sew in silence. In a jumble of languages – Slovakian, German, Hungarian, French, Polish – they chatted about their work, their homes, their families . . . even joked among themselves. Most of them were young, after all, late teens, early twenties. The youngest was only fourteen.

Little Hen, they called her, as she darted about the salon fetching pins and sweeping up snipped threads.

Friends worked together. There was Irene, Bracha and Renée, all from Bratislava, and Bracha's sister Katka, who stitched smart wool coats for their clients, even when her own fingers were frozen with cold. Baba and Lulu were another two seamstresses who were close friends, one serious, one mischievous. Hunya, in her mid-thirties, was both friend and mother-figure, and a force to be reckoned with. Olga, a similar age to Hunya, seemed ancient to the younger girls.

They were all Jews.

Sewing alongside them were two French communists, corsetière Alida and resistance fighter Marilou, both arrested and deported for opposing the Nazi occupation of their country.

Twenty-five women working in total, needles in, needles out. When one was called away from work and never seen again, Marta would quickly arrange for another to take her place. She wanted as many female prisoners as possible to join this refuge in the basement. In this room they had names. Beyond the salon they were nameless, merely numbers.

There was certainly work enough for everyone. The big, black order book was so full there was a six-month waiting list, even for very high status clients in Berlin. Priority for orders was given to their local clients, and to the woman who had established the salon. Hedwig Höss. Wife of the commandant of Auschwitz concentration camp.

One day, a day like any other, there was a cry of dismay in the basement salon and the horrible smell of burnt fabric. Catastrophe. While pressing a dress, the fabric had been scorched by a too-hot iron; the burn mark was right at the front, no way of hiding it. The client was due for a fitting the very next day. The clumsy dressmaker was wild with anxiety, crying, 'What can we do? What can we do?'

The others stopped work, feeling her panic. This was not simply a question of a ruined dress. The clients of this fashion workshop were wives of high-ranking men from the Auschwitz SS garrison. Men notorious for beatings, torture and mass murder. Men with total control over the lives and fates of every woman in that room.

Marta, in charge, calmly assessed the damage.

'You know what we'll do? We'll take out this panel here, and insert this fresh fabric here. Quickly now . . .'

They all rallied.

The next day the SS wife arrived for her appointment in the fashion salon. She tried on her new dress and looked, perplexed, in the mirror of the fitting room.

'I don't remember the design being like this.'

'Of course it was,' answered Marta smoothly. 'Doesn't it look nice? A new fashion . . .'[2]

Disaster averted. For the time being.

The dressmakers went back to their work, needles in, needles out, and lived to see another day as prisoners in Auschwitz.

The forces that converged to create a fashion salon in Auschwitz were also responsible for shaping and fracturing the lives of the women who would eventually work there. Two decades earlier, when the dressmakers were young girls or mere infants, they could have no concept of how their fates would converge in such a place. Even the adults in their lives would have struggled to comprehend a future that included couture sewing in the midst of industrialised genocide.

The world is very small when we are children, yet rich with details and sensation. The itch of wool against the skin, the fumbling of cold fingers on stubborn buttons, the fascination of threads unravelling from a torn trouser knee. Our horizon is first within the walls of a family home, then spreads to street corners, fields, forests and cityscapes. There is no foreboding of what will happen in the future. In time, memories and mementoes are all that remain of lost years.

Irene Reichenberg as a child

One of the faces looking out from the past is that of Irene Reichenberg as a child, date unknown. Her features are pale among shadows; her clothes indistinct. Her cheeks are rounded from a hesitant smile, as if wary to show too much emotion.

Irene was born on 23 April 1922 in Bratislava, a beautiful Czechoslovakian city on the banks of the river Danube, barely an hour from Vienna. Irene's birth came three years after a census that showed the city's population was mainly an ethnic mix of Germans, Slovaks and Hungarians. Since 1918, all had come under the politcal control of the new Czechoslovakian state, but the Jewish community of nearly 15,000 was centred in one particular quarter of the city, a few minutes' walk from the northern bank of the Danube.

The hub of the Jewish quarter was the Judengasse, or Židovská ulica – Street of the Jews. Before 1840, Jews had been segregated to this single, sloping street of Bratislava, part of the local castle estate. Gates at each end were locked at night by municipal wardens, essentially creating a ghetto road, which made it clear that Jews were to be considered separate from other Bratislavans.

In the decades that followed, antisemitic laws were relaxed, allowing more prosperous Jewish families the freedom to move away from the street and into the main part of the city. The once proud baroque buildings of Židovská Street were subdivided into cramped tenements housing populous families. While the area had a reputation for being down-market, the cobbled streets were swept clean, and the stores and workshops were busy. It was a close-knit and supportive community. Everyone knew everyone. They knew everyone else's business too. Residents felt a special sense of belonging.

This was the happiest time in my life. I was born there, I grew up there, and there I was with my family – Irene Reichenberg[3]

Židovská Street was a wonderful place for children, who tumbled in and out of friends' houses and colonised the road and pavements with their games. Irene's home was at number eighteen, up on the second floor of a corner building. There were eight Reichenberg children. As with any large family, different alliances and loyalties formed between siblings, as well as a certain distance between the very oldest and youngest. One of Irene's brothers, Armin, worked in a sweet shop. He would eventually leave for the British Mandate of Palestine, and be spared the immediate trauma of the Holocaust. Her other brother, Laci Reichenberg, had a job with a Jewish wholesale textile company. He was married to a young Slovakian named Turulka Fuchs.

There was no thought of war for the family during Irene's

early life. It was hoped all that horror was done with after the Armistice of 1918 and the birth of the new country Czechoslovakia, where Jews were citizens. Irene herself was too young to appreciate the world outside the Jewish quarter. Her path, like most girls of the era, was to become proficient at domestic work, with a view to marriage and motherhood, following the example of her older sisters. Katarina, known as Käthe, was courted by a handsome young man named Leo Kohn; Jolanda – Jolli – married electrician Bela Grotter in 1937; Frieda was the next to marry, becoming Frieda Federweiss, leaving only Irene, Edith and Grete.[4]

Financially supporting this large family fell to Irene's father, Shmuel Reichenberg. Shmuel was a shoemaker, one of many artisans on Židovská Street. The skill and poverty of shoemakers has been immortalised in fairy tales. There truly was a kind of magic in the way Shmuel cut and moulded supple leather pieces onto a wooden last, stitched seams with waxed thread, and hammered in each nail with care, bent over his work from seven in the morning until late in the evening, all without the help of machines. Money was tight and sales uncertain. For many residents of Židovská Street, new shoes or even shoe repairs were a luxury. The hard inter-war years saw the poorest people go barefoot, or keep their failing footwear tied on with rags.

If Irene's father was the breadwinner, her mother Tzvia – Cecilia – was bread-maker and homemaker. Her working day lasted longer even than her husband's. Housework was hard graft with no labour-saving machines and no servants to help, only her daughters. Every second year Tzvia was pregnant, which meant extra cooking, laundry and cleaning. Despite a large family and a small income, Tzvia did her best to make each child feel special. One year little Irene received a special birthday treat: a whole boiled egg all to herself. She was delighted with it, and her friends on Židovská Street heard about this wonder.

One of this special group of friends was a girl from an Orthodox Jewish family – Renée Ungar. Renée's father was a rabbi and her mother a housewife. A year older than Irene, Renée was bold where Irene was quiet.[5] A portrait of Renée from 1939 shows a calm and intelligent demeanour, off-set by two-tone pom-poms dangling from a Peter Pan collar.

Renée Ungar in 1939

Ten years before this photo was taken, when Irene was seven years old, Irene gained a new playmate who would become a lifelong friend, and a brave companion during the most harrowing journey of her life.

This was Bracha Berkovič.

We had good times there – Bracha Berkovič

Bracha was a country girl born in the village of Čepa, in the highlands of Carpathian Ruthenia. Away from core industrial centres, this part of inter-war Czechoslovakia was mainly agricultural. Rural towns and villages were distinguished by their own local speech patterns and customs, and even local embroidery designs.

The landscape of Bracha's childhood was dominated by the seemingly endless ranges of the Tatras Mountains, which softened down into fields of clover, rye, barley, and sprouting green tops of sugar beet. The fields were worked by gangs of young women wearing bouffant-sleeved blouses, wide layered skirts and colourful headscarves. Goose girls tended their flocks; labourers hoed, gleaned and harvested. Summer was a time to wear cotton prints and lighter colours – checks, sprigs and stripes. Winter needed heavy homespun fabrics and woollens. Clothes were dark against the snow. Warm fringed shawls were wrapped over the head and pinned beneath the chin, or crossed and tied at the back. Bright bands of floral embroidery flashed at cuffs and sleeve seams.

Bracha's later life was bound up with clothing, and, coincidentally, so was her birth. Her mother Karolína had to continue with the labour of clothes-washing even late into her pregnancy. In rural Carpathia, dawn's first light saw women carrying bundles of laundry to the river, where they worked barefoot in the cold water, while children played along the river bank. Other washing was done at home, heaving soapy clothes in tubs, scrubbing them on boards, wringing them with chapped hands, then lugging them to a line for drying. Bracha's mother Karolína was climbing a ladder to hang heavy laundry to dry under the eaves of the roof on a cold, rainy day, when she felt the first pangs of labour. This was 8 November 1921. Karolína was only nineteen at the time. It was her first baby.[6]

Bracha was born at her grandparents' house. Although it was small and crowded, with only a clay oven for heating and water from a pump, Bracha remembered her childhood as a time of earthly paradise.[7]

Family love was at the heart of her happy memories, despite some inevitable tensions.[8] Her parents' marriage had been arranged by a local matchmaker – not an unusual custom in Eastern Europe at the time – and it was a successful partnership of two conscientious, capable people. Salomon Berkovič, born deaf-mute, had been intended for Karolína's older sister, but she refused him on account of his perceived disabilities. Eighteen-year-old Karolína was cajoled to take her sister's place, tempted by visions of herself as a bride in white.

They all did their best under a very trying and difficult life
– Bracha Berkovič

New babies quickly followed Karolína and Salomon's wedding. After Bracha's abrupt birth on laundry day came Emil, Katarina, Irena and Moritz. The small house was so full that Katarina – known as Katka – was sent to live with her childless aunt Genia until she was six. Although Bracha felt close to her little sister Irena, unbreakable bonds were woven when Bracha and Katka were transported to Auschwitz together. Sibling loyalty ensured they shared a common fate in the Upper Tailoring Studio.[9]

Bracha's childhood world included smelling the aroma of Sabbath challah bread, enjoying matzo crackers sprinkled with crystallised sugar, and eating baked apples with her Aunt Serena, in a house full of knick-knacks and doilies. It was sewing that first expanded Bracha's horizons beyond village life. More specifically, tailoring.

Salomon Berkovič was an extremely talented tailor, skilled enough to find work with a high-class firm called Pokorny in Bratislava. His sewing machine was transported from Čepa to the big city and he gradually built up his own loyal clientele, working from home on Židovská Street, with an assistant to help with repairs and alterations. Eventually he grew the business to have three staff – all deaf-mute – along with Bracha's Uncle Herman as apprentice. Each year he travelled to Budapest to attend salon events showcasing the latest styles of menswear.

The success of his enterprise was in no small part due to the tireless help of Karolína, who followed him to Bratislava to act as an intermediary with customers and to help with fittings. Determined not to be left behind, young Bracha produced enough tears to persuade her mother to let her travel to Bratislava too.

It was an exciting train ride for a village girl, mixing with other passengers and wondering what the journey's end would bring. Signs on the train were in Czech, Slovak, German and French, highlighting Czechoslovakia's mix of peoples. The carriage windows gave views of changing scenery. The train arrived in a dazzling new world.

Bratislava was green with trees, bright with new architecture and busy with shoppers, prams, horses, handcarts, motor cars and electric trams. Out on the Danube freight barges, little tugs and paddle steamers moved through placid waters. To Bracha, the apartment on Židovská Street was a place full of wonders compared to village life in Čepa. There was running water from taps, not buckets filled at a pump. In place of oil lamps, electric lights flicked on and off with a switch. An indoor flushing toilet was the ultimate marvel. Even better, there was the possibility of meeting new friends. The girls she met in Bratislava would be her companions through the worst that the war years would bring.

> *I liked everything, everything, everything . . . I liked to go to school*
> – Irene Reichenberg

Bracha met Irene Reichenberg at school. Education was a core quality of Jewish life, no matter how poor the family. Bratislava was not short of schools and colleges. The clothes worn for a 1930 photograph at the neighbourhood Jewish Orthodox school show the pride families took in sending their children to school, even if this meant extra thrift at home. Since the posed picture is a special occasion, some girls wear white socks and shoes, in contrast to the sturdy leather boots that are more sensible for playtime. Many girls are in simple shift dresses, easy to sew and maintain; others have fancier frocks with a range of lace or starched collars.

Jewish Orthodox elementary school photo, 1930. Bracha Berkovič
standing second from the left, middle row.

The 1920s fashion for bobbed hair is obvious, as well as more traditional plaits. There was no school uniform for girls, so fashion could sometimes creep in. One year there was a craze for *volant* collars made of very fine fabrics that were pleated or flounced. Girls vied to wear the most volants at once. The victor was a girl named Perla, who attracted universal envy for many ruffles of delicate muslin. Happy days.

Lessons at the Jewish Orthodox elementary school were taught in German, a language that would have increasing dominance in Czechoslovakian life. At first Bracha floundered to fit in, being new to town, and most comfortable speaking Hungarian and Yiddish; but she soon adapted, forming friendships with Irene and Renée. All the girls became multi-lingual, sometimes switching from one language to another in the same sentence.

Out of school hours the children of the Jewish quarter roamed the streets and stairways playing tig, hide-and-seek, hoop bowling or simply messing about. During summer holidays, too poor to afford vacations out of the city, they swarmed to the Danube to swim in a shallow pool by the river, or to play in the park.

Such games did not stop Bracha feeling homesick for her village friends. Aged eleven, she pestered her parents until she got permission to go home to Čepa for the summer. Wanting to make a good impression as an independent girl from the big city, she planned an outfit far smarter than anything she would normally wear in Bratislava, and proudly took the train ride alone. She wore a beige dress gifted by an affluent friend, a red patent leather belt, black patent leather shoes, and a straw hat with a coloured ribbon.

Details such as these seem frivolous in a wider context of the war and suffering that would follow, but they fix a memory. They stay in the mind when such freedoms and such elegance seem to belong to a vanished world.

These are really very beautiful memories – Irene Reichenberg

The best clothes of all were saved for Sabbath and other holy days. Jewish families followed an age-old pattern of familiar rituals, from the festival of Rosh Hashanah and the treat of apples dipped in honey, to the unleavened bread and bitter herbs at a seder meal at Passover. Jewish high holidays saw the slaughtering of fattened geese, the popping of corn, and chicken noodle soup simmering on the hob. Irene loved how her large family gathered at home for prayers, blessings and the warmth of togetherness.

For the Sabbath, Židovská Street dwellings would be scented with freshly baked challah bread – which Bracha was adept at braiding. It would be mixed at home, then carried to the local bakery to be cooked. Women scoured houses clean and tied on white aprons to light Friday night candles. Although Sabbath was, by law, a period without work – including prohibitions on textile labour such as dyeing, spinning or stitching – there was still a family to feed. Bracha's mother somehow found time and energy to make cinnamon biscuits and *topfenknödel*, a kind of boiled curd ball popular even in chic Viennese cafés.

Weddings were naturally a highlight of family life. When one of Salomon Berkovič's tailoring assistants announced his sister was marrying Bracha's uncle Jenő, a shoemaker, Bracha was given a rare indulgence: a shop-bought outfit. Keen to copy her father, who was always pressing garments in his workshop, Bracha decided to iron the lovely sailor-style dress herself. Bridal preparations came to a halt when everyone in the house noticed a horrible burning smell: the dress was scorched.

It seemed a catastrophe to little Bracha, forced to wear an old frock to the wedding. Years later, when a dress was burned on the ironing board of the Auschwitz fashion salon and Marta the overseer coolly took charge to avert disaster, this childhood memory would have a different, softer sheen. Bracha would recall Uncle Jenő's bride being dressed in a room transformed to a wonderland by the music of a wind-up gramophone, paper decorations and lamps illuminating a small potted tree. When the memory faded, she would have to return to the reality of the Upper Tailoring Studio and the demands of Nazi clients.

We knew from the very first moment that we belonged together
                                                    – Rudolf Höss

The wedding of Bracha's uncle was a world apart from the nuptials in Germany celebrated on 17 August 1929, on a farm in Pomerania, about an hour south from the Baltic Sea. The bride on this occasion would one day have a profound impact on Bracha's life, although it is doubtful she would ever learn Bracha's name.

It was the marriage of an ex-mercenary paramilitary soldier named Rudolf Höss. Not long out of prison after serving time for murder, Höss said his vows to 21-year-old Erna Martha Hedwig Hensel, known as Hedwig. A wedding day photograph shows the bride in a loose-waisted white dress reaching down to mid-calf. Short sleeves reveal slender arms. Long looped plaits make her young face seem small and delicate.[10]

'We got married as soon as was possible in order to start our hard life together,' wrote Rudolf in his memoirs.[11] There was also the awkward fact that Hedwig was already pregnant with their first child, Klaus, conceived not long after she and Rudolf first met.

The young couple had been introduced through Hedwig's brother, Gerhard Fritz Hensel, and it had been proverbial love-at-first-sight: a romance between two ardent idealists and devotees of a fledgling group called the *Artman Bund*, or Artaman Society. The Artamans were *volkish*: they craved a simple, rural life, built around concepts of ecology, farm labour and self-sufficiency. Healthy development of mind and body was a core goal, with a ban on alcohol, nicotine and, ironically for the newlyweds, extra-marital sex. Rudolf and Hedwig both felt at home among what Rudolf called a 'community of young patriotic people' seeking a natural way of life.[12]

Artaman racial theories chimed perfectly with the 'Blood and Soil' rhetoric of right-wing proponents of the *Lebensraum* concept so heavily promoted in Adolf Hitler's grandiose manifesto *Mein*

Kampf: that Germany needed to expand east to create their version of an agricultural, racial and industrial paradise, exclusively for those deemed to have pure German blood.

Hedwig was as committed to these ideals as her husband and eager to begin farming their own land, once it was allocated. They were no passive peasant labourers, however. Rudolf was appointed Artaman regional inspector. A year later he crossed paths for a second time with Heinrich Himmler, whom he had first met back in 1921, when Himmler had been an ambitious agronomy student. Both men became committed members of Hitler's *National Sozialistische Deutsche Arbeiterpartei* – National Socialist German Workers' Party. They discussed Germany's problems. Himmler proposed that the only solution to urban immorality and racial weakening was to conquer new territory in the east.[13] Their future collaborations would have devastating results for millions of Jews.

Back in Bratislava, seemingly safe from the ambitions of either Artamans or Nazis, Jewish life continued as normal into the 1930s. Large families meant big gatherings for weddings and other festival occasions – a chance to meet with relatives living remotely, and to encounter a myriad in-laws. The inter-family networks were complex. Somehow everyone was connected to everyone else – nothing extraordinary about that it seemed. So when Irene's big brother Laci Reichenberg married Turul Fuchs – known as Turulka – why would Irene or Bracha think anything of it, other than being glad for the newlyweds?

The connection would be fateful in ways they could not imagine.

Turulka Fuchs had a sister named Marta.

Clever, capable Marta Fuchs was only four years older than Irene and Bracha, but those four years made her seem a world apart in terms of maturity and experience.[14] Marta's family were originally from Mosonmagyaróvár, now part of Hungary. Her mother was Rósa Schneider; her father was Dezider Fuchs – known as Deszö in Hungarian. The Great War was still far from its death throes at Marta's birth, on 1 June 1918. When Rósa and Dezider's family moved to Pezinok, this village was close enough to Bratislava for Marta to attend a secondary school there, specialising in the arts.[15] After she finished school Marta became a dressmaker, training with A. Fischgrundová between September 1932 and October 1934, after which she worked in Bratislava until deportation in 1942.

Marta Fuchs – standing third from right – at a family celebration 1934

On 8 July 1934, Marta's grandparents, the Schneiders, celebrated their fiftieth wedding anniversary in Mosonmagyaróvár. Marta, with her parents and sisters, went to join the festivities. Close family gathered to be photographed in a shaded courtyard. Marta – third from the right, standing next to her sister Klárika – already showed her fashion flair with a happy bow at the front of her blouse. Marta's face is smiling and relaxed; her warm, friendly nature is obvious. Her sister Turulka – some years from being married to Laci Reichenberg – is seated in the centre holding a little girl. There are other touches of style shown in the well-cut suits, the art deco striped scarf worn by Marta's mother (third from left, seated) and the neat town shoes of the women seated on the front row.

In 1934 Marta was in Bratislava, completing her two-year training as a seamstress. Also in 1934, Rudolf Höss joined the SS – a very different kind of vocation.

After much soul-searching, he had decided his dream of an agricultural idyll with the Artamans would have to wait. Himmler had persuaded him that his talents could be even better served in a more ambitious arena: furthering the goals of National Socialism. Rudolf accepted his first concentration camp role at Dachau, outside Munich. It was supposedly to 're-educate' those who posed a threat to the newly elected Nazi regime.

His wife Hedwig dutifully moved to SS family quarters outside the camp with their trio of young children – Klaus, Heidetraut and Inge-Brigitt. Despite the upheaval, Hedwig was politically committed to National Socialist aims, and did not object to her husband's new work. He was only acting as custodian of 'enemies of the state' after all. At the birth of their next child, Hans-Jürgen, Hedwig specifically requested a caesarean operation, so that a lengthy labour would not interfere with plans to hear Hitler's big May Day speech in Berlin.[16]

In 1934 Bracha Berkovič was far removed from Berlin politics, or even the buzz of Bratislava. During one Rosh Hashanah celebration she had fallen ill. Tuberculosis was diagnosed. A transfer to the renowned TB sanatorium of Vyšné Hágy in the High Tatras Mountains took her away from home for two long years while she recovered. Her world view widened every bit as much as the high-altitude view from the sanatorium. She learned the Czech language, adapted to eating non-kosher food, and even received her very first Christmas present – a lovely new dress. She marvelled at the twinkling greenery of the sanatorium Christmas tree.

Despite all these new experiences, Bracha was still not worldly wise. Having found some toys and clothes abandoned in the sanatorium attic, left there by previous patients, she decided to send them back to her family in Bratislava. She took an armful of things – including a yo-yo and a teddy bear with a growl in its stomach – and marched to the local post office, confidently assuming they would reach her home somehow. The post office clerk kindly made the gifts up into an actual parcel for her, then addressed the package and sorted the postage.

Because of her time in the sanatorium, Bracha was a year behind Irene and Renée once she returned to Bratislava. All the girls continued their education, taking classes that would prepare them for the world of work. Out of financial necessity, most children on Židovská Street left school at fourteen to learn a trade. Their jobs were proscribed by gender. Girls' work was primarily secretarial or in the textile trade, and the income was intended to keep them going until they married and started families of their own.

Irene enrolled at a commercial college managed by Carpathian Germans. Renée undertook training in shorthand and book-keeping. Bracha first got a place on a secretarial course at Notre Dame Catholic High School. Because she looked 'Christian', according to the simplistic, reductive stereotypes of race that proliferated, she was put right on the front row of the 1938 school photograph celebrating the diploma awards. However, her appearance was no defence against intensifying prejudice and segregation in Europe.

As teenagers, the girls were now old enough to be aware of increasing tensions abroad and at home. Nazi anti-Jewish rhetoric in Germany inflamed existing antisemitic tensions in Czechoslovakia. Radio reports were increasingly bleak as the Nazis consolidated their power. The *Prager Tagblatt* newspaper kept everyone abreast of the latest international developments. How to react was a dilemma.

Could Jewish families be complacent and hope the violence would remain sporadic? Was it overreacting to think of leaving the city to take refuge in less volatile rural surroundings? More extreme still, should they think of leaving Europe altogether, to undertake *Aliyah* – the journey to the land of Palestine?

Irene and Bracha both joined Zionist youth groups. It was partly for fun and camaraderie; boys and girls could build friendships or start tentative romances. Underlying the interactions was a deeper purpose: training to do kibbutz work. Bracha and Irene both belonged to the HaShomer HaTzair group – the 'Young Guard'. Irene was also one of the kibbutz hopefuls with the left-wing HaOgen group – 'The Anchor' – set to undertake the challenge of emigration to Palestine in 1938. The illness and untimely death of her mother in the same year, coupled with a lack of money for tickets, stopped her from carrying out the plan.

Bracha Berkovič, seated, second from left, with Mizrachi friends pre-war

Bracha also joined a similar group called Mizrachi. In a photo of her with Mizrachi friends (seated, front left) she looks radiant and relaxed. The clothes of all the teenagers are informal, practical and free from fashionable quirks. It was at Mizrachi meetings that Bracha made a new connection – yet another strand in a web that would eventually link a great many lives. She became friends with a lively young girl named Shoshana Storch.

Shoshana's family was from the town of Kežmarok in eastern Slovakia. Although set against the backdrop of the High Tatras Mountains and far from the cities of Bratislava and Prague, Kežmarok still featured elegant touches. Lines of linden trees made the shopping streets seem more like boulevards than mere roads; stone arches cast shade on cobbled alleyways, which led to pretty courtyards and ancient wells.[17]

The Storch house was near one of these wells. A wide yard at the back gave space in summer. In winter the heart of the home was a large stove with a ceramic front, warming the whole family in one big room. There was an outhouse where rats often lurked, so it was as well to clap loudly before going in. On school days all seven Storch children would be spread out on the stairs to put on their shoes, laughing and joking: Dora, Hunya, Tauba, Rivka, Abraham, Adolph, Naftali and Shoshana. Finances were often tight, but support from one of the grandfathers meant the children at least had shoes and the cellar would be well-stocked for winter, with coal and potatoes.

Shoshana herself escaped from Czechoslovakia to Palestine while it was still possible, as did her parents and most of her brothers and sisters. It was her older sister Hermine – known as Hunya – who would be trapped in Europe, and who would one day join forces with Bracha, Irene and Marta.

At this time I had no inkling of how fateful the choice of this occu-
pation would be for me   – Hunya Volkmann, *née* Storch

Hunya was born on 5 October 1908, the same year as Hedwig Hensel-Höss.[18] She learned hand-sewing from her mother Zipora. Zipora was especially skilled at embroidery, which brides coveted for their trousseaus. (Having a husband of limited commercial sense, Hunya's grandmother had been forced to sell her own trousseau to help feed her family.) At home, Hunya was also taught how to use and service a sewing machine.

Hunya's concentration camp registration card from 1943 lists her height as one metre sixty-five, her hair and eyes as brown. Nose – straight. Slim build, round face, ears medium large. Full set of teeth, no distinguishing marks, no criminal record.[19] The description does not come close to capturing her character, which was unquestionably spirited. She had a strong will, tempered with compassion and generosity.

High spirits meant Hunya could never settle to schoolwork. Her ambition was to be a seamstress. Professional dressmaking was not for dreamers and dilettantes; it required dedication, resilience and years of training. The basics had to be mastered before personal brilliance could be explored. Hunya signed as an apprentice with the best seamstress in Kežmarok. Where better to learn her craft? For a year she was picking up pins, cleaning the workshop and running errands, all the while silently watching experienced sewers transform fabric into garments.

Pattern drafting, cutting, stitching, pressing, fitting, finishing . . . every stage of the process required skills that Hunya was determined to acquire. Even as a lowly apprentice she was kept busy. Back at home she would rush her evening meal, then work until well after midnight on her mother's 'Bobbin' brand sewing machine, repairing and making clothes for family and friends. Two further years in the Kežmarok salon gave her the experience needed to be accepted for a well-known sewing school abroad, the next step in furthering her ambitions. It would mean the usual graft of a trainee dressmaker: working ten to twelve hours a day in a dark and stuffy atelier, six days a week. She was ready for the challenge.

While the Artamans and National Socialists in Germany discussed expanding east to pursue their policies, in the late 1920s Hunya made plans to travel west, to continue training as a dressmaker in Leipzig.

As teenagers, neither Irene, Bracha nor Renée felt the same calling as Hunya had when she was their age. Not one of them thought of taking up dressmaking as a profession. Not at first. They were intent on finishing their chosen vocational training. This seemed something that could be controlled, whatever the political turmoil beyond the borders of Czechoslovakia, as Adolf Hitler ramped up rhetoric against Jews and made ever more emphatic demands for German rights.

In 1938 it became dramatically obvious that lines drawn on a map would be no defence against Nazi expansionist ambitions. Hitler demanded control of the Sudetenland area of Czechoslovakia, claiming it was to protect the people of German descent living there. Hoping to stave off outright conflict, European powers met at Munich to debate the issue. Czechoslovakia was not represented at the conference; it had no say in the decision to annex Sudetenland territory. This was September.

In November, parts of the country were ceded to Hungary and Poland. Bracha felt the effects of this first-hand. Her family had returned to Čepa village in 1938. When Hungary occupied the area, the family once again uprooted and illegally crossed the border back to Bratislava. It was a foreshadowing of future displacements.

In March 1939, Bohemia and Moravia came under German

rule. Slovakia was now a puppet clero-fascist state, with right-wing antisemitic rulers. Czechoslovakia ceased to exist as a country.

In Hunya's home town of Kežmarok, Jews left voluntarily, or were 'encouraged' to go. A Jewish pupil at school in Kežmarok came into class to see the words *Wir sind judenrein* written on the blackboard: 'We are Jew-free'. Long-time classmates became racial enemies.[20]

Back in Bratislava, Irene arrived at school as usual one day in 1939. She hustled along to the regular classroom with her friends, ready for lessons. The teacher came in and without any preamble announced, 'You can't expect German children to sit with Jews in the same classroom. Jews out.'

Irene and the other Jewish girls gathered their books and left. Their non-Jewish friends said nothing, did nothing.

'They were nice girls,' said Irene, bewildered by the passivity. 'I cannot complain about them.'[21]

Childhood was over.

The One and Only Power

Fashion is the one and only power – the strongest of all
– Traudl Junge, Hitler's secretary, quoting Adolf Hitler[1]

Prague fashions from 1940, in Eva *magazine.*

The glamour of fashion and fabrics may seem far removed from politics; a frivolous contrast to the violence of war. What do dressmaking ateliers, or magazine spreads on Spring Style in *Vogue,* have to do with dark-suited men sitting around conference tables deciding the fate of nations, or battle-ready soldiers, or scheming secret police?

The Nazis were well aware of the power of clothing to shape social identity and to emphasise power. They were also significantly interested in the wealth of the European textile industry, an industry dominated by Jewish capital and Jewish talent.

Clothes cover us all, of course. What we choose to wear, or what we're permitted to wear, is far from haphazard. Cultures shape clothing choices. Money shapes the garment trade.

Dressmakers crafted garments that contributed to fashion's idealised world of catwalks, photoshoots and society gossip. In turn, dressmakers would be caught up in the policies of those who used fashion for their own brutal ends.

Fürs Haus *magazine cover, November 1934*

The clothing industry has its roots at a local level. For young girls across twentieth-century Europe, picking up a needle and thread could be a hobby, but it was more likely to be a necessity. Mending and making were considered core female tasks. Those skilled at thrift could turn the cuff or collar of a man's shirt so that the frayed edge was hidden; they could darn stockings with matching yarn so no runs were visible; they could let out seams or add tucks to accommodate a changing waistline. Then there was the actual making of garments – baby layettes, children's clothes, festival outfits, streetwear, and aprons to protect them all.

The festive atmosphere of market day drives away gloom and sadness
– Ladislav Grosman, *The Shop on Main Street*

When Bracha Berkovič stepped out of her front door on Židovská Street in Bratislava and looked left, she would have seen the road switch back on itself, up to the old wooden church of St Nicholas. At the corner of the hairpin bend was Good Shepherd's House, a shop that sold sewing notions such as ribbons, buttons, thimbles and paper packets of needles. A sewer also needed sharp cutting shears, daintier scissors for snipping and unpicking, tailor's chalk for marking lines, and pins – endless often-errant pins.

The shopping streets of Bratislava had many stores similar to Good Shepherd's House, as well as bazaars with trays of wooden goods for customers to rummage through. On market days, traders and pedlars came into town, some setting their wares on tables under coloured canvas parasols, others settling on the kerb with baskets and barrels of wares. Potential customers turned over the goods – laces, crochet strips, buttons, brooches, embroidered scarves – and they prepared to haggle. Sellers called out their patter, or simply sat and kept a watchful eye out for sleight-of-hand theft.

Smaller shops sold ready-made goods. A cobbler might have shoes strung at the doorway in bunches like dark bananas. A tailor could have clothes hung from poles jutting overhead. Their workshops might be in the store's dark interior, or even in the backyard. Bracha's father Salomon was saving for his own clothing manufacturing company, so that he too could have his name painted on a colourful board above a shop entrance.

Then there were the fabric stores – irresistible for anyone dreaming of new outfits. In rural areas there were still villagers who made homespun cloth, but towns sold yardage featuring crepes, satins, silks, tweeds, acetates, cottons, linens, seersucker and many variations, produced in the great textile factories of Europe. Drapers' shops boasted giant rolls of fabric, as well as material folded over shorter cardboard rectangles. Assistants handled the goods for potential buyers, spreading the fabric along a counter to show off designs and quality. Experienced shoppers felt the weight, the weave and the drape, mentally assessing how it would make up.

In the mid-twentieth century there was a great appreciation for the 'wearability' of fabrics: would they shrink, lose colour, be warm enough or cool enough as required? Sewers and shoppers learned the values of natural fibres, as well as appreciating the affordability of artificial fabrics such as rayon. Fashionable colours changed from one season to the next. Novelty prints were jolly for summer; velvets and fur trims came out on show in autumn, followed by winter wools and worsteds. Spring was all about florals.

For both amateur and professional sewers, a machine was a crucial investment. Home workshops and salons mainly used treadle machines. They were beautiful creations, often in black enamel with gold scrolling designs. They were set into a wooden table with wrought iron stands for stability. Brand names included Singer, Minerva and Bobbin.

Lucky the stitchers who could afford purring electric sewing machines. Sewing machine merchants would sell a model outright or on hire purchase, and newspapers carried ads for second-hand sales. Portable machines had a hand crank. They clicked into moulded wooden cases with a carry handle, and were ideal for dressmakers and tailors who visited clients homes to do a batch of work, sometimes staying for several days to complete the orders.

Every town and almost every village in Europe would have a local dressmaker, someone who adapted styles seen in fashion magazines, who altered shop-bought clothes and who did repairs. The best artisans would build up a loyal customer base, even if working from home. Speciality sewers produced luxury lingerie, trousseau linens, bridal gowns or foundation garments. Those with drive and capital would open small salons, with their name in proud letters above the display window. Those with flair and good fortune aimed to deploy their talents at an international level.

Why shouldn't dressmaker Marta Fuchs aspire that high? She was skilled, she was personable, she made connections in the trade. The international fashion scene in Prague beckoned. Marta hoped to follow the call one day.

A woman must be slender and willowy, though not devoid of curves and roundness of figure — *Eva* magazine, September 1940

Prague was the perfect place for an up-and-coming dressmaker. Marta could have counted on self-confidence and a friendly nature to overcome the inevitable sense of intimidation at moving from Bratislava to hone her talents in a capital city famous for its high-quality fashion.

Prague's old town was truly picturesque, with buildings crumpled together and chimneys built high to smoke above the tiles and gables. The new developments of the first republic – between 1918 and 1938 – were a pageant of modernity. From out of building sites and scaffolding white office blocks, apartments and factories showed clean lines and functional aesthetics. Prague's fashions had the same contrasts. There were old-fashioned folk costumes drawing on antiquated styles alongside confident clothes, renowned for their tasteful elegance.

Fashionable hat style, Eva *magazine, 1940*

Anyone window shopping along Prague's chic boulevards – carefully moving through crowds of pedestrians and across streets clogged with trams and cars – would be impressed with the artistic displays of the modern department stores. New designs were shown on stylised mannequins, or strung out in kinetic shapes. There were cascading racks of silk ties and printed scarves, hat stands with every kind of turban, trilby, bonnet, beret or pillbox. Handbags galore, with matching purses. More shoes than could be worn in a lifetime – leather, raffia, silk, cotton and cork.

Prices were marked in eye-catching fonts on attractive cards. Bargain hunters felt their pulse race at the seasonal *Sale* signs. Shopping was an enjoyable leisure activity, perhaps including a spot of café culture and cake indulgence, but it was often based on good sense: most people in the mid-twentieth century owned fewer clothes, maintained them carefully, and accessorised them for variety.

Savvy shoppers idled along the Graben, the German promenade in Prague, which boasted Moric Schiller, a salon and fabric shop embellished with the honour: 'By appointment to the Court'.

Beach fashions from summer 1940, Eva *magazine*

Polished plaques in the most exclusive commercial streets gave the names of elite salons such as the haute couture house of Hana Podolská – famous for dressing film stars – or Zdeňka Fuchsová and Hedvika Viková, who had both worked for Podolská.[2] Fashion was an arena where women could not only compete with men, but sometimes surpass them. Women worked at every level of couture.

Prague's lucrative fashion industry was supported by quality journalism and photography, published in magazines such as *Pražská Móda* (Prague Fashion), *Vkus* (Good Taste), *Dámske akademické módní listy* (Ladies Academy of Fashion Journal), and *Eva.*

Eva magazine was a particularly sophisticated and entertaining read, aimed at younger Czech and Slovak-speaking women such as Marta Fuchs. Along with articles on fashion and domestic creativity, there was plenty of space given over to female achievements in the arts, in business and even in the arenas of flying and motorcycling.[3] Featured models are not only well-dressed in *Eva*, they look full of life and energy, whether modelling smart fur hats for autumn, or depicted in snazzy taffeta beach wear for summer. The magazine offered intelligent, feminist escapism, with luxury that seemed almost achievable, in peacetime at least.

When Marta was aspiring to work in Prague in the late 1930s, fashions favoured long, sleek lines that optimised bias-cut techniques for fluid fabrics, and smart tailoring for suits. Designs with sloping shoulders were being superseded by a squarer shape built up on horsehair or cotton pads. The bold new style suggested strength and capability – qualities that women would need more than ever as Europe was dragged into conflict.

I won a prize for Paris, but ended up in Auschwitz – Marta Fuchs

One of Czechoslovakia's most famous pre-war columnists was Milena Jesenská. She had a keen eye for literary talent – promoting Franz Kafka among others – and for political commentary. Her style tips for women readers drew on her own fascination with quality clothing, her knowledge of international trends, and an admiration for French underwear.[4]

France was certainly the beating heart of European fashion, no matter how strong Prague styles and Czech talents. Marta's skills meant she could have worked in Paris, had stronger forces than fashion not intervened.

Marta was an outstanding cutter: a sought-after prize in any salon. The cutter ensured a paper pattern could be transformed into a working garment. It was the cutter who knew how to press and lay out fabrics so that the weave was straight; who assessed the pattern pieces and pinned them into place; who took up the special shears and cut in a long, low, sliding motion. Once those blades parted the fabric, there was no going back.

Marta never made it to Paris.

Spring fashions in La Coquette *French dressmaking magazine, undated*

The closest Marta would come to French fashion would be from reading Czech journals drawing on French styles, such as *Nové Pařížké Módy* (New Paris Fashion), and *Paris Elegance*.

Paris was the ultimate when it came to fashion. Although Prague was justly proud of its independent salons, there was still an incredible buzz of excitement when French couturier Paul Poiret put on an exhibition in the Czechoslovakian capital in 1924. Parisian ideas were spread in fashion journals, during fashion weeks, through clothing trade fairs and even via film costuming.

During the inter-war years, dressmakers of all calibres worldwide looked to Paris with admiration and envy. If possible, they travelled to Paris to get a feel for the season's new modes and, with the right connections, to obtain a seat at one of the sumptuous couture catwalk shows; where haughty mannequins sauntered through salons with thick carpets and gilt mirrors, and potential clients drank expensive champagne while noting the numbers of outfits they coveted. Sables slipped from their shoulders; light sparkled on pearls, gold and diamonds. The air was scented with roses, camellias, Chanel No. 5 and Schiaparelli's perfume Shocking.

Behind the scenes of a new season's show it was all sweat and concentration for mannequins, dressers, fitters, stitchers, choreographers and sales clerks. French haute couture was sustained by the labour of many thousands of employees, mostly working incognito. Haute couture collections required specialists who might train seven years to focus on sleeves or skirts, pockets or buttonholes. There were cutters, such as Marta, pattern drafters, finishers and embellishers – those who excelled at beading, embroidery and lacemaking.

Fashion's magic was created by work, not wand-waving. And yet, for all the long hours, hard graft and demanding clients, it was still the free world in couture ateliers or lowly sweatshops, not literal slavery in a concentration camp workshop.

For a few years longer, Marta Fuchs worked out of love and for well-earned money in her Bratislavan salon.

You should never become a seamstress. True, it saved my life, but you just sit there and sew   – Hunya Volkmann, *née* Storch[5]

What of Germany? Would it be content to let Paris shine the brightest?

Hunya Storch, working in Germany from the late 1920s and through the 1930s, witnessed first-hand how the German fashion industry not only resisted French influences, but became a willing proponent of discriminative and ultimately destructive policies.

Hunya was still in her teens when she travelled all the way from Kežmarok in Czechoslovakia to Leipzig in east Germany.

The express train across the border from Prague travelled through an ordered landscape of neat towns and well-hedged fields. It looked very flat after the backdrop of the Tatras Mountains. Hunya immediately felt at home in Leipzig. She loved the excitement of high-class theatre and operettas, the lure of well-stocked bookshops, and the fashions on show in prosperous shops. She shrugged off her small-town clothes and relaxed into the role of a city girl, enjoying life in a group of young friends.

Hunya flourished in her Leipzig apprenticeship and eventually opened her own business, a salon based in a room of her father's apartment. When her father returned from the small synagogue nearby he would serve very sugary lemon tea to the women waiting for their dressmaker appointment. One of his perks was to taste the tea. In turn, the clients knew not to shake his hand in greeting, as he was a religious Jew.[6]

Hunya's client base grew by word of mouth, because she was extremely good at her job. She had the ability to browse magazines such as *Vogue, Elegante Welt* (World of Elegance) and *Die Dame* (The Lady), then craft her own patterns. She drew freehand on paper, no instructions required. When her sister Dora was in Leipzig she helped Hunya with finishing work, such as hems and pressing. There was always the idea that Hunya would teach Dora the dressmaking trade, but somehow she never got round to it. Dora revelled in the beautiful clothes and admired Hunya's talents, including the fact that she could dress anyone, whatever their figure.

Although Hunya created tasteful clothes that followed fashion, there was also something unique about each garment. Hunya loved the independence of having her own salon, and thrived on bringing her imagination to each commission. She liked complexity and enjoyed a challenge. If, some years later, she felt jaded about sewing, it was due more to how she was treated as a dressmaker, rather than how she felt about the craft.

Being Jewish and Czechoslovakian in Germany presented plenty of challenges for Hunya. The problem was not gaining clients. Over five years she attracted a loyal customer base, dressing elite women of Leipzig – Jewish and Gentile – including the wife of the chief judge. The fundamental problem was being unable to advertise her salon, since she did not have a visa to work in Germany legally. After 1936, Hunya decided her situation had to change. She reluctantly quit the salon at her father's apartment and began working for clients in their own homes. In addition to earning her own living, she had set herself the task of helping support her family back in Kežmarok, by regularly sending them money.

A portrait from 1935 shows Hunya looking well-styled and strong minded, yet pensive. Her hair is set in fashionable waves, which could be created by clips or a permanent Marcel process. Neat and glossy, the waves frame an oval face. Her top is both modest and attractive – it looks to be a knitted blouse or dress with a crochet plastron, showing a pale slip underneath, fastened at the throat with a dainty satin bow.

Hunya Storch, 1935

The ring on her left hand is prominently displayed. While in Leipzig, Hunya fell in love with Nathan Volkmann – handsome, confident, serious and educated. She knew his family through sewing mourning clothes for his sisters after the death of their parents. Nathan was equally enamoured with Hunya, but they could not marry. He was a Polish national, she was a Jew, and Nazi bureaucracy was too restrictive to permit it. For a while Hunya was so disillusioned she went back to Kežmarok. She found the provincial town stifling and racked her brains for some legal loophole that would enable her to return to Germany.

A marriage of convenience seemed to be the answer. Her sister-in-law's brother Jakob Winkler agreed to do the honours, becoming her husband on paper only. It was hardly an ideal solution, but it entitled Hunya to an *Einreise* – a temporary permit to live in Germany – and a new Czech passport. She returned to Leipzig. After a four-year engagement she married Nathan, to become Hunya Volkmann.

For a while sewing was mostly set aside, with only a few commissions for fun or extra money. She was basking in happiness.

In retrospect, the signs of impending disaster were all there: symptoms of disapproval over female apparel that were part of wider policies designed to mould public opinion, control the fashion industry and dispossess Jews.

Germany between the two wars had a brief, wonderful burst of emancipation in terms of fashions, feminism and artistic freedom. However, crushing economic problems in Germany took the shine out of the Weimar Republic's indulgent self-expression. Hitler's NSDAP seemed to offer an alternative to mass unemployment, dire inflation and a national identity crisis. The new Nazi regime of the 1930s claimed that Paris chic and

Hollywood vamps were degrading for German women. Instead young women were encouraged to scorn high heels in favour of hiking boots, to have sun tans from outdoor work, not pale foundation powders.

Being fresh and appealing had one purpose only: to attract a healthy Aryan male in order to mate and make babies. Older women could be proud of their brood. Their clothes were to be plainer. Sensible. Respectable. Girdles were to control the spread of matronly figures, not to cup the buttocks or make bosoms provocatively pert. Propaganda about women's roles and images in Germany was pervasive and relentless.

Front cover of Mode und Heim *magazine, Germany 1940*

In 1933, German Jewish journalist Bella Fromm noted in her diary that Hitler had declared: 'The Berlin women must become the best-dressed women in Europe: No more Paris models.'[7] That same year Dr Joseph Goebbels, Reich Minister of Enlightenment and Propaganda, put himself in charge of a 'Fashion House', as Fromm termed it: the *Deutsches Modeamt*, or German Fashion Institute. Goebbels recognised the power of the fashion industry to shape image, which he knew was crucial for controlling behaviour.

Publications sympathetic to the Nazi regime, such as *Die Mode* (Fashion) and *FrauenWarte* (Women's Viewpoint), readily conformed to Nazi Party ideals.[8] German women were encouraged to associate with traits allied with the fundamental roles of mother and housewife. Their professions would preferably reflect stereotypical 'female' areas such as kindness, catering, nurturing and textiles.[9]

The drive for German-centric fashions was no bad thing in itself. In Leipzig, Hunya wanted the freedom to create her own confident styles, even as Marta Fuchs in Bratislava aimed for world-class quality that derived from Czechoslovakian influences. It was perhaps right for the German Fashion Institute to be scornful of the idea that only Paris could dictate a season's hem length or silhouette.

Unfortunately, beyond the seemingly innocent German magazine articles on cheerful spring cottons and ballgown tulle, there were relentless forces at work. Goebbels not only wanted to dictate how women presented themselves (supporting roles only), he also wanted to control the power of the clothing industry.

This meant ousting the Jews.

Removal of Jewish people from the fashion industry and clothing trade as a whole was not an accidental by-product of antisemitism. It was a goal. A goal that would be achieved through blackmail, threats, sanctions, boycotts, extortion and forced liquidations. Marta, Hunya, Bracha, Irene . . . none of these young Jewish women had any part in the governments and organisations that pursued this ruthless goal. They would all suffer because of it. They would endeavour to survive despite it.

One of the most powerful tactics to achieve control of Jewish people and their assets was to draw on primitive tribal mentality: mistrust of the 'other'. In emphasising a difference between Jews and non-Jews (rebranded as 'Aryans' in nationalist terminology), the Nazis deliberately manufactured divisions between 'us' and 'them'. To emphasise the 'us' element of cohesion, they cleverly exploited the power of belonging created when groups wear a uniform.

Whether a Storm Trooper, Hitler Youth boy or member of the German Girls League, there was a uniform to bond the group together – a paramilitary costume show often staged in staggering theatrical events. Uniforms minimised obvious differences between different classes, giving the impression of equality within the ethnic group.

The Nazi movement was so readily identified with clothing before coming to power, their men on the streets were known as 'Brown Shirts'. Journalist Bella Fromm noted in 1932 how the men 'strutted around like peacocks' and seemed to be 'intoxicated by their own masquerade'. Even more sinister was the psychological power of uniform to help the wearer live up to the image.[10] The Brown Shirts would play a big role in growing violence directed at the clothing industry, although their power was soon to be surpassed by those who wore the darker fabrics of SS uniforms.

Even without a uniform, the Nazi swastika symbol – black on red – transformed neutral clothes into a statement. As well as lapel badges and armbands, there were socks knitted with an elaborate swastika design on the ankle clocking. Hitler received endless gifts sewn by adoring women, including swastikas stitched onto pillowcases, sometimes accompanied by a vow of 'eternal loyalty'.[11]

Every level of sewing was corrupted by politics: a young girl's sewing sampler from 1934 – a piece of work demonstrating a learner sewer's skill with stitch techniques – has the usual alphabet, name and date, and a red-thread embroidered swastika.[12]

Folk costume was also co-opted to widen the us/them divide. *Trachtenkleidung* – traditional folk costume – was supposed to reflect Germany's rich cultural heritage, and so it was widely praised and portrayed in nationalist media. Inevitably this excluded foreigners. Nor were German Jews to wear *tracht*. It was for Aryans only.[13] The message to German Jews was clear: you are not *us*.

Further division was emphasised when the Nazis deliberately conflated 'foreign' fashion with Jewishness. Attacks on so-called decadent women and Paris fashion served the dual purpose of creating antipathy towards the French and stoking antisemitism. Somehow it was made to seem the fault of Jews if German women wore 'tarty' red lipstick and were slaves to fashion's whims. The contempt was misogynistic as well as antisemitic: it perpetrated the idea that unless women conformed to externally policed standards of dress and behaviour, they were automatically sexualised and demonised as whores.

The reason Goebbels' propaganda juggernaut could so readily make the connection between fashion and Jews was because the clothing industry was heavily reliant on Jewish talent, Jewish connections, Jewish graft and Jewish capital.

Textile production across Europe is often overlooked in economic histories, despite the fact that it generates huge revenues, employs millions and is a major factor in international trade – a crucial element for Nazi Germany in particular as it attempted to build up foreign currency in the 1930s.

Roughly eighty per cent of department stores and chain-store businesses were owned by German Jews in inter-war Germany. Almost half the wholesale textile firms were Jewish too. Jewish workers made up a huge number of those employed in designing, making, moving and selling clothes. Berlin was an acclaimed centre of women's ready-to-wear apparel thanks to the energies and intelligence of Jewish entrepreneurs, over a century of development.

It was not enough for popular Nazi propaganda magazines such as *Der Stürmer* to publish images of Jewish textile workers as parasites in the industry, or sexual predators corrupting innocent Aryan maidens and contaminating goods worn by Aryan Germans. Nazi tactics would move from words to deeds.

Indescribable excitement in the air

– Joseph Goebbels diary entry, 1 April 1933[14]

On 1 April 1933 at 10 a.m., there began a national boycott of German Jewish businesses by Aryan Germans. It was carefully orchestrated by the Nazi Party. Hitler had been made Chancellor in January of that year. The Nazis had only been fully in power since March. Clearly anti-Jewish measures were a major priority for the new regime.

Kauft nicht bei Juden! – Don't buy from Jews!

The message was plastered on posters, daubed with paint on windows, and scrawled on signs used to block shop doorways, along with crude yellow-black Stars of David.

The sight of men in paramilitary uniform lined up outside department store windows was a powerful contrast to the plaster mannequins on the other side of the glass, displaying elegant spring fashions; a contrast too, to crowds of pedestrians gathered to observe, or to enjoy the spectacle. Their faces tell the story. The Brown Shirts are stern, infused with righteousness. Onlookers are bewildered, amused, compliant, annoyed.

A courageous minority defied the boycott to make symbolic purchases in deserted Jewish shops. Some were irritated at the inconvenience, deciding they would not have their shopping habits dictated to them.

'I tried to get in because I was so outraged,' said one woman. 'I knew the owner, I knew these people. We'd always gone there.'[15]

One Aryan seamstress was actually radicalised against the Nazi regime having witnessed this state-sponsored treatment of Jews. She said Jewish garment workers were 'always the best. Virtuous, industrious. I began only to shop at Jewish stores.'[16]

When intimidation turned to violence – including missiles breaking the windows of the elegant Jewish-owned department store Tietz, in Berlin – police rarely intervened. Broken windows were symbolic of the fragile sense of security that Jewish traders now had.

After twenty-four hours of harassment, the boycott was called off. Intermittent violence continued. It had proved that in 1933 most non-Jewish Germans were still relatively apathetic about antisemitic actions, and it had antagonised foreign governments, who protested against the intimidation. Nazi leaders were exasperated at the foreign response: they had emphasised that 'only' German Jews were to be harassed, not foreign Jews. Complaints about the boycott were dismissed by the government as Jewish atrocity propaganda. If there had been issues, Nazis explained, the Jews were told they had brought it on themselves.[17]

Even though the boycott was called off, it had laid the groundwork for increased pressure on Jewish businesses, and it paved the way for ever more sophisticated ways of controlling trade. Countless Jewish garment workers in Germany, including Hunya in her Leipzig salon, would next have their livelihoods threatened with an initiative launched in May 1933 – only a month after the boycott – with the long-term aim of making every aspect of the clothing trade Jew-free. This was ADEFA.

ADEFA label from a 1930s floral crepe day dress

ADEFA: an acronym for *Arbeitsgemeinschaft deutsch-arischer Fabrikanten der Bekleidungsindustrie* – Federation of German-Aryan Manufacturers of the Clothing Industry. The word *Aryan* was inserted to emphasise precisely what was meant by 'German': no Jews. ADEFA was nothing more than a bullying lobby group intended to push Jews – seen as competition – completely out of the market. ADEFA publicity sought to 'reassure' German buyers – trade and public – that every single stage of a garment's manufacture was untainted by Jewish hands.[18]

The ADEFA label was added to these 'pure' Aryan garments, sometimes with the acronym stylised as a Reich eagle, sometimes with full text and the addition of *Deutsches Erzeugnis* (German Product), so there could be no confusion about the exclusive correlation between Aryan and German.[19] In commercial and artistic terms, ADEFA was a failure. The clothes were nothing special. Design and distribution were weakened by the loss of Jewish talent and connections. ADEFA's fashion shows were not well-attended, despite extensive advertising, which included a brusque 'Heil Hitler' after the promotional blurb. The main benefit to National Socialism was that it provided yet another level of legitimisation for the concept that Aryans could profit from Jews.

ADEFA was dismantled in August 1939, job done. ADEFA tactics came to seem relatively benign, compared to the brutal violence of November 1938.

A band of rowdies goes and destroys an enormous fortune in a single night. And Goebbels just eggs them on   – Hermann Goering[20]

On the morning of Wednesday 10 November 1938, Hunya Volkmann opened a window to look out over the Leipzig street where she lived. She was surprised to see people rushing past, some dishevelled, some clutching hastily wrapped bundles.

'What's happened?' she called out to them.

She caught shards of news. Synagogues burned. Houses graffitied. Windows smashed. Jews beaten to death.

Was it safe to go out? Leipzig's Jews were a diverse group, mainly integrated, certainly not ghettoised, even though there was a Jewish quarter. Could they be such obvious targets?

Jews had been dismissed from German positions of influence since 1933. Then came the Nazi Nuremberg Laws of September 1935, which effectively revoked the German citizenship of Jews, even through marriage to a non-Jewish German. 1935 also saw Jewish people banned from public swimming baths and discouraged from public parks and theatres because *Volksgenossen* – 'racial comrades' – did not want to share these spaces with Jews.

Leipzig experienced its fair share of virulent antisemitic propaganda, as well as the seemingly more civilised media promotions by ADEFA. The *Leipziger Tageszeitung* – a daily newspaper – shamelessly printed promotional lists of purely Aryan shops and artisans.[21] All the while, NSDAP political influence had steadily grown stronger in the city. And yet who would want to believe fellow Leipzigers would turn so vicious?

Hunya and her husband Nathan stayed at home together in silence that Thursday morning, waiting for whatever would happen next. Groups of rioters had spread out across town, yelling *Raus ihr Judenschwein!* – 'Come out you Jewish pigs!' When Hunya heard a knocking at the door she braced for the arrival of Storm Troopers, or Gestapo, or violent Leipzigers.

It was her father. A non-Jewish neighbour had warned him to leave the synagogue where he was studying because 'bad things are going to happen'. A few minutes later the synagogue was vandalised – one of three in Leipzig to be destroyed – and the Torah scrolls torched.

There were similar distressing stories across Germany and Austria: seemingly 'spontaneous' outbreaks of anti-Jewish violence, which were in fact carefully orchestrated by Nazi officials, who removed their uniforms so they looked like regular Germans. Their actions incited other thugs to join in.

Although thousands of Jewish properties were smashed and defaced, Jewish department stores were particularly attractive targets for attack. Grünfeld's linen store in Berlin had already been defaced with obscene cartoons depicting torture and maiming of Jews, back in June. On 9 and 10 November, other department stores suffered the same and worse. Nathan Israel, Berlin's equivalent of Harrods, was badly vandalised, as were Tietz, KaDeWe and Wertheim. Almost all the city's department stores were Jewish-owned.[22]

Looters crunched on glass shards from the shattered windows, grabbing whatever took their fancy from racks and shelves. Brown Shirts tossed goods out of windows, and trampled clothes in the streets. Worse, Jewish people were harried from their beds, pummelled, humiliated and arrested. Many were dragged off for their first taste of concentration camp existence.

Rudolf Höss had been promoted that year to SS Captain, and transferred – with his family – to an adjutant role in Sachsenhausen concentration camp, north of Berlin, where many victims of pogroms were sent, including a group of Jews from Leipzig.[23]

In the following year, Höss would become administrator of prisoner belongings in Sachsenhausen, and second-in-command at the camp. He and his wife Hedwig would grow only too accustomed to handling such property in his next posting. At Auschwitz.

In Leipzig, the famous department stores Bamberger's, Hertz's and Ury's were set ablaze in the early hours of 10 November 1938. The local fire brigades rushed to make sure flames did not spread to non-Jewish buildings. They did nothing to save the shops themselves.

In Germany as a whole, an estimated six to seven thousand Jewish businesses were looted and trashed.[24] It was open, shameless, government-sanctioned behaviour. The German public were too frightened to intervene, or too eager to benefit. Rolls of fabric stolen from drapery departments could be quietly cut and stitched into new clothes – who would be any the wiser?

The mass devastation of 9/10 November 1938 became known as *Kristallnacht* – Night of the Broken Glass. It is an evocative term, but so very telling that events were viewed in terms of property not people. Broken glass not broken lives. Reichsmarschall Goering complained to Goebbels, 'I wish you had killed two hundred Jews instead of destroying such valuables.'[25]

Although Kristallnacht had shown German citizens the ugly reality of life for Jews, perhaps they took selfish comfort from the thought that it was happening to other people – that families harried through the streets in their night clothes must have done *something* wrong to be treated in such a discordant way.

While Jewish Germans feared for their livelihoods and homes, Aryan women could still leaf through magazines of 1938 to admire a new style of hat, consider booking a river cruise or city break, dream of a swimming pool in the back garden, banish unattractive armpit smells with Odo-ro-no deodorant, make an appointment for massage and beauty creams at an Elizabeth Arden salon, pick a pattern to make a lace blouse, or choose a furrier for winter pelts. In short, indulge in escapism. Magazine adverts offered Cutex nail polish, Guterman's sewing silks in a rainbow of shades, and Schwarzkopf dyes for suitably Aryan hair blonding. Dirty hands could be scrubbed clean with Palmolive soap.

In one 1938 article rhapsodising over fresh fashion colours, column-effect gowns and marabou jackets, *Elegante Welt* magazine proclaimed the mood on the horizon was 'predominantly cheerful'. Any anxieties were dismissed by the journalist with the admonition, 'economic crises are none other than the indestructible will to live and optimism of a people.'[26]

As Plenipotentiary of the Four Year Plan, Hermann Goering was responsible for gearing up the German economy for war. He certainly saw Kristallnacht damage as a crisis, complaining that there was no point in him crafting frugal policies when pogroms caused massive losses to the economy.[27] His response to the Kristallnacht vandalism was brazen. He presented German Jews with a staggeringly high bill to cover the damage.

Emmy Goering, Hermann's adoring wife, was a devotee of fabulous clothes that set off her generous figure. In her memoirs she admitted to feeling uneasy at antisemitic boycotts, making it clear that she had done her small bit to support some Jewish friends who'd had *Jude* – Jew – daubed on their shop windows. However, she also confessed to feeling uncomfortable going into Jewish shops, afraid it would mean trouble for her husband.

Joseph Goebbels meanwhile gloated in his diary that Berliners were enraptured at the loot of Kristallnacht. Significantly, he highlighted the fact that clothes and soft furnishings were the main prizes acquired: 'Fur coats, carpets, valuable textiles were all to be had for nothing.'[28] Magda Goebbels, Joseph's immaculately styled wife, was a devotee of good style, and very upset about the impact of the November pogroms. She lamented the closure of a Jewish salon: 'What a nuisance that Kohnen is closing . . . we all know that when the Jews go, so will the elegance from Berlin.'[29]

SS wives such as Emmy, Magda and Hedwig, seduced by privilege, were witness to the visible victimisation of Jews, but they decided the best way to cope with such discomfort was to turn away from it. Absorbed with fulfilling their roles as National Socialist women, they were learning that the world could be refashioned to suit their image of it, and to fulfil their needs.

Hunya's clients had included the elite women of Leipzig. She had dressed Jews and non-Jews. Her creations draped the bodies of bystanders and victims of the hooliganism. She had been asleep during Kristallnacht; now she had to stay alert to face the continuing calamity. All her energies turned to escape.

We were happy to survive the day and somehow keep our head above water   – Irene Reichenberg[30]

Back in Bratislava, young Irene Reichenberg was frantic. From March 1938, hundreds of Jewish refugees arrived in the city, escaping Nazi persecution in Germany and newly annexed Austria. When Czech territories came under German rule there were more refugees fleeing to Slovakia, which became autonomous in October 1938. Pro-Nazi gangs felt free to attack Jewish property as well as any Jewish people simply out in public. Jewish charities did what they could to help and house those in need. There were riots and fights on Židovská Street.

Irene could not get her father to see that the brutality would not lessen; that it was not simply another spike in antisemitism, it would not all blow over. Even if Irene was clear-sighted enough to recognise the danger, what could they actually do about it? Where would they go? In all her life she had been too poor even to take a trip to Vienna, a mere forty miles away.

Escape? Impossible.

'Emigration, anything that cost money, we could not afford at all. That was not possible. We couldn't,' she said.[31]

Together with her friend Bracha Berkovič, Irene planned a different mode of survival. One that involved needles, fabric, thread and pins.

3

What Next, How to Continue?

Well, we stood there, several girls from the class, Jewish girls.
We stood there on the street, and did not know what next, how
to continue   – Irene Reichenberg[1]

Spring 1939.

Fashion magazines anticipated lighter styles and brighter fabrics – rayon florals, chiffon scarves and hat veils.

The reality of March was far harsher.

Hitler wore a long, double-breasted military coat for his visit to Prague on 18 March 1939, perfectly complemented by an entourage of marching Wehrmacht soldiers, light tanks and heavy guns. He inspected his new conquest from under the brim of a peaked cap. Storm clouds and rain cleared for a moody sky. The crowds of civilians who welcomed him into the subjugated territories of Bohemia and Moravia stretched gloved hands out in salute. A few faces under the hats and caps showed bewilderment. Four days before, on 14 March, the country of Czechoslovakia had been dissolved. On the same day Slovakia declared independence.

Anyone with access to a wireless could listen to Hitler's speeches broadcast across the new Greater Germany. One young Czech girl remembers that the radio shook as Hitler screamed '*Juden raus!*' and the family had to put their hands over their ears.[2]

'Jews out!' It had been an aim from the early days of the

NSDAP, following carefully planned stages of defining Jews, pushing them to emigrate, marking them as 'other', rendering them powerless and forcing them into poverty. These Nazi tactics would be adopted by almost every territory that came under the aegis of the Reich swastika. In tandem was an impetus to profit from Jews in whatever way possible.

Both processes would culminate in the travesty of a fashion salon in Auschwitz.

Fashion was far from Irene Reichenberg's thoughts in spring 1939.

Irene's sister, fourteen-year-old Edith, had taken over the role of homemaker since their mother's untimely death the year before. Home was no longer much of a haven. Anti-Jewish violence was swiftly legitimised in the new republic of Slovakia. Windows in Bratislava's Jewish quarter were smashed. Threatening graffiti continued – taunts such as 'Jewish pigs!' and 'Go to Palestine!'

Renée Ungar in Slovakia, 1938

Irene's friend Renée had to escort her father, the rabbi, through the streets to the closest synagogue, since it was not safe for him to be out alone. Religious Jewish men were particular targets for harassment.

A 1938 photograph of Renée shows her looking smart in streetwear – a fitted jacket and modestly long dark skirt. When dressed confidently, there was always a chance of individuals 'passing' as non-Jewish, even though such judgements were entirely subjective.

In fact, the Slovak government decided that more must be done to distinguish Jews from non-Jews, to enable more thorough exploitation and persecution. From 1 September 1941, all Jews would be compelled to wear a large yellow Star of David on their outer clothing. If coats and jackets were removed, the next layer needed a star also. From sewing boxes and sewing kits came the needles and thread to complete this humiliating task. Some fastened the star with loose tacking stitches so it could be unpicked in a hurry when 'passing'.

Clothing became contaminated by state-approved stigma. With a yellow star, Renée's jacket would no longer be simply part of a teenage girl's outfit, but a garment that made her a target.

The journey to such visual segregation was not only condoned by the Slovakian government, it was vigorously enacted, following the lead of Third Reich policies. The Slovak People's Party was headed by its president, radical Catholic priest Josef Tiso, and the even more extremist Prime Minister, Dr Vojtech Tuka. They were fuelled by a potent mix of nationalism, anti-semitism and self-interest. Their attacks on Jewish life and livelihoods were not organised solely out of hatred. They unashamedly wanted to enrich themselves at the expense of Jewish citizens.

When Hitler looked out over Prague in March 1939, he was surveying an acquisition. Now Germany had control of Czechoslovakia's important industrial bases, and access to the country's many other assets. The plunder that would quickly follow was not only the spoils of war, it was a very urgently needed source of income to keep the Reich from teetering into bankruptcy.[3] Nazi territorial conquests were as much for revenue as for bragging rights.

Greed was behind the 1940 legislation to authorise the Slovak government to do whatever was necessary to exclude Jewish people from the country's social and economic life. Greed predominated in the ongoing meetings between Tuka, Tiso and SS Hauptsturmführer Dieter Wisliceny, an emissary of Adolf Eichmann; sent from Germany ostensibly as an advisor on Jewish affairs, in actuality to work out the logistics of profiteering from Jewish assets. Greed motivated their direct actions against Jewish businesses.

The impact of such greed would be devastating for the victims, but gloriously enriching for the perpetrators.

I intend to loot and to loot thoroughly – Hermann Goering[4]

The idea of using war to pay for war was nothing new. Both German soldiers and locals took advantage of the upheaval of invasion to seize what they could. This was entirely contrary to the 1907 Hague Convention on the Rules of Land Warfare, which made it perfectly clear that invading armies could not seize private property unless they paid compensation. Germany had been a signatory of the Rules, but as a Nazi nation it became intoxicated with victory after erasing one European border after another.

Wehrmacht troops were actively encouraged to consider each successive conquest as a glorified shopping spree. An orgy of consumerism followed each country's surrender. In particular Goering enabled easy acquisition of furs, silks and luxury goods by the Wehrmacht. There were to be no limits on purchases made by troops, and no limits to the parcels they could send back to Germany.

After the customs border between the Czech Protectorate and Germany was abolished on 1 October 1940, there was a purchasing frenzy by soldiers and visiting civilians that cleared shop shelves of furs, perfume, shoes, gloves . . . anything that could be posted home or carried away. Similarly, when Paris fell, occupying Wehrmacht troops bought up such a gross amount of goods they were nicknamed 'potato beetles' by the French, because they departed round-backed and loaded.

What did it matter if excess spreading of Reichsmarks and promissory notes devalued the local currency? If inflation made shopping a financial nightmare for locals? The main thing was to keep Germans – *Aryans* – happy. Hitler had first-hand experience of the discontent caused on the Home Front during the Great War, when food and other essentials ran out. He had no intention of letting his own subjects become mutinous. He would keep them happy with booty from other, 'lesser' people.

Germans expanding east across Europe did not observe the nicety of paying for goods they took. Their rapacity in Ukraine, for example, earned them the nickname 'hyenas'. Inevitably Jewish businesses were the most vulnerable to looting, as they had the least protection. In fact, police and Wehrmacht soldiers in German-occupied Poland merely observed when Jewish shop windows were smashed so locals – impelled by antisemitism and avarice – could help themselves to goods.[5]

Back in Germany, mothers, wives, sweethearts and siblings received surprise packages from menfolk abroad, and they were delighted at the abundance. In their own domestic way these women became war profiteers. Perhaps they were genuinely unaware that their gains were other people's losses.[6]

There was even extra plundering carried out in time to fill German shop window displays for Christmas.

Jews were specific targets in other methods of benefiting both German civilians and Wehrmacht troops. After the invasion of Russia in 1941, there was a gradual realisation that German supply stores were dangerously inadequate for winter combat. Hitler and Goebbels called on patriotic Germans to volunteer donations of any furs and woollen clothing that could be spared for the Eastern Front.

For Jewish Germans, the confiscation of furs was compulsory, no compensation. Checks were made for Jewish wardrobes still containing fur coats, capes, muffs, gloves and hats. Even fur collars were to be unpicked and handed over. Non-compliance was severely punished by the state police.[7] This was not simply a question of wealthy people giving up a luxurious pelt only worn to show status. Fur in some form was worn by all social classes, out of necessity in winter, from humble coney skins to svelte mink.

Nationwide collections of winter clothing and kit for troops were referred to as a Christmas present from the German people to the Eastern Front. Hundreds of thousands of items were received. No doubt men of the Wehrmacht appreciated the new warmth. And the Jews who shivered in bitter weather – what did their suffering matter?

The Jews had to hand over all their furs, jewellery, sporting equipment and other valuable items. Everything the Hlinka guards liked, they confiscated — Katka Feldbauer[8]

It would take more than foreign shopping sprees and confiscated furs to finance Hitler's wars and keep Germans fed and clothed. German-controlled territories were to be rendered Jew-free. *Entjudung* – 'de-Jewing' – was to be achieved through a process of dispossession, deportation and eventually mass murder. Dispossession was an integral part of what would become known as the Holocaust.

In November 1938, *Das Schwarze Korps* – an SS magazine – ran an article claiming that Jews were 'parasites', 'incapable of doing work itself'.[9] Clearly this was propaganda. However, the radical robbery of Jewish property and businesses was part of a drive to fulfil the accusation, and so justify abuse. Essentially, Jews were to be rendered destitute and desperate. Easier to control. It was no coincidence that despoiling Jews enriched others.

In all Nazi-occupied territories, Jews became fair game for every kind of theft and intimidation for pay-offs. There were bribes to avoid harassment, bribes to obtain visas, bribes to keep off deportation lists to labour camps and ghettos. Germany set a template of how the enrichment would work. Other regimes were happy to watch and learn, Slovakia included. From low-level Hlinka guards – the paramilitary of the Slovak People's Party – to officials at the highest level, everyone wanted to cash in.

Hunya Storch, now married as Frau Volkmann, felt the impact of dispossession in Leipzig when the November 1938 *Decree of Eliminating Jews from German Economic Life* became law. It stated that all Jewish businesses had to cease on New Year's Day 1939. The decree followed six years of disenfranchisement and exclusion.

For Hunya it would culminate in a stripping of all assets, and a literal stripping of clothes while being processed in Auschwitz. The young women she would later meet in the camp fashion studio – Marta, Bracha, Irene and the others – all had their own recollections of similar dispossession. They would eventually experience the absolute minimum of what is required for life to continue. It was a long and degrading downfall, beginning with brazen state-sanctioned theft.

Under the 1938 decree, Jewish assets were to be regarded as *Volksvermögen* – collective assets of the German people. 'German' was synonymous with 'Aryan'. This did not only apply to valuables such as jewellery and art, houses, land and cars. It also included bicycles, radios, furniture, clothes and sewing machines.

Hermann Goering presided over a multitude of initiatives in Germany to use Jewish money to bulk out the Nazi budget.[10] The most obvious strategy of dispossession was enacted throughout the 1930s. This was 'Aryanisation' – forcing the takeover of Jewish businesses for the benefits of so-called Aryans, or non-Jews. The main goal of Aryanisation went far beyond simply causing distress and hardship. The prize, for the perpetrators, was actual ownership of Jewish businesses, as well as elimination of competition.

Under the new laws an 'Arisator' – an Aryan manager – was awarded the right to take over a business, usually for free or on payment of a nominal fee; not to mention bribes for corrupt officials who managed the Aryanisation bureaucracy. The bullying tactics were disguised in corporate language: the business ownership was to be transferred to a *Treuhänder*, or liquidation trustee. This could be anyone non-Jewish who fancied a new enterprise on the cheap, or someone the Trustees' Office authority wanted to reward.

In the fashion industry, eager Nazis seized the opportunity to acquire their own Aryanised clothing enterprises. Magda Goebbels even used her influence to help Hilda Romatski, Aryan owner of Romatski fashion house on Berlin's popular shopping street Kurfürstendamm, who had complained about the 'unfair competition' of the Jewish fashion salon Grete, a few doors along the boulevard. With breathtaking hypocrisy, Magda wrote to the German Labour Front in 1937 to demand the closure of Romatski's Jewish rival, declaring, 'it is personally disagreeable to me and unbearable to be suspected of being dressed by a Jewish fashion house.'[11]

In contrast, Hedwig Höss would brazenly choose to establish

a salon in Auschwitz, where the majority of her coterie of dressmakers had been imprisoned for no other reason than for being Jewish.

There's plenty of people have grown fat at the Aryanisation trough, as fat as pigs – Ladislav Grosman, *The Shop on Main Street*[12]

In Berlin alone there were approximately 2,400 textile-related businesses under Jewish ownership, all vulnerable to predators. In Leipzig, Hunya Volkmann's base, 1,600 businesses were forcibly sold under Aryanisation by November 1938. The remaining 1,300 businesses in Jewish hands would not last much longer.[13] Everything Hunya had worked so hard to build up could legally be snatched away from her.

One of Hunya's aunts was married to a Mr Gelb, who owned one of the many department stores in Leipzig. Hunya's sister Dora had worked there for a while. The Gelb family asked Hunya and her husband Nathan to help deal with the Aryanisation, a hugely stressful process. Hunya and Nathan did what they could. The store was acquired by a non-Jewish German owner, for a pitiful sum.

It was a buyer's paradise. Arisators knew Jews had to sell, and sell quickly at that. They snapped up enterprises for forty per cent or even as little as ten per cent of their actual value. If stock was liquidated before the sell-off, shoppers might innocently browse clothing sale rails and fabric remnant baskets, delighted to find a bargain. Plenty of people were not so innocent, but happy to make the most of Jewish misfortune.

It was not only the pressure of Aryanisation laws that forced speed sales: Jews were also desperate to get out of Germany as soon as possible. Hunya felt this pressure. Stretching meagre resources, visas and tickets were arranged for her parents to escape to Palestine. Meanwhile she made daily rounds of foreign consulates, joining crowds of other anxious applicants to apply for emigration documents. There were endless interviews and complex questionnaires. Few countries were accepting unlimited emigrants; most were indifferent to the plight of Jews in Europe.

Hunya had no luck with her applications for Palestine and Argentina, her first choices. Finally she succeeded in obtaining entry permits and two tickets for Paraguay. It was daunting to think of sailing halfway round the world to another culture on another continent, so very different from her sheltered upbringing in a small town in the High Tatras, but if it meant she and Nathan would be safe, it was worth the upheaval. Her dressmaking skills would surely be appreciated wherever they ended up.

It was not to be. At the last moment the consulate in Germany cancelled permits so hard-won by Jews. Hunya was trapped in Germany.

In Bratislava, Irene Reichenberg experienced the demeaning process of dispossession first-hand. From 2 September 1940, all Slovakian Jews were required to register their assets. Irene's father Shmuel Reichenberg dutifully gave details of his shoemaking business. A pre-war photograph shows a portrait of Shmuel with his youngest daughter Grete – Irene's sister. He seems calm, a little worn perhaps, but smart in a shirt, tie and jacket. His life had been centred on work, family and synagogue worship each Sabbath. Like many, he hoped that if he did as he was told and followed the rules, restrictions could be endured.

His was one of over 600 Jewish businesses in Bratislava, many of them based around the textile trades. Any optimism he might have felt about continuing to trade was entirely misplaced. Under the first Aryanisation law in force from 1 June 1940, Shmuel Reichenberg's work licence was revoked. This law essentially meant that Jews could not conduct independent business of any kind. He came home to the small apartment at 18 Židovská Street. Without work there would be no income. Without income – starvation and homelessness.

Irene had no choice but to adapt. Over time she gradually became worn down by escalating traumas, to the point where only Bracha's unstinting friendship and the rhythm of needle and thread would save her. For now she watched her father set up a stool and a small table under the window in the apartment. He set out his tools. All along Židovská Street Jewish friends and acquaintances brought him odd jobs, which he completed with his usual skill, assuming he could acquire leather and sewing notions.

It was incredibly difficult to keep going. His work was now illegal, but how else could he earn money? Jewish charities were unbearably stretched, particularly in caring for the thousands of desperate refugees who had fled to Czechoslovakia thinking it would be safer than Germany.

Among unscrupulous Slovaks there was a scramble to bag the best Jewish businesses for themselves, with no consideration for the actual owners. So it was that the tailoring business Bracha Berkovič's father Salomon had worked so diligently to establish was stolen and handed over to a Catholic competitor – clients, stock, reputation and all.

In the course of a year, Tiso's Central Economic Office – *Ústredný Hospodársky Úrad* – transferred over 2,000 Slovakian Jewish businesses into Aryan ownership, including the Berkovič tailoring shop. It was very easy for someone who fancied a Jewish business to obtain it via Aryanisation. Sometimes the original owner was kept on as an employee, particularly if the Arisator had no clue how to run the business. Sometimes they were simply shown the door. Bracha's father was not given an option – he was out.

A staggering 10,000 Jewish businesses in Slovakia were ultimately liquidated under Aryanisation rules. The massive profits acquired were transferred to a special account run by SS representative Dieter Wisliceny. Out of these 10,000 businesses, more than one thousand were stores selling textiles. All those bolts of fabric, so proudly displayed and so admired by shoppers – gone. Arisators sold off the stock. Those who bought the fabric might never have known which business it originally came from. They might never have cared.[14]

Prague suffered a similar rapaciousness, following the same tactics of segregation, registration and robbery. Before the imposition of the yellow star, Jewish people had been well assimilated into Prague society. Now, any property worth more than 10,000 *koruna* was confiscated and deposited in a special bank account in Prague. Receipts were duly given, to maintain the illusion that it was a temporary holding. Then came Aryanisation of businesses, including Prague's fabulous fashion industry, from high-class couture to humble home-workers.

As late as 1939, non-Jewish clients were assuring their favourite Jewish-owned salons that Nazi antisemitism would not affect their loyalty. They were still eager to have Jewish seamstresses make up garments inspired by Chanel of Paris, or designed by home-grown talent. Regardless of clients' wishes, once an Arisator appeared at the salon door, asking to see all accounts, all stock, all employee records, there was no way to resist takeover. Businesses were sometimes sold to a faithful employee, under the assumption that this was a precautionary tactic only. It was entirely up to the new owner to decide how much they would honour the spirit of the transfer, or how much they would try to profit from it.

In fashion magazines, adverts for Jewish shops and services simply disappeared without comment. Brick and mortar shops remained in place after Aryanisation, with the same clothes, the same shoes, but Jewish shop names were painted over and Jewish clothes labels removed.

Dressmakers such as Marta Fuchs now had no legal

opportunities for running a sewing business. Like Hunya in Leipzig, Marta's focus from 1938 onwards was to escape Europe entirely. Canny enough to realise that while Jewish goods were coveted, Jewish life would, conversely, become worthless, Marta stayed at Hotel Juliš on Prague's famous Wenceslas Square. This beautiful boulevard was home to the National Museum, a multitude of modern offices, the Bata shoe store and a pre-Great War shopping centre.

This was not why Marta had chosen to stay at Hotel Juliš. She needed to be near transport hubs and foreign embassies. Her desperate plan was to catch a train to a port and leave by sea for Latin America. She now spent her spare hours with a Spanish dictionary, not fashion magazines; queuing for visas not sale bargains. By the time a visa for Ecuador was miraculously granted, it was too late. The Germans were evolving new policies to trap Jews, rather than bullying them into leaving.[15] Marta was forced to return to Bratislava.

After autumn 1941, 'Jews out!' would signify deportation. A ghetto was established in the Czech town of Terezín – called Theresienstadt by the Germans – allegedly a 'model town' for only Jews, in reality a transit camp for a far darker destination.

On the spur of the moment I decided to learn to sew a little bit
– Irene Reichenberg[16]

What could young people do in the face of such powerfully oppressive forces?

Marta, Irene, Renée and Bracha were among the many tens of thousands who paid the human cost of greed. To them the relentless anti-Jewish legislation was not just stark words on a page. It was a robbery of rights and possessions.

The more that was taken from them, the more they bonded in resilience.

Dressmaking was a financial resort for so many women in European economies, and worldwide. It was considered suitably 'female' as a profession and needed relatively little equipment. In German-occupied territories, women were forced to turn to their needles to earn money for daily bread. By daylight, lamplight or candlelight, between housework and caring duties, they bent over their work, making outfits, doing alterations, re-knitting unravelled woollens and creating colourful embroidery patterns.

One Bratislavan Jew, Grete Roth, began weaving classes in the late 1930s, when it became clear that her husband's law office would be liquidated. She was able to dress her entire family in tailor-made outfits, made up from her home-based loom.[17] In the Protectorate, seventeen-year-old Katka Feldbauer was a straight 'A' student until the school principal called her into the office to tell her to pack her belongings – *Jews out*. Deeply stunned, she took up work with a seamstress, who was actually an Arisator for Jewish businesses. She earned a pittance, hidden in a back room.[18] Grete and Katka would both one day share a dormitory with the Auschwitz dressmakers.

Forced out of school, Irene Reichenberg had time on her hands and a need for a new skill. She chose sewing. Her older sister Käthe, married to handsome Leo Kohn, had already trained as a seamstress. Her friend Renée was also sewing in secret, as well as Renée's sister Gita. As a Jew, Irene was barred from vocational college and regular training. However, she knew a dressmaker, a Polish woman married to a Bratislavan Jew. This woman's work licence had been revoked, but she was willing to teach clandestinely for only five *koruna* a day. Bracha also joined the lessons.

Bracha had not learned to sew from her mother and did not take to it wholeheartedly, unlike her younger sister Katka. Katka Berkovič was very adept. She picked up tailoring techniques more quickly than Bracha, and became especially proficient at coats. Both sisters had extra lessons with their father, who was deeply concerned about the deterioration of life for Jews in Slovakia, and desperate to find some way to protect his children. He made time to train his oldest son Emil as a tailor, since Emil was not permitted to continue with his regular education.

Sisters Bracha and Katka Berkovič, pre-war

A photograph of Bracha and Katka from this time gives no hint of the hardship that had almost been normalised in daily life. Bracha embraces her sister and faces the camera with bright eyes and a nice smile. Katka seems a little more guarded, shyer. Both have glossy hair and lovely long plaits.

The girls befriended another young apprentice at the 'underground' seamstress school. She was a Jewish girl named Rona Böszi. Rona had emigrated from Berlin to escape Nazi persecution. She was a wonderful friend, always ready to help the others when they got into difficulties with their sewing.

Alles verwenden nichts verschwenden

– Everything used, nothing wasted[19]

On the home front it fell to women to make the best of things in reduced circumstances. The apron became the housewife's uniform equivalent. Portrayed as cheerful and feminine in pattern books and women's magazines – even when engineered from an old shirt or tablecloth – there was no getting away from the fact that an apron was fundamentally a protective garment, not a fashion item.[20] Surviving aprons from wartime Germany are stained, patched and darned: evidence of their needfulness.[21] Propaganda could not hide the reality of hard work and shortages.

Aprons featured in a 1941 German sewing magazine,
Deutches Moden Zeitung

Long before full military mobilisation, Germany had been diverting finance and material resources to accelerate rearmament programmes, leaving scant supplies for civilians. Plunder and dispossession were meant to make up the shortfall. Even so, food rationing was first introduced in Germany in August 1939, shortly before the invasion of Poland.

Clothes rationing followed two months later, on 14 November.

Clothing coupons were backdated to the first of September and gave regular civilians one hundred points in their *Reichskleiderkarte* – clothes coupon book – for the year ahead. With a coat or suit costing sixty points, this did not leave much freedom for wardrobe replenishing. Nazi women's organisations laboured to persuade housewives to take advantage of the synthetic fabrics being churned out as replacements for scarcer natural fibres.

To ease pressure on factory production of mass-produced clothing, home visits from a tailor or dressmaker were encouraged, as long as they were not Jewish, of course. Various women's groups offered training courses in core skills, including sewing. Women were also advised to remodel existing clothes and to make their own where possible, to avoid pressure on the ready-to-wear industry. Every scrap of fabric was to be saved, with nothing wasted. A general shortage of sewing silks and cottons meant pulling threads from fabric selvedge or reusing tacking threads.

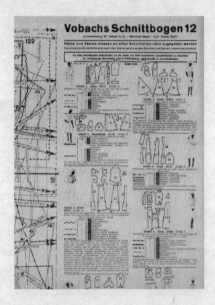

Paper pattern detail from Deutches Moden Zeitung, *1941*

Dressmaking magazines often included free patterns for home sewers. Paper quality declined noticeably as the war dragged on. To economise on paper, multiple garment patterns were overlaid onto one sheet, requiring keen eyesight, geometrical cunning and endless patience to decode.

Of course, not everyone was affected equally by clothing shortages. Elite Nazi women felt no compunction in abusing the ration system. In January 1940, Magda Goebbels had her private secretary argue against having sixteen points deducted from her allowance, to cover three pairs of stockings. Magda objected on the grounds that she needed the stockings for her work as a nurse. The following month, Master Court Shoe Manufacturer Wilhelm Breitsprecher, who counted the Kaiser as one of his former clients, found the courage to write to Frau Goebbels to say he could not begin work on her crocodile leather shoes until she forwarded the necessary ration cards.[22]

Wives of high-ranking Nazi leaders not only felt above the law when it came to ration points, they continued to patronise Jewish seamstresses on the sly.[23] Such a sense of privilege would eventually motivate Hedwig Höss to create her own coterie of personal sewers, once established as a camp commandant's wife in Auschwitz. She had no intention of letting standards slip. No matter who did the stitching, she would still look smart. In a 1939 family photograph she stands with her brother Fritz Hensel, confident in a pale suit and shoes. No patches, darns or dirt on *her* clothes.

We have put together Jewish workshops with the help of skilled Jewish workers, with which goods will be made which will greatly ease the position of German production   – Hans Frank[24]

One of the great ironies of *Entjudung* policies and Aryanisation was that industries in Germany and Nazi-occupied territories promptly found themselves without the necessary skilled labour to operate their newly acquired businesses. The shortfall of labour across all industries that were supposed to be 'Jew-free' was exacerbated generally by the insatiable appetite of the German military for more recruits to fight on multiple fronts. And so, having legally squeezed seamstresses such as Hunya and Marta out of work, the Nazis were faced with a shortage of tailors and dressmakers. In some areas intensive tailoring training courses were set up for non-Jews, but it was hardly an adequate solution in the short term.

The answer was simple and brutal: forced labour and slave labour.

The summons for compulsory labour might arrive in a civilised manner, by letter or public posting of names. Or a person might simply be dragged from the street or rounded up at home while the rest of the family looked on, helpless. They began with men and boys.

Bracha's brother Emil, training to be a tailor with his father, received notification that he was to report for work at a collection point for male Jews at Žilina, a Slovakian town over a hundred miles from Bratislava. Beyond that, scant information. The family never saw him again. He was only eighteen years old. He did not live many months longer. There is no known grave marker, only the sombre memorial to all those who perished at Majdanek extermination camp [25]

Irene's father joined thousands of other Jews at the hastily constructed labour camp of Sered', about an hour north-east of Bratislava. There were other camps run by Slovak fascists at Vyhne and Nováky. Thanks to 'Jewish Codex' laws crafted by Dieter Wisliceny and the Slovak government, all Jews aged between sixteen and sixty could be put to work according to ministerial whim. Under Hlinka authority, Shmuel Reichenberg made boots and shoes at Sered' camp. Other workshops at

Sered' created furniture, clothing and even toys. Shmuel's work was of such high calibre that the camp guards adopted him as their own personal, unpaid, bootmaker. They provided equipment and raw materials, then strutted in the camp and town in bespoke footwear.

There were children imprisoned in the camps, with their own rudimentary schoolroom and occasional breaks for play. Irene's youngest sister, fourteen-year-old Grete, who was disabled, was able to stay with her father in Sered'. Because of his protected status she was safe too – a miracle considering how people with disabilities were targeted by Nazi euthanasia programmes.[26]

Photographs taken to document tailoring workshops in Slovakian camps show neatly dressed women and men bent over gleaming sewing machines. Their feet work the treadles, their hands guide the fabric, and yet their minds must be on loved ones left behind, and fears for the future.

When she parted from her father and sister Grete in 1941, Irene had no way of knowing she too would end up using her skills to survive, and for far more prestigious clients.

Nathan Volkmann, Hunya's husband

Meanwhile, in Germany, Hunya Volkmann felt fairly safe with a Czech passport, but she was terrified that her husband Nathan would be taken. He was a Polish national and they were considered fair game for German labour round-ups. She determined he should make his escape, and planned a route for him, crossing through Italy to Switzerland and being smuggled over all borders, which were closed to Jews. It was a wrench to see him leave, but Nathan was not gone long. He returned home, unable to bear the thought of abandoning Hunya.

They stayed together for six weeks longer. When round-ups began in the Jewish quarter, Nathan was taken. Soldiers guarded the columns of men, Nathan among them, using their batons to hit any women who got too close. No one was officially allowed access to the barracks where the men were initially being held, but somehow Hunya – no timid soul – managed to convince a guard to let her see Nathan. She hid her shock at seeing him transformed from a smart, groomed man to an unkempt prisoner. Their meeting was short and heartfelt. Powerless to change laws or break open the barracks, Hunya settled on the one thing she could do to help her husband. She determined to get him a decent pair of shoes.

This was not an indulgent fashion fix. Nathan would need strong footwear for heavy-duty work. Mustering her self-esteem, Hunya returned to the Gelb's department store once owned by her aunt's family, and asked the new proprietor to help her out. It took a great deal of pride-swallowing, persuasion and an outrageous amount of money for the Arisator to agree to sell her some shoes. Hunya hurried back to the barracks and arrived in time to see the last columns of shaven-headed men being led out of town. Nathan had gone, marching away in worn-out shoes, while she was left holding the perfect pair.[27]

Not long afterwards her turn came for deportation.

The making of fur coats is an art of its own, and should not be attempted by anyone but a furrier. But there are small articles of fur which the average needlewoman can manage
      – The Pictorial Guide to Modern Home Needlecraft

Fur fashions featured in Eva *magazine 1940*

Hunya did not have far to go for her first bout of forced labour. Along with other Jews as well as the non-Jewish spouses of so-called 'mixed marriages', she was ousted from her home and sent to a new *Judenstelle*, 'Jewish area', in Leipzig, where residents were allocated cramped quarters. She got a single room at the Carlebach school. It had been partly torched during Kristallnacht. The impressive stone entrance steps of the school no longer welcomed scholars and teachers, most of whom would be deported and murdered over the coming years.[28] Nathan addressed his letters to Hunya here. The letters became shorter and less optimistic as months passed. He was sent to Sachsenhausen concentration camp on 26 October 1939. It would not be his final destination.

Hunya's new compulsory job was with the firm of Friedrich Rohde, which provided furs for the Wehrmacht. Leipzig was internationally famous for its fur commerce, centred around an area called the Brühl. Through fur the city had built particularly strong links with London and Paris. An annual trade fair called the *Messe* attracted visitors from all over the world. Warehouses and workshops in the Brühl were full of skins bought in bulk by auction, then cleaned, dyed, tanned and graded.

Once processed the pelts were made up into bundles, which were then stitched into fur garments. Fur work was highly skilled and overwhelmingly a Jewish speciality. Skins had to be cut with a razor, never scissors, and sewn with a three-sided needle that had a very sharp point. Temperature control was important, to ensure skins did not rot or dry out. Infestations were alarming. When lined and brushed, fur garments could be sensuously glamorous, and seriously warm.

This then became Hunya's new world. Having war-essential work at least gave her the freedom to leave the Jewish quarter. She used this relative freedom to help families back at the Carlebach school, by seeking out shops that would agree to sell food to a holder of Jewish ration coupons. Hunya then smuggled the food back into the ghetto.

In contrast to the avarice and brutality of Aryanisers and other antisemites, she discovered that many of her German friends were generous with their support and angry about the crimes against Jews. Hunya also nurtured excellent relationships with her worker companions and the German managers at Rohde's factory, who were surprisingly respectful. It was clear that whatever the national legislation, people still made their own decisions about how they behaved towards Jews. They could actively abuse them, passively observe the abuse, or quietly choose to help.

Hunya was loyal to those in need and in turn inspired loyalty from her friends, qualities the Nazis consistently underestimated among those they persecuted.

Sewing uniforms for the men who were out to kill us all
— Krystyna Chiger, Lvov Ghetto[29]

Friedrich Rohde's fur factory in Leipzig was one of many thousands of workshops using forced labour, spread over all territories under German rule. Famous textile industry centres in Nazi-occupied Poland were radically restructured to extract maximum hours and effort from a captive Jewish workforce, who were bricked into ghettos and offered a choice of sweated labour or starvation.

Germans such as Hans Biebow, a former coffee merchant, became fat cats of ghetto enterprises in the General Government area of the Reich, covering former Polish lands. Biebow lorded it over Łódź ghetto, known by the Germans as Litzmannstadt ghetto. He cultivated cordial relationships with businessmen across the Reich and advertised the ghetto's potential for whole-sale garment manufacturing.

Uniforms were a core product at forced labour factories. Hunya would be familiar with Wehrmacht pelt requirements, including sheepskin jackets, full fur coats, and rabbit-fur under-bodices. Reich military services also needed black leather coats, fur-lined flying jackets, woollen greatcoats, camouflage gear, desert kit, fancy formal 'number one' uniforms, and the regular grey-green combat outfits. There were also workers making plaited straw overshoes to be worn in the snows of the Eastern Front. They might protect the wearers from frostbite, but the makers had bleeding fingers from twelve hours manipu-lating dry straw.

Other workers, in *Trennabteilung* – 'separation' – departments, had the grisly job of sorting used German uniforms – louse-ridden, bloodstained and possibly bullet-torn – deciding which bits could be salvaged and reconditioned for future soldiers to wear.[30] Hugo Boss's company infamously used slave labour to fulfil contracts for NSDAP uniforms and SS garments. Some companies cashing in on Wehrmacht contracts were originally Jewish businesses summarily Aryanised, such as Többens & Schulz tailors in the Warsaw ghetto.

In return for twelve hours non-stop uniform production, sewers received a little soup and the right to live.[31] This right to live – *Lebensrecht* – was no metaphorical term. As the war progressed, having a work permit was one way to avoid being transported to mysterious destinations with initially unfamiliar names that were soon to become synonymous with mass murder – Treblinka, Chełmno, Bełzec, Sobibór. Machinists at Schwartz Co. uniform factory in Janowska camp, near Lvov, for example, were well aware that if they did not work they could be killed.[32]

Perhaps some ghetto business owners justified their uniform production profiteering on the grounds that it was for the Fatherland – furthering the fight for ultimate victory. However, even more lucrative than cut-rate goods for the Wehrmacht were bulk orders for the civilian clothing trade. Clothes for the high street had a much bigger profit margin. Many big Berlin companies knowingly used Jewish slave labour, including child labour. Among them were household name C&A, and the lingerie company Spiesshofer & Braun, rebranded as Triumph after the war. Nearly a quarter of C&A's annual revenue for the year 1944 apparently came from Łódź ghetto garments.[33]

Łódź ghetto proudly advertised the volume of goods made for the civilian market. Correspondence between clothing companies and ghetto managers expressed mutual satisfaction at the arrangement whereby Jews were ousted from their own jobs and homes to create clothes for Germans, who might well have been congratulating themselves on running Jew-free department stores and shopping for Jew-free fashions.[34]

Aprons, frocks, bras, girdles, baby clothes, menswear . . . High fashion and functional wear . . . Not one of the garments had a label that would link them to the ghetto, or the stiff hands of hunched workers guiding mile after mile of seams through a sewing machine.

Forced labourers worked in cramped, stuffy, dirty conditions, with requisitioned equipment and improvised yarns. Even so, they produced beautiful work, which attracted elite clients who would be chauffeured past distressing scenes of ghetto suffering in order to be fitted with elegant bespoke outfits. Hans Biebow encouraged these enterprises in Łódź ghetto, showing special favour to expert Jewish tailors and dressmakers.[35]

Brigitte Frank, wife of Hans Frank, the Governor-General of the occupied Polish territories, even took her little son Niklaus with her on shopping trips into the ghetto. Niklaus later recalled looking from the window of the Mercedes car and seeing 'skinny people in flapping clothes and children who stared at me with goggle eyes.' Brigitte answered his question, 'Why aren't they smiling?' with a cross, 'You wouldn't understand,' before instructing the driver to pull up at the corner for a fur shop and some 'rather good' corselettes.[36]

Brigitte's sister-in-law Lily liked to go to Płaszów concentration camp near Kraków to trade, telling Jews, 'I am the sister of the Governor-General; if you have some precious thing to give me, I can save your life.'[37]

Hedwig Höss's fashion salon in Auschwitz was not without precedent.

While Brigitte Frank shopped for furs and was fitted for new foundation garments, her husband presided over a fascist regime specialising in oppression and exploitation. All Poles under German rule were treated as subhuman, fit to be brutalised, robbed and executed. Jews in Poland suffered extra levels of persecution, sometimes from antisemites in the local population, who did not need any encouragement to smash Jewish shops and stalls and scare away customers. When the ghettos were created, some Poles pitied the suffering of their Jewish neighbours, others readily took over Jewish businesses.[38]

Surviving records detail the crimes of Poles, including some police units, who joined German 'Jew hunts', seeking out Jews who had gone into hiding. Their bounty might be a small sum of money, but more often a successful hunter was rewarded with the clothes of Jews who had been handed over for execution. At its most sordid level, the theft of goods from Jewish people came down to stripping executed corpses for their clothes. A peasant ordered to bury Jews who had been shot by collaborator police took a dress, shoes and headscarf for the trouble, but later complained, 'Only afterwards did I find out that there was a bullet hole in the back of the dress.'[39]

These were sporadic murders. Across the East highly organised and well-equipped Nazi killing squads moved from town to village to hamlet, massacring entire Jewish communities. The tens of thousands of victims were forced to strip first. No point wasting clothes in the burial pits.

This was all under the aegis of Hans Frank. The Frank family would become part of Hedwig Höss's social circle once Hedwig and Rudolf moved from the Berlin area to the General Government and a new concentration camp at Auschwitz.

Going one step further than Brigitte Frank buying corsets in the ghetto, Hedwig would eventually acquire her own 'pet' corsetières, although these women were, blissfully, unaware of their fates in the early 1940s. As ghettos were being constructed and sewing machines whirred in textile factories, the two corset specialists who would one day measure up Hedwig's figure for foundation garments were still more or less safely at home.

One was Herta Fuchs, cousin to Marta Fuchs, a very good-looking young woman from Trnava in Slovakia. Herta was only just finishing her specialist training in corset-making when fate took her on a different journey to a very different set of clients.[40] Then there was Alida Delasalle, a French communist from Normandy, who would be arrested in February 1942 for distributing anti-Nazi leaflets, hidden within the pink coutil fabric layers of her client's corsets.[41]

If it were not for the war, for Nazi oppression, for Hedwig Höss's desire for a trimmer silhouette, Herta and Alida would never have met. Trains from very different parts of the Third Reich brought together these two women, along with Bracha, Irene, Marta, Renée, Hunya, and millions of other bewildered captives, to a perverted new kind of civilisation – the structured horrors of a concentration camp.

One day we received a shipment of beautifully embroidered children's furs from Rumania or the Ukraine. We all choked and many a tear fell on those furs – Herta Mehl, Ravensbrück concentration camp[42]

Jews in Trnava, the home town of Marta's corsetière cousin Herta, were among the Slovakians told in 1939 that they would not be allowed to shop during the same hours as non-Jews, and that they had to give up jewellery and furs.[43]

In the German Reich, furs collected from charitable donations and requisitions had to be sorted and remodelled for military use. One of the centres for this unpleasant work was Ravensbrück women's concentration camp, about sixty miles north of Berlin. Here, prisoners arrested for anti-Nazi crimes and for prostitution and violent offences were sent; ostensibly for re-education, in actuality to prop up the German economy and the German Wehrmacht through forced labour in Waffen-SS workshops.

Ravensbrück became something of a textile centre, because officials such as SS General Oswald Pohl, chief administrator of all SS industry, considered textiles to be female work.[44] Pohl – future guest at the Höss residence in Auschwitz – was perfectly at ease with the use of slave labour. In 1941 he boasted, 'The very fact of our cultural goals leads our companies down certain paths that a purely private businessman would never dare.'[45]

Between 1940 and 1941 the SS founded businesses in Majdanek, Stuthoff . . . and Auschwitz, the new domain of Rudolf Höss.

Fur coats featured in the French Bon Marché *shopping catalogue, winter 1939/40*

The furrier's cutting workshop at Ravensbrück was a dusty, grubby place. Furs stolen from all over the expanding Reich were recut into jackets, gloves and liners for soldiers at the front. Some were vermin-ridden on arrival. Many of the garments boasted labels from the finest furriers in Europe and beyond. Women splitting seams to 'up-cycle' fox, sable, mink and muskrat frequently found jewellery and foreign currency sewn inside. This was handed to SS women at a separate table, and eventually forwarded to a special Reich bank account specifically for loot.

Why such hidden treasure? Because increasingly the furs being sorted were not simply stolen from Jews at liberty. They were robbed from Jews systematically being deported to concentration camps and extermination centres. These deportees hid valuables, innocently supposing they would be useful at their destination. Unaware of plans being developed by bureaucrats at every level of the Nazi administration, they believed they were only being resettled for work.

Work was partly a motivator for emptying ghettos of Jews. Heinrich Himmler toured Ravensbrück workshops in spring 1942. He gave orders for the Waffen-SS uniform production line shifts to be increased from eight hours to eleven. When Nazi bosses in the Reich and General Government complained that emptying ghettos would mean production would come to a standstill, they were reassured that tailoring, furrier and shoe-making workshops would be re-established in concentration camps.

Life was nearly impossible, but the worst was still to come
– Renée Ungar[46]

For the young dressmakers in Bratislava, there were disquieting rumours about the camps. Czech Jews were being deported to ghettos in Łódź, Minsk and Riga, and to the nearer camp at Terezín. It was re-assuring to hear that Terezín had thriving workshops, including sewing factories that churned out cheap dresses for Germany. One of the Terezín factories was headed by the former owner of a large Prague fashion salon, who was able to pick out seamstresses she recognised from among new arrivals and give them sewing work.[47]

Work was one thing. The camps ultimately had a far more ambitious and horrific purpose. Top secret discussions between Hitler, Himmler and select SS men generated the overall structure of a plan. Details were finessed in meetings such as the conference at the villa by the lake in Wannsee, on 20 January 1942, where methods to implement the 'Final Solution' of the 'Jewish Question' were discussed. Europe, Great Britain and Russia were to be completely Jew-free, and not only because of economic expulsion, ghetto concentrations or emigration: step by step genocide was implemented. For a while, work would give the right to live. Anyone considered a 'useless mouth' would be eliminated permanently. To survive a little bit longer, productivity was key.[48]

Whatever the rumours about ghettos and concentration camps, it was hard for the young dressmakers and their families in Bratislava to take them seriously.

If they need our work, they won't let us die of starvation, thought Renée Ungar, the rabbi's daughter.

There were those who fled to Hungary, those who had money to save themselves for a while. The majority had to wait for their fate. The summons for Marta, Bracha, Irene, Renée and other Slovakian women came in March 1942.

4

The Yellow Star

*From September 1941, I wore the Jewish Star until my deport-
ation* — Herta Fuchs[1]

In the archives of Yad Vashem, there is a particular collection of faces: hundreds of identity cards of Holocaust victims from Slovakia. The faces are memorialised in black and white. Some are studio portraits with a neutral background and flattering lighting. Some are informal snapshots – a street scene, a back-yard, a wall with windows. The photos are cropped into squares, many with pinking shears that have left wavy edges.

Unlike the idealised outfits depicted in contemporary fashion magazines, these ID cards have captured real people in everyday clothes – all ages, all body shapes. For the women, their individuality shows in the clothing details as well as the faces. A neatly buttoned collar, a twisted turban knot, cheerful plaid squares, pretty puffed sleeves. There are polka-dots, two-tone colour blocks, pleats, drapes, bows, cravats and chevrons. Tilt hats, sweaters, cardigans, coats, ornamental hankies in breast pockets. Hair is hidden, pulled back, piled high in a pompadour style, or tamed into pinned curls, rolls, waves and buns.

Half smiles, full beams, pensive looks.

Although each card shows a unique being, the stamp on the corner of every photograph is a reminder that to the fascist Slovak state they are not regular citizens: they are Jews. Unlike other Slovakians, who had regular ID cards, Jews were told their State identification papers were not valid. They were to get new documents from the Jewish main office in Bratislava. The photos are stamped with *Ústredňa Židov Bratislava* and the initials *ÚŽ* – Jewish Centre.

One of the archived ID cards shows a young woman with a fun, slightly toothy smile, bushy hair and a white crochet collar added to her dress. There is a name carefully inked with a fountain pen above the printed phrase, *Vlastnoručný podpis majitei'a* – 'Handwritten signature of the owner'. The name is Irené Reichenberg. Appearances can be deceptive. While the handwriting on the surviving ID card seems to belong to Irene Reichenberg, daughter of Shmuel the shoemaker, the picture certainly is not her, but of another young woman from Bratislava with the same name, who would sadly perish in the Holocaust.[2]

Seamstress Irene Reichenberg of 18 Židovská Street had duly registered as ordered at the Jewish Centre, despite concerns about why the lists were necessary. There were rumours in town about earlier deportations to labour camps, or to the ghetto of Terezín. There was even talk of a place called Auschwitz.

'Nobody really knew what that was, we had no clue,' Irene later said.

People knew enough to be aware of arrests and disappearances, which was why there were many underground movements throughout the Third Reich that were involved in clandestine document falsification in order to obtain 'safe' identities. In fact, Irene's sister Käthe was married to Leo Kohn, a printer who made counterfeit ID cards during the war. Leo intended to avoid all arrests and round-ups by crafting fake IDs for himself, his wife and his brother Gustav. He altered his name slightly from Kohn to Kohút, meaning *rooster* in Slovak, because it was less Jewish. This subterfuge served him well for several years while he worked within an underground cell of

Slovak Jewish communists, alongside a young Jew named Alfred 'Freddie' Wetzler.[3]

Käthe Kohn/Kohút née *Reichenberg*

New names and counterfeit cards were one way to attempt to avoid arrests and deportations. The 'Irené Reichenberg' of the ID card shared a name with Irene the dressmaker, but the similarities in handwriting are a coincidence.[4]

Irene herself was living openly in the Jewish Quarter, along with many other Jewish families forced out of other areas in the city. Not only was Irene's name and address now registered at the Jewish Centre, from September 1941 her Jewishness was made obvious by the compulsory wearing of the yellow Star of David on the left side of the chest. A few people had the courage to wear their star with pride. Others felt it was a humiliation. It was one more way of marking Jews out as different, as 'other'.

In Leipzig, dressmaker Hunya Volkmann thought of her yellow star as a mark of disgrace. She carried her handbag so it covered the star, despite harsh penalties for hiding it. When passing as 'Aryan', she had to remember to keep spare change for the tram handy, so she did not shift the bag to get at her money.

It was not only shame that made Hunya cover up the star. During her long months working at the Rohde fur factory, she was doing informal underground work of her own. While out in town, she charmed shopkeepers into adding to her carefully garnered supplies of forbidden off-ration food. This was then distributed among her friends in the Jewish quarter, including two desperate teenage boys – Jews from Kraków – who had escaped deportations on fake Aryan papers, but who needed to get across the border to safety. Remarkably, the foreman at Rohde's factory not only gave Hunya a huge sum of money so the boys could bribe border guards, he also arranged fake IDs and German uniforms as a disguise.

Hunya's journeys across the city were also to help deliver money, gold, diamonds and documents belonging to her Jewish friends to German allies, who promised to keep these possessions until the war was over and they could be reclaimed. On one terrifying occasion Hunya was stopped by the Gestapo, who followed her home. She just had time to hide incriminating bags of valuables with the building concierge before she was questioned. They asked why she had a few hundred marks on her.

She kept calm as she replied, 'I earned it honestly. I have a job at a workshop making soldiers' uniforms. My salary is good. There's nothing to spend it on.'

Miraculously, her name was not added to any of the transport lists of Jews regularly being deported from Leipzig. This relief was quickly extinguished by the arrival of a telegram. After three and a half years of separation from her husband, during which time he had sent a clandestine letter from a place called Auschwitz-Monowitz, Hunya now had news that her beloved Nathan was dead. Official documents later listed his death as 4 March 1943, in Auschwitz Extermination Camp, a place that would soon be all too familiar to Hunya.[5]

Hunya's next message was from the two Polish boys she had helped to escape. They wrote to say that they had no clothes. She sent them things from Nathan's wardrobe, which she had been keeping safe. He would not need them anymore.

People left their apartments, bought false identification papers for
astronomical sums, but nothing helped – Irene Grünwald[6]

At the end of February 1942, large posters appeared on billboards and street kiosks in Slovakia announcing that unmarried Jewish girls over the age of sixteen were to report at certain assembly points for service in a work camp. In March, Hlinka guards began appearing in homes and apartments to reinforce the demand.

Irene, Marta, Bracha, Renée – all of them were vulnerable.

What was the best option to escape deportation?

Live openly and honestly, trusting that somehow the worst would not happen, even while not yet knowing what the 'worst' could mean – or maybe obtain a precious 'exemption' certificate declaring the bearer to be a Jew of value? Go on the run with false papers, perhaps even crossing borders to find a country untainted by fascist policies? Or give up what was left of a normal life to squeeze into cellars, under floorboards, or behind false walls, relying on the kindness – or cupidity – of those persuaded to offer concealment for an undetermined length of time?

The dressmakers and their families faced this muddle of imperfect choices.

Thousands of Jews went into hiding in Slovakia. Hundreds of thousands in Europe and Russia. Those who hid them faced the difficulties of feeding extra mouths on limited food supplies, as well as avoiding discovery. The penalty for hiding Jews was arrest or death. For some the fear was too great; even when their neighbours begged for support, they could not or would not offer it. In every country there were people eager to get a reward for reporting hidden Jews, or to cream off bribes for keeping quiet. Who could be trusted?

After the first waves of deportation, when news of mass murder was more widespread and credible, desperation made the decision for Jews in fear for their lives and freedom: they hid, and suffered extreme hardships while hidden, because they felt they had no other option.

Aside from Käthe Kohút, who went into hiding with her husband Leo, Irene's older married sisters Jolli and Frieda hoped they would not be chosen for deportation because the initial round-ups were for single women only. Irene herself was at home with her youngest sister Edith, who turned eighteen in 1942. Irene's sister-in-law Turulka – married to her brother Laci; sister to Marta Fuchs – pre-empted any call-ups of married women. She slipped away to Budapest, and later escaped to the Slovakian mountains with partisans, along with Laci. Hungary was a popular destination for Jews attempting to avoid fascist round-ups. At the time it seemed safe.

One of Hunya's sisters – Tauba Fenster – hid with her children in a wooden farm outbuilding for six months during the winter of 1944–45, in the village of Lapšanka Zidar on the Polish/Soviet border. Hunya's little nephew Simcha, aged four, was dressed as a girl, to avoid anyone curious demanding to examine evidence of a Jewish circumcision. The children were told endless stories to keep them quiet.

Many decades after the war, Simcha and his family made a 'roots' visit to Lapšanka, where they met the family of Silon – the man who had helped smuggle the Fensters to the village. Silon's grandchildren were touched to realise the part he had played in saving Jewish lives. Silon himself wrote that there were 'some good people among the many Slovak murderers'.[7]

If so many Jews at risk attempted to hide, why didn't Irene and others take the opportunity when the summons came for their own deportation?

Firstly, it was a question of money: if you had none, you could not pay for food, shelter or bribes. Secondly, the women told to report for deportation genuinely believed they were only being sent to labour camps. The government assured them they would only be away working for a set amount of time. Finally, most importantly, they were told that if they did not report at the required time and place, their parents would be taken instead. Marta's cousin Herta Fuchs was in hiding on a farm when her distraught mother asked her to come home, so the whole family would not be deported in her place.

The threat was too powerful to ignore.

We did not expect a picnic, but what we found was the beginning of sheer horror — Rivka Paskus[8]

Hlinka guards knocked on the door of 18 Židovská Street. Irene and Edith Reichenberg were to report to Patrónka factory by 8 a.m. on Monday 23 March. All around the Jewish quarter in Bratislava there were similar summons, staggered through the week.[9]

What to pack? What to wear?

These were not frivolous considerations. Looking smart meant the women might feel more confident, and even be treated with more respect. There were girls who prepared for the journey by wearing their best clothes and getting their hair freshly set.

This had to be balanced against practicalities.

'Take the most essential things,' Hlinka guards told Irene.

If they were going to work, they most likely needed hard-wearing, sensible gear. They had been advised to take a change of work clothes, strong shoes and warm blankets, to a total of no more than forty kilos. It had been a bad winter with heavy snow, and March was still cold: overcoats were essential.

New fashions for spring coats 1942, from the German fashion/dressmaking magazine Mode und Wäsche

Fashion magazines for spring 1942 show images of carefree, smiling women stepping out with belted waists, flared hems or fabulous 'swag' back pleating. This was entirely jarring with the reality for the Slovakian deportees, who dressed with trepidation, adding woolly caps, scarves and gloves in anticipation of work in bad weather. Some girls layered up with extra clothing as a way of carrying it all.

The luggage limit was enough to fill a backpack or small suitcase. Having suffered so much impoverishment under the fascist regime, there were plenty of girls and women who barely owned spare clothes to pack.

Tucked among the change of underwear and clean stockings were mementoes from home and simple personal effects such as combs, mirrors, soap and sanitary towels. Where money could be spared, the girls carried a purse. Worldly-wise women had hidden notes and coins within their clothes to keep their valuables extra safe. Packets of food for the journey were wrapped in paper and tied with string.

Then came the final hours before leaving home. The last Shabbat with family. The last walk through quiet streets before curfew. The last meal. Last messages, embraces and kisses.[10]

Irene and Edith kept close together, jostled by the crowds of women gathered at Patrónka , an empty munitions factory near Lamač railway station on the outskirts of Bratislava. Renée Ungar, the rabbi's daughter, was also there. Forty women were billeted in each of the narrow factory rooms. The lucky ones had stuffed sacks as mattresses, the rest slept on scattered straw or the bare floor. Toilet facilities were unhygienic and clearly inadequate.

For the first couple of days a charity kitchen in Bratislava was able to provide kosher food. After that, it was a question of eat what you were given and like it. To attempt some kind of order in the chaos, Hlinka guards gave an armband to one woman in each room, to signify she was in charge. It was a small preview of how future camp life would be regulated by orderlies picked from among the prisoners.

Younger women were perhaps physically robust enough to cope with the conditions, but they were still traumatised at being torn away from their homes. Some girls screamed and cried desperately. Hlinka guards beat them as an example to the others to keep silent. The windows, doors and gates were blocked. Escape was not possible.

Among the older women struggling to adapt to the discomfort was Olga Kovácz, in her mid-thirties when deported from Patrónka. Olga would be on the same transport as Marta Fuchs. Olga was a seamstress.[11]

★

Bracha Berkovič could perhaps have risked hiding in plain sight to avoid the transports. Her looks were considered suitably 'Aryan', so she could pass as a Catholic Slovakian rather than a Jew. She was away from home when she heard about the deportations. 'Home' in March 1942 was actually quite far from Bratislava, because her family had been forcibly relocated to a small town near the northern border with Poland, less than a hundred miles south of Auschwitz, as it happened.

The Berkovič family were among over 11,000 Jews evicted from their homes in Bratislava to make room for Aryans. Relocated to Liptovský Svätý Mikuláš they all shared a single room in the attic, with the bathroom several floors down. With no jobs, meagre food and all savings lost, it was a humiliating existence.

March 1942 Berkovič family photograph. Bracha is standing, second from right; Katka is standing first from the left.

In early March, only two weeks before the transports, Bracha's immediate family posed for a group photograph. For all the degradation of the new restrictions imposed on them, their identities as respectable, capable, intelligent people are captured by the camera. Salomon Berkovič's skill as a tailor is abundantly evident in the suits he has created for himself and his two sons. He sits with his wife Karolína, with their youngest boy Moritz between them – a loveable and clever boy and a keen chess player. The Norfolk jacket and tilted hat give Moritz an air of adulthood.

The oldest boy Emil stands just behind Moritz. He would be taken for forced labour. For the rest of his too-short life he would have no need of shirt, tie and tailoring. The youngest Berkovič daughter, Irena, was nicknamed Pimpi. She had been a delicate child, nursed through a near-fatal bout of pneumonia. For all that she was delicate, she had a keen brain and was a keen student. It must have seemed a stroke of luck that she and Moritz were both too young for the first round-ups from Slovakia. Pimpi and Bracha were very close.

Bracha, looking fabulously confident and mature with her up-do, has an affectionate arm around Pimpi. The collar of a polka-dot blouse is a pretty contrast to her suit. On the far left is Katka, the middle sister and talented tailor in her own right, wearing a modest checked dress.

It was the last time the family would be photographed together.

In mid-March, Bracha had decided to take off her yellow star and travel down to Bratislava to visit Irene. When she got back from the city, she found out that her younger sister Katka had already been arrested by Hlinka guards and taken to a holding camp at nearby Tábor Poprad – Poprad Camp. Bracha believed all the promises that it was for a work placement. Why wouldn't she? So many labourers were genuinely required in Germany and the occupied territories.

Unwilling to let Katka face the unknown alone, Bracha

voluntarily went to the local police station and turned herself in. She was promptly escorted to the assembly point in Poprad by a regular policeman.

'Don't run away,' he half-joked. 'Or I'll get into trouble.'

Poprad was full of hundreds of girls and women already. Also passing through Poprad was a nineteen-year-old girl Bracha would meet further along the journey, Alice Strauss. Alice was a dressmaker.[12]

Bracha was late arriving and almost missed the transport out.[13]

It's time for Slovaks to get rich! – Ferdinand Ďurčanský, Slovak Minister for Home and Foreign Affairs, February 1940

It was not enough to roundup young Jews for labour. Hlinka guards at Patrónka holding camp also robbed them. Renée the rabbi's daughter commented that these Slovak Nazis 'were good students of the German teachers'.[14] On arrival the girls and women were relieved of jewellery, watches, pens, money . . . even spectacles. Their suitcases and bags that had been so carefully packed were also confiscated. They formed big piles in the yard at Patrónka. Some women were made to sign a document relinquishing all rights to their property and promising they would never make claims for restitution.[15]

Rivka Paskus, who would eventually end up living alongside the Auschwitz dressmakers, had the wits to use her watch as a bribe so that she could send a message warning her brother to 'sacrifice everything and escape'.[16] Michal Kabáč, one of the Hlinka guards, later confessed – apparently without remorse – that the guards were allowed to choose whatever clothes they wanted from the women's luggage. He took a pair of shoes, wrapped them and sent them home.

Inevitably the men used their power over the women as

leverage for sexual barter. Some of the Hlinka had been at school with the girls they were now guarding and abusing.[17]

These bribes and confiscations were small-scale compared to State initiatives to profit from Slovakian Jews. Having made Jewish people impoverished outcasts, they now blamed Jews for being parasites. The Slovak government generated a win-win scenario for themselves: they could fulfil German demands for labour at the same time as dispossessing Jews further. So when the Germans demanded 120,000 Slovakian labourers in February 1942, President Josef Tiso countered with an offer of 20,000 Jews. The offer was accepted – hence the round-ups.

SS officer Dieter Wisliceny was the broker for deals regarding Jewish deportation and dispossession. By March 1942, Wisliceny had been made aware of the ultimate plans for European Jews, as finessed at the infamous conference in Wannsee villa that January. His boss, Adolf Eichmann, had met with Wisliceny in Bratislava and revealed the Führer's verbal order – and Himmler's written order – for a Jewish *Endlosung*: final solution. Wisliceny was very impressed by a red-bordered document signed by Himmler himself, 'which gave him as much power to use as he saw fit.' He arranged that the 20,000 Jews would be divided, with half sent to Majdanek concentration camp, and half to another place, designated Camp A.[18]

The Wannsee conference meeting minutes detail estimates of Jewish populations in each country occupied by the Germans, or coveted by them, including 88,000 Jews in Slovakia. It was stated in the minutes that there was no question of the Slovak government refusing to cooperate with implementation of the new stage of *Endlosung* – the deportations.[19] President Tiso, Prime Minister Tuka and their collaborators were happy to oblige. So much so, they agreed to pay the Germans 500 Reichsmarks for each Jew deported. The sum was ostensibly to pay towards Jewish 'vocational training.'[20] A fortune in Reichsmarks was handed over, all collected from Jewish assets. And here was the crux: if Jews were sent elsewhere, their homes and goods would be abandoned, and ripe for redistribution.

Once the first wave of single workers were deported, including the first few thousand girls and women, Tiso said it was degrading for the remaining families to be dependent on State support, so they would follow next. Before they went, these deportees had to complete a *vermögenserklärung* – a declaration of possessions. Essentially, they had to list everything they owned, no matter how humble. It was the same pattern across German territories. There were even instructions on how to label house keys and where to leave them on quitting home for the last time. Jewish assets became national property.

Neither Irene, Bracha, nor the other women being held in Patrónka and Poprad had any idea that their families would be betrayed so callously; that everything and everyone they had left at home would be organised so completely for disposal. Within just over four months, the Slovakian government would deport 53,000 Jews.[21] The young dressmakers were among the first to go.

Tactics of deportation and dispossession were finessed by the Nazis and their allies, always hidden behind euphemistic language, such as 'administered', 'handled', 'remitted' or 'confiscated'; never looted, plundered or stolen. While Jewish goods were piling up in multiple warehouses, halls and even churches in Prague and Bratislava, there were similar collections building in every country tainted by Nazi greed. It was no haphazard undertaking. Hitler authorised a special taskforce led by

Alfred Rosenberg called ERR – *Einsatzstab Reichsleiter Rosenberg.*

In addition to acquiring as much art and gold from occupied territories as possible, ERR's purpose was to strip abandoned Jewish households, redistribute the property and make a fat profit.[22] There was even pressure on the German Security Service to deport Jews more quickly, so more goods could be seized. In some cases, neighbours did not wait for homes to be vacated before they appeared with carts to start their own unauthorised appropriation of whatever took their fancy. Of course, the authorities frowned on this. They wanted all the good stuff for themselves.

ERR plunder in France was sorted by interns from nearby concentration camps, dressed in white overalls or aprons. The work was well documented in posed photographs, discovered after the war. Women in particular were tasked with making bundles of textiles. Nazi officials selected the best quality fabrics, comforters, linens and carpets for themselves, although Hitler and Goering had first choice of the art. It was Hitler's plan to fill a new museum in Linz with the greatest European treasures. Goering simply coveted luxury goods for himself and his family. His residences were crammed with Jewish acquisitions. His wife Emma chose not to enquire about their provenance.

At his post-war trial, Goering told the Nuremberg court, 'I deny most emphatically that my actions were dictated by the desire to subjugate foreign peoples by wars, to murder them, to rob them, or to enslave them.'[23] The evidence to the contrary is overwhelming. Alfred Rosenberg had Hitler's personal approval for redistributing Jewish belongings among party members and Wehrmacht staff.[24] And it was not only Nazi bigwigs who benefited from the robbery.

Warehouses of looted goods were laid out almost like shops, without the price tags. In fact one of the big plunder warehouses in Paris was nicknamed 'Galeries Lafayette' after the famous department store. Shoppers could stroll the aisles admiring neat displays of dismantled lives.

Furniture featured in the popular French shopping catalogue
Bon Marché *winter 1939/40, reminiscent of room sets of*
plundered goods set out for appropriation by new owners.

Here, groupings of bedroom furniture or dining room sets; there, a vast selection of dinner services, and prams, and toys, and pianos stacked on their sides to save space. Along racks of shelving could be found every type of silverware, glass goods, jewellery and ornaments. There were sewing machines, sewing boxes, haberdashery and darning kits. For those with literary tastes, empty bookcases . . . and a choice of books to fill them.[25]

Other repositories resembled glorified thrift shops and jumble sales. Here everyday objects such as egg cups, cricket bats and lampshades were collected. Of no particular financial value, they were termed *ramschlager* or 'junk' items. Oddments of daily life; things found in bedside cabinets, at the back of drawers or from attic corners. They had not been junk to their rightful owners. Parisian dressmaker Marilou Colombain noted how 'shocked and demoralised' the French were when the looting began.[26]

More than the financial and cultural losses, it was the reduction of safe home lives into a series of impersonal objects that most demonstrated the thorough elimination of Jewish existences. Plundered goods were worth more than the people who had first bought, made or cherished them.

The looted items were certainly packed to travel with greater care than their Jewish owners would be when their turn came to take the train.

Every week hundreds of loot trains left hubs in occupied lands for Germany. Within the freight cars were crated goods nestling in straw, all labelled most efficiently: Lace Curtains, Lined Curtains, Pillows, Sheets . . .'[27] ERR liaised with Goering, who was in overall charge of the Reich railway traffic, to enable train after train to take loot from France, Holland, Belgium, Norway, the Protectorate, Polish lands and more, back to the heart of the Reich.

Non-Jewish civilians were only too happy to receive 'new' furniture, furnishings, textiles and clothes. Some items were auctioned off with no attempt to conceal their provenance. Auction houses in Europe's major cities worked in close collaboration with ERR officials, and made enormous profits selling off plunder. Those with aspirations for antique furniture, imported rugs and fancy candelabras could go and bid to their hearts' content. Jewish belongings quickly found new homes. Their sheets went on new mattresses, their lingerie graced new bodies, their coffee pots poured brews for new owners to savour.

In Leipzig, Hunya would have seen bill posters and newspaper adverts informing citizens of the auctioning of Jewish assets. Even the furniture of Jewish hospitals, schools and orphanages was taken and sold to other municipal bidders.[28]

The German Red Cross, a de facto Nazi organisation separated from the International Red Cross, welcomed all donations. In fact, the German Red Cross helped co-ordinate the distribution of staggering amounts of plunder, for the benefit of Aryans only. A housewife bombed out of her home could start over with welfare gifts of curtains, tablecloths, bedding, towels, shoes, clothes, cutlery and crockery. The German Wehrmacht also benefited, receiving watches and warm clothing.

What did it matter to them that a new wardrobe or shirt or plates had travelled all the way from Prague, or anywhere else in the Reich? There were mutterings among Germans that the war had better be won, or else the Jews would be back, wanting their things.[29]

The first Jewish deportees from Slovakia were told they would be back home soon enough. As girls and women were brought in from towns and villages in west Slovakia to Patrónka holding camp, the overcrowding grew severe and for many of them it was almost a relief to be told to muster for a transfer. Irene Reichenberg was not so confident when she looked down from a dormitory window to the courtyard below. Their guards had a bonfire burning and were throwing documents into the flames: identity cards. Her own ID photograph and signature with the Jewish Centre stamp would be blackening to ash with the rest.

Irene knew then that the journey ahead of them was not a return trip. They were not expected back again.

The Jews are now being deported to the east. A fairly barbaric procedure – Joseph Goebbels diary entry, 27 March 1942[30]

Train lines across German territories were busy day and night during the war. Combatants went out to join battle lines; injured men returned. Plundered goods travelled to new homes; their former owners left home for the last time.

1941 atlas page showing German expansion into the
former Czechoslovakia. At the bottom of the map,
Bratislava is renamed Pressburg.

Every deportation of people to concentration camps and extermination centres was precisely timetabled, down to the minute.
All stations along the route had copies of these timetables.
Long, long trains of freight wagons were a familiar sight.
Sometimes there were cries for help or water from behind the
wooden slats. Sometimes hands appeared at the single ventilation hole criss-crossed with barbed wire. Sometimes notes were
thrown from the train; sometimes corpses.

For Jews and other enemies of the Nazi regime, all train
routes converged on ominous destinations.

The Jewish women and girls at Patrónka holding camp still assumed – hoped – they would be working in Slovakia somewhere. There was talk of a labour camp supporting the famous Bat'a shoe manufacturers: T&A Bat'a company, owned by entrepreneur Jan Antonín Bat'a.[31] Irene Reichenberg's father was a shoemaker; she would surely be able to take to cobbling with time and training. Darker rumours suggested they could be heading for the Eastern Front to 'raise morale' for German troops. That did not bear thinking about.

Irene and her sister Edith stayed together during the mustering at Patrónka. They were ordered into rows and marched to nearby Lamač station, surrounded by grassy fields. The train that waited on the rails was built for transporting cattle, a not so subtle indicator that they had been demoted to the status of beasts, albeit beasts still in their best clothes and carrying a few rucksacks and handbags. Forty women and girls were loaded into each cattle car. Two buckets were in place. No food or drink. The doors slid shut and were locked. Hlinka guards and Slovak police were their escorts to the border. As the locomotive set off, couplings went taut, and the cars jerked into motion and followed along.

Irene and Edith were on the second transport of Jewish women from Patrónka, two of 798 women heading for the same destination, though not all towards the same fate. Many of them were Irene's classmates from school.[32] They did not know where they were going; nobody told them anything. Postcards were shared out. In the half-light the young women wrote messages to their loved ones, throwing them out into the snow in the hope that railway workers would find them and put them in the post.[33]

Travelling on the same train, with the same fear and discomfort, were dressmakers Marta Fuchs and Olga Kovácz.

Glimpses out of the tiny window hole showed a landscape

of cold fields, wooden houses and snow-capped hills. Irene guessed they were heading north. The train went through the town of Liptovský Svätý Mikuláš, where Bracha's family lived in their attic apartment, then through Žilina, where there was a brief stop, and on to the town of Zwardoń, about forty minutes from the Polish border. Here, in darkness, the guards changed: Hlinka for SS. The Slovaks now relinquished all responsibility and travelled back home, ready to load the next transport.

During this journey of roughly 250 miles, the travellers figured out what the two buckets were for: there were no toilets.

From Zwardoń the train continued another fifty miles into occupied Poland.

Bracha's route north began in Poprad. With her sister Katka she travelled on the fourth train of Jewish women to leave Slovakia, 997 of them in total, departing 2 April 1942. Some of the cattle cars from Poprad had chalk hidden inside, so the passengers could write their destination, once it was known, to help spread information back to Slovakia. Also on Poprad transports were dressmakers Borishka Zobel and Alice Strauss. Borishka was a highly skilled pattern cutter. One of Alice's travelling companions was a girl from Poland, who was able to spy out their route. She said it seemed they were going to Auschwitz. Her assessment was correct.[34]

The trains kept arriving. The lives of the dressmakers of Auschwitz gradually converged.

By the time French seamstresses Alida Vasselin and Marilou Colombain were deported from France in January 1943, Auschwitz was more than a rumour. Alida, the corset specialist, had endured long months in various prisons, and interrogations by the Gestapo. She consistently denied any involvement with the resistance, even after the shock of her husband Robert's execution. Marilou, a Parisian partisan fighter, had been in prison since her arrest on 16 December 1942.

On 23 January, both women joined other French political prisoners – all female – for a transport from France to Auschwitz. Unlike RSHA transports organised by Adolf Eichmann's department, these women were not arrested for being Jewish. Of the 230 women, 119 were communists or left-wing affiliates, and so considered a political threat to Nazi right-wing ideology. Their incarceration and deportation came under the aegis of a policy known as *Nacht und Nebel* – night and fog: they were meant to disappear into nebulous obscurity, shunted from one prison to another.

The women of this winter convoy endured a hideous journey of several days in bitter cold. Those Frenchwomen who had received packages while in prison dressed as warmly as possible, in some cases wearing everything they owned at that time.

Alida was still mourning her husband's death. Marilou grieved for her young son, not long dead of diphtheria. She did not know the fate of her husband Henri, who had also been arrested. Camaraderie was all that kept the French women going until their arrival at Auschwitz on 26 January. Their train stayed on a siding overnight. In the morning, the cattle cars were lined up along the wooden platform of the freight station and the doors were unlocked.[35]

Hunya Volkmann, one of the feistiest of the future group of dressmakers, arrived at Auschwitz on a baking hot day in June 1943. Hers was the very last train of Jews to leave Leipzig. The police came for her in the ghetto at 5 a.m. on 15 June 1943. She'd had the chance to evade arrest. A hiding place had been on offer for the sum of 1,000 marks, and Aryan friends had said they would shelter her for free. Ground down by years of tension, she decided to go with the others. She did not want to be the only Jew left alive in Leipzig.[36]

Unlike the violence and tumult of earlier round-ups in Leipzig, where long lines of adults and children were bullied onto the trains, by the time it came to the last round-up, Jews were calm, almost resigned. The ghetto was emptied and rooms waited for new tenants. A few lost objects were left as rubbish in the street.

Hunya joined others at Leipzig jail on Wächterstrasse, the gathering point. The last transport included staff from the Jewish hospital and other employees of the Jewish community. Their previous homes in the ghetto seemed luxurious compared to the dirty floor they now had to crouch on – barely room to stretch out or sleep. Hunya recognised many faces in the crowd. Friends gathered together, talking and even joking to pass the time. She felt confident she could summon the resilience to face anything. Her strength was contagious, and it would be needed.

After two days of discomfort and dread, they were harried from the jail to the main Leipzig railway station where their train waited. Hunya could not help thinking back to when she had first arrived at the city, as a young girl from Kežmarok, fresh and ambitious, ready to learn her trade. Now the station was filled with the drab colours of uniforms, not a variety of peacetime clothes.

She found a space in the cattle car with a friend, dentist Ruth Ringer, and Ruth's husband Hans, who had been a doctor at the hospital. For a moment she was reminded of a ghost train at a funfair, which took its passengers through shocks and surprises. But this was no amusement park ride.[37]

The miles passed. It was all rather civilised at first, despite suffocating heat during the day. Hunya was luckier than most: shortly after her arrest, an apprentice from the fur factory where she had worked delivered a basket of food, courtesy of her former factory manager. The unlooked-for kindness was as welcome as the provisions. She shared them around and attempted to rally her companions. There would be enough sorrow at the end of the line; they could at least be cheerful for a few hours. Her good nature diluted some of the bitterness. They almost forgot where they were and where they were going.

At one stop, a convoy of disabled and elderly people from a care home was added to the train. Their helpers felt powerless when their patients suffered severe maladies and disturbed episodes. Two men had to wrestle with one nurse when she attempted suicide in despair. The sick grew worse; the dead were bundled out and the toilet buckets emptied whenever the train stopped.

The train slowed one final time. A lamp illuminated a huge sign: Auschwitz. Now there were no jokes, no genteel conversations, only dread. The latest transport had arrived, and of the hundreds of Jews on board, only two would survive to liberation.

Just before men were separated from women, Dr Ringer turned to his wife Ruth and said, 'Stick together with Hunya. I have a feeling she'll make it.'[38]

Irene, Bracha, Katka, Marta, Alice, Olga, Alida, Marilou, Borishka, Hunya . . .

Whichever train they travelled on, new arrivals at Auschwitz all faced the sickening moment when the doors opened and the screaming began: *Los, los! Heraus und einreihen!* – 'Move it! Get out and form lines!'

5

The Customary Reception

The customary reception was waiting for us: lots of screaming and beatings
          – Hunya Volkmann[1]

Bracha Berkovič before deportation. Well-dressed, glossy hair, bright smile for the camera.

Bracha Berkovič was worried about her luggage. She had a suitcase in the cattle car, safeguarded all the way from Poprad, but they were shouting at her – *Raus! Raus!* – to jump down from the car. She could not reach her case and there were people everywhere, angry dogs on leashes, men in SS uniforms, and her sister Katka to watch.

'Don't worry,' called an SS guard. 'We'll bring everything after you.'

How would they sort everything out properly? she wondered.

It was a long jump down from the train to a wooden platform roughly 500 metres long. A wooden staircase connected the 'ramp', as the platform was called, to the road. Transports for the concentration camp were brought to this side line.[2] Not far from the ramp were railway houses built for staff working on the busy main line through Auschwitz that connected Vienna in Austria with Kraków in Poland.

Fourteen-year-old Bogusława Głowacka lived in one of these houses. She worked as a maid for one of the SS men, and would sometimes meet prisoners from the tailor's and cobbler's shops when running errands in the main camp at Auschwitz. Bogusława said it was impossible not to see the trains being unloaded: 'The moment the train stopped, an incredible uproar broke out, with the screams of the SS men, the sobbing and howling of the people being unloaded, the barking of dogs and the sounds of gunshots.'[3]

For a few moments the new arrivals stood in free air, as civilians. Normal people. Looking around, they noticed men wearing striped suits working in the fields. 'We thought they were mentally deranged,' said one of the new girls, assuming the shaved heads and uniforms meant they were patients from a mental institution.[4]

Bracha kept her chin up, even though all she had left in her possession now were the clothes she stood up in, and some vitamins in her pocket – a precious parting gift from her mother. Then began the march, every step taking them further away from normal. They soon turned south within a perimeter of wire fences and guard towers, then along a road lined with brick and wooden buildings.

Later transports, which included families and elderly people,

were greeted by the reassuring sight of big trucks with the sign
of the Red Cross. 'Where there is the Red Cross it can't be so
bad,' thought one Slovakian girl arriving in July 1942.[5] She did
not know then that Oswald Pohl, the head of concentration
camp administration, was also chairman of the German Red
Cross board of administration. This created a hideous collaboration. The trucks that inspired arrivals with confidence were,
in fact, to drive people straight to the gas chambers: by July
measures were in place to murder new arrivals considered
surplus to labour requirements. From July onwards, Jewish
transports to Auschwitz were sorted on the platform, for life
or death.

In March and April 1942, when the Slovakian transports
first arrived, there were no selections for the gas. The women
had come to work. They were marched past quarries, kilns and
brick dumps towards the gate of the *Stammlager*, or main camp,
also known as Auschwitz I. The gate, forged by inmate-black-
smith Jan Liwaz, had originally been the entrance to Auschwitz,
but the camp complex had long since outgrown this initial
security perimeter. Seamstress Alice Strauss looked up at the
sign as she passed beneath it. Arching over the gate was the
wrought metal declaration *Arbeit Macht Frei* – Work Sets You
Free. [6]

Bracha's transport from Poprad came too late in the day on
3 April to undergo immediate processing. Instead the women
were marched through the camp to a line of red-brick barrack
blocks. These buildings had originally been constructed for
industrial workers, to be near the town's railway hub, then they
were used by the Polish army. From 1940, under the aegis of
newly arrived commandant Rudolf Höss, a second storey and
attic had been added to each block. Now they could hold
hundreds more prisoners. Ten of the thirty blocks had been
designated for women of the first ever Jewish transports to

arrive at Auschwitz. Bracha, Katka and the others were hustled into one of them.

Along one face of these ten blocks was a high concrete barrier – only just built – dividing the women from the men's area of the camp. On the other side, a brick wall divided the women from the outside world. Beyond this wall was the commandant's comfortable house, on Legiónow Street. The house had been built in 1937, shortly before the war, by a Polish soldier named Sergeant Soja, who was evicted with very limited notice on 8 July 1940, under the watchful eye of armed SS. The whole neighbourhood was to be cleared for the German occupiers.

Hedwig Höss made a home for herself and her growing family in the Soja house. A Höss villa guest-book was begun in 1942. Visitors could uncap a fountain pen and write their messages of appreciation for Rudolf and Hedwig's hospitality.

There was no gracious hostess and no kind welcome for new arrivals in the camp prison blocks. Instead the Slovakian women found themselves under orders from other prisoners called *kapos* – bosses, or squad leaders. These were mainly German women – non-Jews – incarcerated as criminals or 'enemies of the state' and transferred from Ravensbrück concentration camp shortly before the first Slovakian transport arrived. They had experience of how to survive in the camp system and knew that being a prison functionary was one way to gain advantages. For many concentration camp prisoners, and for people in post-war society, the word *kapo* became synonymous with cruelty and violence. Survivor testimonies make clear that kapos who were degraded by temperament and/or intolerable circumstances did indeed become perpetrators as well as victims. Even so, not everyone forced into the role of kapo abused the position. When she was eventually chosen as kapo of the Upper Tailoring Studio, Marta Fuchs would be one of those who used her privileged prison status to secure relative safety and dignity for the women of this work squad.

On arrival at Auschwitz Marta was just one more bewildered inmate, hustled into a hostile environment.

Bracha and her sister found themselves in an empty building with straw on the floor. Somehow a message got passed around: hide your things or they will be taken from you. Bracha and Katka joined a chain of girls passing belongings up to the eaves of the barrack, including combs, soap and handkerchiefs. Incredibly, Bracha realised she was next to an SS woman in the chain. SS guards had been sent from Ravensbrück at the same time as the first female prisoners. Now Bracha found herself bargaining, 'If you help me, I'll let you have some of my vitamins.'

It was a surreal moment, but Bracha found everything about the experience bizarre. She saw one of the Slovakian women had somehow brought a tin of sardines into the block with her. Immediately a kapo seized the tin and began to wolf down the contents. Bracha watched, astonished. She could not understand how anyone could get so excited about a tin of fish. She would learn.

That first night there was somewhere to wash, and working toilets, but the washroom was filthy and the toilets quickly proved inadequate for such a large group. There was even a dole of food – a thick porridge called *kasha*. Bracha could not manage to finish all hers, so she put the bowl of leftovers on a windowsill. It was stolen. Again, she was amazed at such behaviour.

In the morning, after a drink of murky warm water, Bracha looked out of the window at the next block along. A figure in a Russian army uniform was waving at her, making strange gestures about the head as if mentally deranged. Was there something familiar about the face? Bracha was once again hit by disbelief. It was her best friend Irene Reichenberg.

Irene's transport from Bratislava had arrived a few days before, on 28 March. Now she tried to explain to Bracha what had given her such a strange appearance. She mimed a pair of scissors on her scalp: *Your hair will be cut . . .*[7]

Keep quiet and don't lose your sense of humour! – Edita Maliarová,
to friends from Bratislava undergoing the camp induction[8]

Bracha Berkovič was one of over 6,000 Jewish women and girls brought from Slovakia in nine transports between 26 March and 29 April 1942. They were the first specifically Jewish transports organised by Adolf Eichmann's RHSA department (*Reichssicherheitshauptamt* or Main Security Office) to arrive at Auschwitz. Along with the one thousand prisoners transferred from Ravensbrück, they were the first female inmates. They had been selected to work, and their initial processing at Auschwitz was calculated to render labourers compliant. It was also a deliberate process of humiliation, both physically and emotionally brutal.

Survivors were asked, post-war, *Why didn't you resist?* Those who endured the procedure and lived could only say they could barely believe what was happening. As one of Bracha's companions later explained, 'The enemy had guns and we were stripped naked and everything went so fast.'[9] What could the young women from Slovakia do, when led to a washroom and commanded to undress?

The immediate response was confusion. Kapos and SS were on hand to emphasise the order with shouts and punches – *Faster! Faster!* Jewellery was to be removed too. Bracha's sister Katka could not get one of her earrings out quickly enough, and an SS guard slapped her so hard, the earring broke. On future transports, impatient SS would actually saw through rings that got stuck on trembling fingers, leaving hands torn and bleeding.[10]

And so the layers came off, removing evidence of life before the camp and taking away obvious markers of individuality.

Winter coats, an important investment and carefully treasured, now unbelted and set aside. Sweaters and cardigans, often home-made, with patches of wool fluff where the arms rubbed against the body, peeled off. Then, more hesitantly, the front buttons of blouses, and neat side zips of dresses and skirts, all creased from the journey, possibly marked with sweat.[11] Shoes and boots – off, placed together out of habit, their insoles gently curved to fit the owner's feet, the heels scuffed from all the steps their owners had walked. Socks rolled off, perhaps new, perhaps darned. Stockings unclipped from girdles and garter belts. Legs bare. Feet cold on concrete.

All the while eyes darting to other women for validation that this was truly happening; that they were really being forced to strip in public.

The ritual of undressing is usually reserved for the privacy of a bedroom or a doctor's surgery, perhaps in a swimming pool cubicle, or shop changing room behind a curtain. Unmarried women and girls on the transports to Auschwitz would have almost no experience of undressing completely under the gaze of others, unless, perhaps, with a sister who shared a bedroom. The undressing process in Auschwitz not only stripped identity as clothes came off, it also stripped away dignity.

In mid-twentieth-century Europe, there was a very definite 'language' of clothes for public and private. There was streetwear such as suits, smart frocks, coats, handbags, hats and school uniform; then in the house there could be a little more informality – soft slippers, knitwear, aprons and housecoats. Underwear was definitely reserved for the most private, most intimate space of the bedroom, not a cold hall in a concentration camp.

Although all new arrivals undergoing processing felt the humiliation of being stripped, for women and girls there were added layers of shame. Modesty was still a core female value in society, for all that there were icons who flaunted sex appeal and women who dressed defiantly. 'Nice' girls were decently turned out, with no thigh-high hems or plunging necklines, and shoulders were only bare in high summer. There was a complex series of subtle social rules to follow, ensuring clothes were attractive but not too alluring. For Orthodox Jewish women, sleeves covered the arm to the elbow or wrist, and there were no bare collarbones or knees.

Clothing was always under scrutiny. Peer pressure informed choices as to whether an outfit was dowdy or fashionable. Older women criticised clothes that were considered provocative rather than pretty; men decided whether a woman looked available or off-limits. In real world scenarios, women and girls were quickly censured for not dressing appropriately. In Auschwitz, they were screamed at for not stripping quickly enough.

All too soon, the last layer. The underwear.

Unhooking bras and tentatively sliding slip ribbons off shoulders in front of men would ordinarily be judged a striptease: seductive and most certainly not modest. The undressing in Auschwitz was a perverse distortion of either seduction or modesty. There was no choice; no agency. Bras had to come off. Under orders, girdles were unpeeled.

For teenagers still uncomfortable with their post-puberty bodies, it was excruciating to reveal their curves, or perceived lack of them. The unmarried young women may have felt just as ambiguous about sexuality. The naked body was an aspect of intimacy only to be shared with a husband, and even then there could be the defence of bed sheets and nightgowns. For older women, peeling off foundation garments had the added issue of exposing bodies changed by years of childbearing, hard work or indulgence.

The final garment – the final illusion of protection – was the hardest to remove. Pants. These could be 'Directoire' drawers, gathered above the knee with firm elastic; camiknickers fastened at the gusset with three tiny buttons, or French knickers with lace edging and floral embroidery. White, pink, blue, yellow; old, new, pretty, practical, pristine, darned – all had to come off and be folded with the rest of the clothes, still warm from the body, the last vestiges of a life now being set aside.

Some women held this last garment, their knickers, in front of their genitals, a desperate gesture of decency. They'd had it drummed into them that how you dressed affected how men treated you; that modest clothing was a protection from catcalls and groping in public to the secret, unspoken horrors of sexual abuse and rape.[12]

As the women on one of the Poprad transports huddled together naked, an SS man snickered, 'Oh boy, they must be coming from a nunnery. All of them are virgins!'[13]

How did he know? Because the women were manually raped as guards searched internally for hidden valuables.

This then was the context of undressing for newly arrived women and girls, as SS guards swore at them, calling them whores and pigs. There was an additional humiliation: public menstruation. Sanitary pads and napkins of the 1940s were either worn pinned inside the knickers, or looped onto an elasticated waistbelt. Either way, it was utterly taboo to show such things to anyone, let alone a crowd of people. To have to remove the used pads and bleed freely, all the while being abused for your lack of hygiene, was a torment that all menstruating females would have to endure, until stress and starvation

– and alleged use of powders in their food – stopped their menses entirely. On the day of the induction, menstrual blood flowed down bare legs, along with bleeding from brutal internal searches.

All the while SS men and SS women watched. With hatred. With indifference. With malicious pleasure. SS doctors assessed the naked women like cattle at a market – were they strong, were they healthy, could they work? The women drew together, finding comfort in friends and sisters, even though each nude figure was a mirror for the other. There was defiance, in spite of the trauma; a resilience that would counter the shock; a compassion that would reach out to despairing women contemplating a wild run to the electric fence.

One 21-year-old from the Carpathian Mountains chose her own response to the SS onlookers, stating, 'I decided not to feel ashamed, humiliated, degraded, defeminised and dehumanised. I simply looked through them.'[14]

In the space of a few minutes I had been stripped of every vestige of human dignity and become indistinguishable from everyone around me   – Anita Lasker-Wallfisch[15]

When Bracha was sixteen, she decided to have her two long braids of hair cut off. She was pleased with the new look; others lamented the loss. It was a visible transition from girlhood to more mature styles of young womanhood.

Hair was considered one of the definitive signifiers of 'femininity'. While men's hair was cropped, clippered and subdued with oils, women's hair was to be more abundant. Home hair styles could be achieved with plaits, pins, clips and heated tongs – taking care not to singe the hair as it was waved or curled. Hair salons created even more sophisticated effects, using extraordinary electric perming machines that looked like a

rubber Medusa. Fashionable hairdos wer...
stars and accessorised with ribbons, fancy sli...

German women, in mock-honour of air raids,
that became known as the 'All Clear'. Hair dyes were a...
if unsubtle, way to cover grey, or to transform 'Jewish'
hair into 'Aryan' blonde. This was a common if desperate
strategy for Jews hoping to avoid round-ups.

False hair was worn for fun. Shops sold ringlets sewn onto
bands, or curls sprouting out of hair pins. False hair could also
be a core element of Orthodox Jewish women's appearance,
due to the tradition of married women shaving their heads
smooth and replacing their own hair with wigs, known as a
sheitl. In some Jewish religious narratives, female hair was
viewed as a powerful lure to men, hence the need for married
women to avoid tempting any man except their husband by
covering the head with a scarf or turban, or by removing the
hair altogether. Full-head hairpieces could be shop-bought, or
made from the woman's own pre-marriage hair, or even her
daughter's cut-off plaits.

On arrival at Auschwitz, natural or false, light or dark, curly
or straight, styled or plain, all the hair was cut off.

From her block window Irene had mimed to Bracha that
this would happen, snipping her fingers like scissors. The blades
and clippers used were quickly dull. Inmate-barbers – all men
– seized handfuls of hair from the naked women and chopped,
leaving random tufts sprouting from the scalp. When Irene had
first arrived in Auschwitz and spotted girls from the first transport already shorn, she had wondered, 'God in Heaven, what
kind of crime did they commit, how do they look, what have
they done with them?'[16]

Worse followed. 'Spread your legs!' shouted the guards. Many
of the women wept silently as their pubic hair was hacked off.
It was an utter violation. They had been stripped of identity,

dignity and modesty. A survivor of this ordeal attempted to draw the scene. Her crude sketch shows hairless nudes with lines of bewildered speech – *Is that you? You have a pretty figure! Where are you?*[17]

Sisters and friends walked past each other without recognition, such was the power of hair to give identity. Some women burst out laughing, they looked so comic. They joked how now they looked like their brothers. Others found comfort that they were all suffering together. A few stood grasping locks of their own ruined hair, as if holding onto a last piece of humanity.

When Bracha cut off her two braids aged sixteen, she was paid for the hair. It was a commodity; it fetched a price. When women were forcibly shaved in concentration camps and extermination centres it was primarily for hygiene purposes – to avoid lice – but the hair did not go to waste.

As early as 1940 Richard Glücks, one of Himmler's subordinates, gave the order that concentration camp hair was to be utilised, separated into male and female hair.[18] The shorter staple of men's hair could be felted or spun into yarn. Longer tresses from women was spun and knitted into socks for submarine crews and stockings for German railway workers, felted into bootees or matted to render torpedo warheads watertight.

The hair was washed then hung on lines in lofts above the camp crematoria. Heat from the corpse-burning ovens dried the hair, tended by teams of 'hair combers': a terrible conjunction of activities.[19] Wool carding companies paid 50 pfennigs a kilo for the hair, which was graded in the camps and stuffed into sacks ready for shipment. Hair was a good earner for the Auschwitz administration; accounts of deliveries were drawn up on the fifth day of every month.[20]

The German textile industry had long been competitive in the field of textile innovation. During the war years they oversaw processing of French hair, which was blended to become a fabric used to make slippers, gloves and handbags.[21] In the space of eleven months administrators at the extermination camps Treblinka, Sobibór and Bełzec contributed twenty-five truckloads of female hair to Berlin.

It was not the worst form of human recycling. In 1946 Czech doctor Franz Blaha, an inmate at Dachau, testified on oath about the loathsome practice of tanning human skin to be used as leather in riding breeches, gloves, slippers and bags.[22] Himmler's mistress Hedwig Potthast was said to have a copy of Hitler's book *Mein Kampf* bound with human skin.[23]

This was the mentality moulding the universe Irene and Bracha had entered.

Everything was so unreal that I could not comprehend it . . . No one gave us any explanations as to what was happening and what was about to happen — Bracha Berkovič

Time to wash.

In their hundreds, the naked women dunked themselves into a square bath about a metre and a half deep. No soap. No towels. Irene found it a horrible experience. Bracha was entirely bewildered. The camp version of talcum powder was a dusting of DDT for *Entlausung* – delousing.

By the time Hunya Volkmann reached Auschwitz from Leipzig in 1943, the bath had been replaced with showers. Hunya found herself in a dirty washroom, termed 'Sauna', newly built in Auschwitz II: Birkenau. While naked the new prisoners had been divided into two groups, one of older women or those with obvious health issues, the other for younger, fitter women. Hunya implicitly understood the significance of the division. The two groups separated – one for life, one for death. Although she had folded her clothes as ordered, in defiance of orders Hunya kept her boots on her feet for the shower, thinking to guard them from theft. She stood under a shower head and waited for water.

None came out.

The gas chambers of Nazi extermination camps, disguised as shower rooms, are now known as perhaps the most notorious element of industrial mass murder. However, the evolution from mobile killing squads shooting victims individually to these modern systems of destruction took time. The process had very sinister, significant links with clothes and undressing.

Having decided that shooting civilians on the edges of trenches and pits was an inefficient use of bullets and manpower, the Nazis turned their focus to more streamlined methods of murder that would be less traumatic for the murderers. Initial experiments began with so-called euthanasia injections, followed by gas-van poisonings, using deadly exhaust fumes to kill people trapped inside the sealed trucks. Neither system could handle the logistics of genocide. A breakthrough came in Auschwitz itself, and it was partly down to garment processing.

The problem was lice, or more specifically the deadly disease they carry – typhus. Lice thrive in warm, dirty, crowded conditions. The women arriving in Auschwitz in March and April 1942 found their barracks were alive with lice and bedbugs, which had feasted on the blood of previous inmates. One reason for the primitive head and body shaving on arrival was to try to control lice breeding grounds. Lice seek out creases of skin, or folds in clothes. They proliferate under collars, deep in pockets, within seams and hems. They were so dangerous to health that some members of the Auschwitz underground attempted to use typhus-infected lice as murder weapons against the SS, placing them under collars of shirts and jackets.[24]

Camp commandant Rudolf Höss was rightly concerned about the danger of a typhus epidemic. It was a ludicrous situation: camp conditions were filthy and dangerous both because there was not the infrastructure to provide hygienic facilities and also because the prisoners were considered comparable to vermin themselves – and so unworthy of decent living arrangements. Yet the SS did not want to be contaminated by the very conditions they thought fitting for inmates.

While Hedwig Höss and other SS families living outside the camp could enjoy ablutions in hot water with soap, with their clothes and linens laundered by servants from the nearby town, the women of the transports had no such luxury. Bracha, Irene and the others emerged from the cold, dirty trough of the bathhouse to find their clothes had vanished, taken away for treatment. It was this treatment that would evolve into the system used in the gas chambers.

To stop camp lice infecting the idyll of SS home life there were frequent quarantines and delousings, and a special fumigation centre was set up in Block 3 of the Auschwitz main camp. From 1940, when Höss became the camp's first commandant, a prisoner named Andrzej Rablin was put to work in this chamber.

The room was filled with inmates' clothes, thick with lice. Crystals of highly toxic hydrocyanic acid were added – trade name Zyklon B – and the door sealed. After a twenty-four-hour wait, Rablin and his helpers entered wearing gas masks, with an extractor fan running. Eventually the process was refined using better heat and ventilation systems, so the clothes were safe to wear only fifteen minutes after the gas had dispersed. Lagerführer Karl Fritsch was in charge of camp fumigation and disinfection. It was his idea to try Zyklon B on human 'pests' – Russian prisoners of war. Höss gave him the go-ahead.[25]

Meanwhile, Fritzsch's wife benefited from the forced labour of a Polish teenager named Emilia Żelazny to scrub her clothes clean so lice would not breed.[26]

Fritsch and his team learned through experience that it was hard to take clothes off a corpse; far more efficient to compel the victims to undress before death. How to achieve this compliance without unruly behaviour and revolt? Tell people they are going to get washed. An elaborate system of deception was contrived.

In late 1942, SS Untersturmführer Maximilian Grabner stood on the roof of one of the new crematoria in the Auschwitz sub-camp Birkenau and shouted to a transport of Jews, 'You will now bathe and be disinfected, we don't want any epidemics in the camp!' He instructed his audience to fold their clothes neatly and place their footwear together in pairs, 'so that you can find them after the bath.'[27]

Two buildings requisitioned from Poles in the nearby area of Brzezinka – *Birkenau*, in German – had been re-purposed as gas chambers. The Little Red House went into operation in March 1942; the White Farmhouse was ready for gassings in June of that year. There were blueprints for more ambitious plans: four purpose-built state-of-the-art death centres. Bracha and Irene would come to know them well: they would be part of the crews compelled to build them. SS Sturmbannführer Karl Bischoff was head of gas chamber and crematoria construction in the Auschwitz camps. SS Hauptscharführer Otto Moll was responsible for ensuring that people undressed in an orderly fashion.[28]

Frau Moll and Frau Bischoff were very likely clients of the Auschwitz fashion salon soon to be established by Hedwig Höss. Hedwig's villa was a stone's throw from the original crematorium in Auschwitz 1, re-purposed from the old Polish Army barracks turnip store. Planted with flowers, grass and young trees, it was pleasantly non-menacing. Victims undressed in an outer hall. People were killed in batches of ten.

In Birkenau's new purpose-built gassing facilities, antechambers were cunningly designed to look like changing rooms for genuine showers. Two of the undressing rooms could hold four thousand people at once. Arrivals were reassured by signs in many languages that read, 'To the Baths and Disinfecting Rooms', and 'Cleanliness Brings Freedom'. There were numbered clothes hooks fixed around the undressing rooms.

In the gas chamber itself, there were dummy shower heads. Some victims were handed towels and soaps to continue the deception. Gas pellets were inserted into the chamber from the roof, not from the shower heads themselves. As the victims waited for shower water that never came, the poison spread. Beyond the thick concrete walls of the gas chamber, their clothes were being collected by specialist work squads, called *Sonderkommando*.

> *We received camp clothes and our good shoes were replaced by wooden clogs*
>   – Hunya Volkmann[29]

Hunya Volkmann, standing under a dry shower head, was actually one of the lucky minority selected to live and work in Auschwitz-Birkenau. She was in a genuine washroom, not a gas chamber. The reason no water came out was because the sauna showers were broken that day. She wiped herself with a damp rag and, still wearing nothing but her boots, went to be issued with camp clothes.

Ironically, for all the efforts to kill lice in the fumigation blocks, the clothes handed out to prisoners were still crawling with them.

There were no female camp uniforms waiting for the first Jewish transports of spring 1942. Instead Irene, Bracha, Marta and their companions were handed military gear. Some got dark green winter uniforms of wool; others cotton khaki summer issue. Irene noticed a hammer and sickle design on her jacket buttons, and realised the uniforms were Russian. They still bore evidence of their previous owners – bullet holes, dried blood, faecal stains. The kit might have been fumigated, but it was not washed.

As early as 1940, textile shortages meant clothing quotas for prisoners could not be met. Consequently relatively few female prisoners received the iconic blue-grey striped dresses associated with Nazi concentration camps. Those who did found little comfort in the coarse canvas shifts that left the legs bare – unlike the male striped suits with trousers – and had no pockets. The uniforms were made by prisoners themselves in camp sewing workshops.

When seamstresses Alida Delasalle and Marilou Colombain arrived with the first group of French political prisoners in January 1943, they were issued an entire camp ensemble, from striped dress to sleeveless vest, grey knee-length knickers and rough grey socks. They took what they were given: large women squeezed into too-tight sacks; small women were swamped by the striped burlap. As non-Jews, Alida and Marilou were 'lucky' to have a complete wardrobe: Jewish women were not usually permitted underwear.

There was a ceaseless influx of new inmates in the months and years following the first Jewish transports. Demand outstripped supply. By the time Hunya Volkmann reached Auschwitz in July 1943, the clothes of previous arrivals were being recycled for distribution. Commandant Rudolf Höss lamented the fact that 'not even using the clothing and footwear from the extermination of the Jews could sufficiently improve the clothing shortage.'[30]

Clothes distribution was a chaotic and even painful experi-ence. To a chorus of shouts, insults, whistle shrieks and whip cracks, women ran alongside trestle tables and were thrown one garment and two shoes. Sometimes guards perched like goats on mountains of clothes and tossed them out randomly. Women who had been used to dressing with care, even elegance, found they now had to make do with only a silk blouse, or a chiffon evening gown, or a child's jacket; a heavy wool suit in blistering heat, or a summer frock in winter blizzards.

It was yet another layer of humiliation. Shoes and boots were also flung without order, often in odd pairings. There were satin slippers, brogues, sandals, high heels. The fit was too long, too short, too wide, too narrow. Festooned with such a grotesque disregard for size, style or practicality, the women now looked like performers in a surrealist theatre show.

Whether in Russian uniforms, striped shifts or rag-tag civilian clothes, all the women had a red or white stripe painted down the back of their garments to mark them out as prisoners.

Truly unlucky women had only heavy wooden clogs. This was the fate of Bracha and Irene and the other women of the first transports. They stumbled out into the snow, bare feet already rubbed raw and freezing.

Hunya tried to keep her own decent boots after she was kitted out in camp gear in July 1943, but they were spotted by one of the veteran prisoners, who demanded, 'Give me your shoes, I want your shoes!'

Hunya stood her ground, 'No, I need them for work.'

'Work?' came the mocking reply, 'You've got five days to live then you'll be covered by earth!'

Hunya's anger got the better of her and she cursed in German and Yiddish, not bothering to lower her voice, 'May *you* live no longer than five days then the earth will cover you!'

Around her, other prisoners stared in astonishment. It was unthinkable that anyone should be so defiant. Unfortunately, even Hunya's admirable confidence could not keep her boots on her feet, and she was compelled to swap them for wooden clogs. However, Hunya was not cowed. She asked a young guard when there would be a chance for new arrivals to relieve themselves. In Auschwitz even such a simple question was worthy of brutal punishment, but surprisingly the guard did not lash out. Instead, attempting to defuse the conflict, she turned to a higher-ranking officer, commenting, 'She hasn't yet been taught to pay respect to those in charge.'

Once again, Hunya let her anger show. 'And how can *you* be teaching *me* about respect? You're far younger than I am. You should learn respect from your elders!'[31]

Miraculously, the young guard backed down – the words must have touched a nerve – and Hunya led the way to the latrines. These were so vile Hunya almost regretted her request. Afterwards, safely out of earshot of the guards, the other prisoners laughed at the whole ridiculous scene. It was laughter born out of relief, and admiration for Hunya's boldness.

An unheard-of treasure, prized beyond gold – a needle! This needle became our salvation   – Zdenka Fantlová[32]

In ordinary circumstances, the woman who took Hunya's good work boots might never have stooped to theft and intimidation. Good manners and morals were often perverted in Auschwitz, as inmates scrabbled to stay alive. Good footwear was necessary to survive, as Hunya had already suspected. Barefoot prisoners risked a beating, or even a death sentence. Some women took to sleeping with their shoes as a pillow, to ensure they were not taken during the night.

Stealing from other inmates was viewed with contempt; stealing from the SS was not considered a crime by the prisoners. There was a special word for it in camp slang: *organising*. Organising was not necessarily a selfish action. It could benefit expanding ripples of inmates. Many female prisoners instinctively wanted to co-operate. Organising played a part in binding friendships closer and making connections in a hostile environment that sought to reduce people to the basest instincts.

Small acts of kindness and generosity had great significance in the camps. Examples shine all the more brightly for taking place against such a terrible backdrop of deprivation. There was the teenager who was able to swap hankies, scarves and gloves gleaned from a waste bin, for extra food. She then shared this food with others, while the recipients of the bartered goods were delighted with their new treasures.[33] There was the inmate-doctor who was gifted two pieces of rag – a precious commodity – which she used for a handkerchief and a tooth cleaner;[34] or the women working in a demolition squad in winter who shared a single woollen mitten passed hand to hand.[35]

Then there was a Czech inmate who picked up a pair of thick, warm stockings deliberately dropped by a local Polish peasant woman, who had seen female prisoners on work duty outside the camp in snowy weather 20°C below freezing. The girl's friends decided each one of them could wear the stockings one day at a time. 'I could have hugged and kissed her hand,' she remembered. 'It was a wonderful present and so unexpected. We could hardly get over the shock.'[36]

Women already used to thrift turned their ingenuity to the task of improving their dreadful apparel. The rough fabric of camp clothes would soon absorb the history of the new wearers. It would be frayed and torn during heavy construction work, sodden and rotten from swamp clearing, cracked with dried mud, fouled by sweat and dysentery, stained by pus from weeping sores, or darkened with blood. Somehow, against the odds, inmates had to try to hold onto a sense of self-respect.

When a woman miraculously got hold of a needle, it would be shared generously among friends. Inmates were absolutely forbidden to own such things, and yet sewing was a skill that could make a significant difference to a prisoner's self-esteem, through the simple act of altering clothes to fit better. Waistbands were added to sloppy skirts; hems were let down to get an inch more leg covering; oversized frocks were taken in.

Since theft was rife, where possible women organised an

old sock or cap to fashion cloth bags known as 'pinklies' or a 'beggar's bundle'. These forbidden portable pockets tied around the waist under the clothes, just large enough to keep a ration of bread or, for the truly 'wealthy' prisoners, a tooth-less comb.

Organising underwear was a priority for many women who had enough strength to think about such things in the coming months. It became horribly uncomfortable to undertake heavy labour without a bra, particularly when wearing rough fabrics. Inmates fashioned bras from shirt remnants, rag scraps and threads of blankets. If they could not obtain a steel needle to sew, they used a rigid piece of straw.[37]

It was not merely a question of making tiny gains in comfort and practicality. A clean, smart prisoner had clear advantages over a filthy prisoner in patched rags: it showed initiative in organising, willpower to wash despite appalling conditions, and a salvaged sense of dignity. Even the SS reacted more positively to prisoners who had outward signs of inner confidence.

Clothes are a mark of humanity – Tzvetan Todorov[38]

One of Hunya's memorable sayings was *Kleider machen Leute, Hadern machen Läuse*, or 'Clothes make the person, rags make lice.' A less picturesque version of the sentiment in English might be, 'Clothes maketh the man.' Hunya knew from bitter experience how clothes and dignity are linked, and how they show status – or lack of it. The expression 'rags make lice' means both that lice thrive in filthy conditions, and that people in rags are treated as lice.

Concentration camps were a distorted microcosm of fashion and class. Privileged kapos might acquire decent footwear, the best uniforms, and luxury accessories such as aprons, stockings, scarves and underwear; their underlings usually wore the worst clothes. At the lowest level of the hierarchy was nudity, which meant vulnerability, humiliation, violation, and eventually death.

At the top of the hierarchy – the equivalent of haute couture in the camps – were the guards. For them, the SS uniforms, stitched by slave labour, were evidence that they were superior beings. Some of the female guards arriving in Auschwitz would have become accustomed to wearing a uniform through their time in the *Bund Deutscher Mädel* – BDM – League of German Girls, a female branch of the German youth movement.

The actual SS uniform was an impressive incentive for new recruits, even if female guards were only ever auxiliaries in the male-centric Nazi world and had no impressive rank badges and braids like the men. Even so, striding out in military style was empowering. Male or female, guards could set aside their consciences with their civilian clothes. In uniform they were simply 'following orders'.

Haggard, hungry prisoners inevitably admired the compara- tively superhuman, healthy SS in their terrifying magnificence. This, in turn, made it easier for guards to swell with superiority and treat the 'subhumans' as they seemingly deserved. Guards found it far easier to mistreat prisoners if they did not look fully human; if they fitted the insults of *vermin, scum* or *pigs* that were flung at them. It was important that guards did not identify with prisoners. The wider the chasm between guards and inmates, the easier it was to justify brutality and even mass murder, as if they were only destroying parasites after all.

The fact that guards and inmates would all look the same when naked was irrelevant: *clothes* made the difference. This difference had the power of a theatrical performance. The perpetrators strode out in bold black and green; their 'audience' were thin, drab silhouettes. While prisoners shivered during long hours of roll call, SS women had thick overcoats, and black waterproof cloaks with hoods. As prisoners endured agonies of frostbite, the SS had leather boots, wool stockings and gloves. When prisoners despaired of mud, shit, blood and lice, the SS were scrubbed, laundered, polished and groomed.

Appearance was everything.

The guards would tolerate a certain amount of peacocking from inmate-functionaries, such as the embroidered hand-made aprons in vogue among privileged kapos, but they were disturbed by too much distortion in the 'natural' order of things. One way of punishing prisoners was to confiscate clothes. When inmate-workers at a munitions factory in the Auschwitz complex began to sew pretty pink and blue collars onto their uniforms, an SS woman tore them off violently. The workers made replacements and named them *Petöfi* collars, after a revolutionary Hungarian poet.[39]

Back in the early days of Auschwitz's existence, when the first Jews arrived, Bracha Berkovič's appearance confused one guard, who told her, 'You don't look at all Jewish. Why don't you just say you're Aryan?' It could have meant better treatment, since Jews were at the very bottom of the camp hierarchy. Bracha refused. She would face whatever happened alongside her sister Katka, and in the company of friends such as Irene and Renée.

Bracha's first garment-related task in Auschwitz was not mending or altering the awful Russian uniform she had been given. Along with all the other new arrivals, she was handed two scraps of fabric with four digits on them. One scrap was to be glued to the front left of her jacket, the other was to be kept ready to be shown as identification, or to receive food rations.

Having taken away their visible identities, the Nazis now replaced them with numbers.

Irene had already noticed the Ravensbrück transfers had inverted triangles called a *Winkel* displayed under their numbers.

She was to learn that a red triangle signified a political prisoner, green was for criminals, and black meant 'asocials' – mostly sex workers. Letters on the triangle denoted nationality, such as P for Pole. Now Irene got a number of her own, 2786, followed by her little sister Edith with 2787. Also in this batch were dressmakers Marta Fuchs with 2043 and Olga Kovácz, 2622.

Bracha and her sister Katka, on the fourth transport from Slovakia, were 4245 and 4246. Marta's cousin Herta Fuchs, on the fifth transport, received number 4787. Frenchwomen Alida Delasalle and Marilou Colombain were 31659 and 31853 respectively, showing how the camp population had grown by January 1943. By the time Hunya Volkmann arrived in July of that year, the Auschwitz complex was engorged. Hunya became prisoner number 46351. Eventually, in May 1944, inmate numbers were listed from 1 again, prefixed with 'A' or 'B', to conceal the extent of the turnover of human cargo. Deportees selected for death on arrival did not receive a number, only instructions to form orderly columns ready to march towards the undressing areas.

For women on the first Jewish transports, physical numbering on the skin came three months after their induction, in June 1942, when guards found they could not keep track of inmate identities as there were so many deaths. Tattoos on skin were easy to log, even on a corpse.

The women who had survived until June queued in front of two Slovakian boys, who inked their left arms. Number 2282 – formerly known as Helen Stern – asked her tattooist, a young man named Lale Sokolov, to take his time pricking in the ink, because she wanted to ask him if he knew anything of her relatives in the men's camp. As a result, her digits looked larger than most.[40] Bracha also had oversized numerals staining her skin, in this instance because the tattooist wanted to ask about his female relatives in the women's barracks.

The numbers were all registered in a complex card filing system administered by SS staff and inmates. Communist inmate Anna Binder, from the first Ravensbrück transport, was assigned to the office detail. One by one she filled out data sheets for each prisoner, listing name, birth date, occupation and so on. Among the countless new arrivals she registered seamstress Marta Fuchs. It was their first contact, and, significantly, not their last.

In the snowy end days of winter 1942, several thousand blossoming, healthy young women were transformed into unrecognisable, trembling creatures, almost ageless and sexless. There they were, formed in rows of five, stripped, violated, shaved, numbered, lumbered with used military clothing.

They were no longer students, homemakers, dressmakers, secretaries, sweethearts, shop-workers, daughters, milliners, singers, farmers, gymnasts, teachers, nurses . . . they were simply *zugangi* – incomers – despised, numbered, nameless objects.

'This,' said Irene Reichenberg, who stood with her sister Edith and her friends from Bratislava, 'this is how we went to work.'[41]

Only if they lived through the first year would work become their salvation, not their nightmare.

You Want to Stay Alive

All knew and recognised the conflicting emotion when your
neighbour's hand is the only thing on earth you can lean on
and at the same time you want to stay alive, even if your
friend is selected to die — Hunya Volkmann[1]

Bracha was an optimist.

Even after months of trauma, she insisted on telling others
– Irene, Katka, Renée – to keep going, to endure. 'You'll see,'
she said. 'After the war we will all get together for coffee and
pastries.'

Irene laughed at such a crazy idea. 'The only way out of this
place is through the chimney,' she answered bitterly.

They all saw smoke rising from the crematorium just beyond
their barracks in the main camp. Sometimes it blew over the
roll call square in front of the camp kitchen, where they stood
in rows for hours whatever the weather, to be counted until
numbers tallied; sometimes it dropped feathery ashes into the
garden of Hedwig Höss, the commandant's wife, landing on
the leaves, lawn and rose buds.

As for coffee and pastries, these were dreams of a vanished
world. Back in Bratislava, the art nouveau Carlton coffee bar
was one of the smartest places to meet up, with elegant clientele, rich burgundy furnishings and gilded furniture. It could
not have been any further from the current reality. For
Auschwitz inmates morning 'coffee' was simply dark water,

brewed from ground chicory or acorns, or less identifiable sources. Lunch was turnip water, referred to as 'soup'. It was served from a deep cauldron during a half-hour work-break. If you had no bowl, you could not collect your ration, simple as that.

For the first few days in camp Irene refused to eat it. 'It stinks!' she said in disgust. Even though she came from a poor family where the gift of an egg on her birthday had been a truly special treat, she was used to good food lovingly prepared, not slops barely fit for pigswill. The whole day's bread ration was allocated in the evening after seemingly endless hours at roll call, a mere 200 grams. It was coarse and heavy bread, hard to digest. Low grade jam or margarine completed the menu, with occasional portions of sausage.

Irene was told the sausage was made from horse meat, definitely not kosher. Stressed and disgusted, she completely lost her appetite. In time, hunger won out. In fact, they were all driven mad with it. Renée the rabbi's daughter was horrified to watch women fight to snatch extra portions of bread in the lamp-less shadows of evening dinnertime at the barracks. Stronger women preyed on the weak, who were left with nothing to eat. Renée did not approve of this savagery and did not participate, but she certainly understood the primitive urges behind it.

As weeks passed the women lost their bloom, their curves, their health. Chronic diarrhoea, known as *Durchfall*, was a debilitating and humiliating side-effect.

Meanwhile, Johan Paul Kremer, an SS doctor newly arrived in Auschwitz, wrote a diary entry in praise of his first meal at the Waffen-SS Club House near the railway station. It included duck livers with stuffed tomatoes and salad. Dr Kremer noted, 'Water is infected, so we drink seltzer-water which is served free.' Two days later he prescribed himself gruel, mint tea and charcoal tablets against a bout of diarrhoea. The inmates had no such remedies.²

Hedwig Höss fed her family on home-grown vegetables from the garden and good cuts of meat. She also pressured inmate-servants in her house to smuggle food out of the camp stores and into her larder.

One day Bracha passed a gaunt girl walking along the main street of the camp. She recognised her friend Hanna, a former classmate from Bratislava. Hanna's family had been well-off and quite refined. Before the war Hanna's mother had often wished that her plump daughter conformed to the slender silhouette idolised in fashion, lamenting, 'If only she would lose ten kilos or more, then she'd be pretty.'³ The mother would have been horrified to see her daughter so skeletal.

Renée the rabbi's daughter observed the fights for food and felt the anguish of semi-starvation, commenting, 'I can no longer judge a person committing a crime as a result of hunger.'⁴

To conjure up a time when the group of friends would be free to sit in a café and indulge in coffee and pastries, when food was there to be savoured not fought over, was Bracha naïve or resilient – or both?

Bracha's memories of her mother stewing kosher chicken, or sprinkling raisins into strudel pastry were only that – memories. She could no more taste such flavours than she could embrace the woman who created them. In the first, harsh months of camp life there was absolutely no reason to be hopeful. The induction process at Auschwitz had stripped the Jewish women of clothes, dignity, identity and delusions.

And yet Bracha still wondered, 'When will we be going home?' She still set her will to survive against the relentless Nazi policies of profit and extermination. What is more, she was determined to look after her sister Katka and her best friend Irene too. In turn, Irene clung to her sister Edith.

Support groups like these were essential for survival and a humanising element of experience for many female inmates, in spite of the hardcore minority who looked out for their own fate alone – both understandable responses to such extreme circumstances. Friends and relatives shared bunks and blankets. They scrambled for the washroom together at the 3 a.m. reveille. They stood shoulder to shoulder during hours and hours of roll call, catching anyone who fainted, whispering words of encouragement to anyone who was beaten. They marched alongside each other at dawn, through the *Arbeit Macht Frei* gateway. They sought each other out at the end of an exhausting day's work, to share meagre crusts of bread and scrapings of margarine.

On 17 July 1942 they waited together, lined up along the camp road, ready for inspection by Heinrich Himmler, VIP guest at the camp. Himmler had come to view his assets. Himmler and Höss were driven through the camp gate in a black, open-top Mercedes car. Multiple cameras were set up to record them as they assessed the camp and chatted together, while the camp orchestra played the 'Triumphal March' from Verdi's opera *Aida*. The prisoners had been told to smarten up, with clean clothes and clogs. Medals, braids and insignia stand out against the SS officers' black uniforms.

The SS were star performers, with prisoners and barbed wire as a backdrop.

Did they even notice the prisoners standing to attention in drab Russian kit? Even if they had, they would not have registered them as individuals, as humans. The prisoners were workers, plain and simple.

One prisoner was pushed forward from the ranks of women. A seamstress friend of Bracha's called Margaret Birnbaum, nicknamed Manci. Manci still had flesh on her bones despite the starvation rations, so she was made to strip and stand naked before Himmler as an example of a healthy, able-bodied worker. The first function of Auschwitz was as an industrial complex after all. The huge *Interessengebiet* – zone of interest – with multiple satellite camps was originally intended to generate fat profits for the SS, supporting Heinrich Himmler's power-saturated ambitions.[5] Jewish slave labour from prisoners such as Irene, Bracha, Katka and Manci was an essential factor in the Auschwitz industries, generating both products and profit.

How did Himmler square economic needs with over-arching Nazi plans for a Jew-free Europe? He resolved the conflict by actively promoting increased transports of Jews to Auschwitz and working Jews as long as possible in inhumane conditions until they died or were unable to work and were murdered. Himmler's orders to camp commandant Rudolf Höss were to exterminate Jews unable to work, to make room for others.[6] His thoughts on seeing dressmaker Manci Birnbaum exposed are not recorded. After his VIP inspection, Himmler went off for dinner with Rudolf and Hedwig, and other Nazi bigwigs.

In the same month as the inspection, Höss met with Dieter Wisliceny – Eichmann's emissary in Slovakia. They discussed the Slovakian Jews, described by Höss as his most expert workers, specially selected.[7] Höss himself claimed he followed proper policies ensuring the proper deployment of prisoners, according to their professional background and labouring abilities. He singled out those with 'an important and rare professional background', such as diamond cutters, lens grinders, toolmakers and watchmakers, labelling them as 'like a historic treasure, protected at all times.'[8] Other valued professions were builders, bricklayers, electricians, carpenters and locksmiths.

These were all traditionally male professions. Where did that leave transports of women? Their gender worked against them. What use were mothers and milliners in a world of grit, brick and cement? Hands that were familiar with needles, typewriters, cow-milking, dough-kneading and bandage-wrapping were now set to full-on manual labour that was usually considered men's work.

> *I received a pickaxe. I did not know how to use it and could hardly*
> *lift it; a blow with the butt of a gun taught me how*
> — Dr Claudette Bloch[9]

If Bracha's optimism was to pay off, the women would have to survive the physical and mental challenges of work in the most brutal conditions, to fulfil the industrial and agricultural fantasies of the SS. The foundations of the Thousand Year Reich, promised by Hitler in his grandiose rhetoric, were laid by slaves. Some can be seen in the background of photographs taken to commemorate Himmler's inspection. In the black and white images they are nameless forms in shapeless clothes. In their hearts they are women. To observers they are a means to an end.

At 7 a.m., once morning roll call was complete, the women waited to hear which work squads – called *kommandos* – they would be assigned to.

Instead of sewing, the dressmakers dredged stagnant ponds, dug drainage ditches, fortified river banks and drained swamps. Back in their days with the Artaman Society Himmler and Höss had discussed ambitions for 'pure-blood' Germans to create deep roots in the East through colonisation and agricultural development. Now their rural dream was to be realised, but the back-breaking work would be carried out by 'subhuman' Jews, not the robust Aryans of Artaman ideology.

Partly naked, the women waded barefoot through contaminated sludge to wrench ditch vegetation up by the roots. Half of this weed-pulling kommando were killed by malaria. Many were submerged in exhaustion and could not be rescued from drowning in time. Unterscharführer Martin, SS leader of the swamp kommando, boasted about how many had died doing the work. 'Only wearing panties,' he grinned, savouring the memory.[10]

Guards were not just passive observers. A Jewish dressmaker from Transylvania watched an SS woman demonstrate how to drown a prisoner in a small puddle.

Kapos often doled out their share of violence too. Bracha's little sister Katka, not robust at the best of times, got a leg wound at work that quickly became infected. When her pace inevitably slowed, she was brutally beaten across the back.

Bracha both witnessed and experienced the suffering. It did not shake her conviction: *It can't happen to me.*

No less dangerous than the swamp kommando were the demolition squads. With their bare hands women pulled down houses that had been hastily abandoned by their rightful Polish owners when ordered to leave the Auschwitz zone of interest. SS woman Runge was in charge of the demolition kommando. She had trained her dog to attack on command. Usually the threat was enough to spur workers on. If not, the dog was let loose, with agonising and even fatal results.

The Polish houses were pulled apart with pickaxes. Irene was staggered at the effort it took. After all the mortar was chipped off, bricks were loaded onto a horse cart, but there were no horses. Irene and nineteen others were harnessed to the cart and they lugged it to a construction site. Bricks and other salvaged materials would be used to make new prison buildings. Irene also laboured building roads to connect the many different zones of interest sites – all under a baking summer sun. Other inmates floundered in the vast pits of sand, digging it out and shovelling it onto trucks, which were then pushed by hand out of the quarry.

The fight for survival was so all-consuming that few women had thoughts of defiance or resistance. That did not mean there weren't occasional, satisfying acts of sabotage, such as the young woman from Poland, doused with the contents of shit-buckets by an SS man, who deliberately dug trenches so they would collapse immediately.[11]

Every day depleted numbers of women marched back to camp. The deaths were registered by office clerks as *Auf der flucht erschossen* – shot while escaping – which was clearly a fiction. SS guards deliberately goaded prisoners to move towards fences, often tossing items of clothing for them to fetch, then shooting them dead when they complied.[12] Renée Ungar said it was obvious the Nazis did not care about their actual work, the important thing was that ultimately the workers would be destroyed.[13]

The roads the women marched on connected several villages that had been levelled to make way for new tilled fields, fish farms, glasshouses, animal pens and aviaries. Rudolf and Hedwig Höss had now actualised the rural paradise dreamed of in the early days of their courtship and marriage.

One road led to the site of a village known as Brzezinka in Polish, and Birkenau in German. The women came to know the landscape well. Starting on 10 August 1942, they were transferred from blocks 1 to 10 in the Auschwitz main camp to a new compound at Birkenau, Sector B-1a, which had only been opened to inmates five days previously. After the women's departure, the blocks in the main camp were disinfected with Zyklon B. Those who could walk went on foot – about a forty-minute journey – to find themselves in a new hell.

The barracks at Birkenau were sordid and shoddy, with only

one thickness of brick and sealed windows, built by long-dead Russian prisoners and set in a desolate landscape. Irene, in Barrack 9, stared at the three-storey bunks built of brick and cement. Each berth in the bunk, called a *koje*, had to fit six women. Could six of them sleep in a space less than two metres across? No point asking. No alternative. Nearly a year later, Hunya Volkmann was put into the same barrack block. By that time a *koje* might have to hold up to fifteen women. Pre-fab buildings intended for only one hundred people now housed a thousand women.

Birkenau means birch wood. There were graceful copses of these silvery-barked trees around the area. In their shade, two abandoned buildings. One, a peaceful-looking red farmhouse, renamed Bunker 1. The other, a white cottage, renamed Bunker 2. A Slovakian woman raking hay in nearby fields that July looked into one of the little houses. She saw a large room with pipes along the walls and ceilings, ending in what looked like shower nozzles. Later in the day she found out it was a gas chamber. Nearby she saw pits being dug for human remains.[14]

The first victims of these converted buildings were Jews considered 'unfit for work'. This included all the young women loaded onto trucks for transfer from the main camp: they had ridden to their deaths. By summer 1942, Jews were being transported directly to Auschwitz for extermination, having been told they were starting an agricultural life in the area.

Inmates, including the dressmakers, were tasked with expanding the Birkenau sub-camp. Himmler had decreed that it would have to hold 200,000 prisoners. The difference in status between prisoners and SS was literally built into the camp architecture: more expertise was applied to designing and equipping gas chambers than a functioning sewage system or washing facilities. Bracha's sister Katka, frail and injured, laboured on new purpose-built crematoria with her bare hands.

At the end of a day's work she had to wash in a puddle, or jostle for a place at a faucet. There was one tap for every 12,000 inmates, and yet modern water pumps were fitted to the crematoria to ensure a full supply.[15]

Eventually prisoners built a new rail spur, connecting the Vienna–Kraków main line with a direct route into the Birkenau complex. They laid ballast and sleepers for two stretches of track, so that one train could be unloaded while another arrived.[16]

In Auschwitz all routes seemed to lead to death. If sickness and hunger did not kill them, brutal work conditions would. Was it any wonder Irene believed the only way out was 'through the chimney'?

As the women stood in line waiting for their work assignments, Katka's heart was heavy – she always seemed to get the worst jobs. Bracha knew they could not go on indefinitely. The question was, how and when could they get assigned to something better? Would it even be possible to use their professional dressmaking skills? There were rumours of less arduous work kommandos, even of a place where, since 22 August 1942, the kommando workers were housed in tolerable conditions. This was the SS administration building, called the *Stabsgebäude*. Here female inmates working at the camp registry office lived, along with women chosen to be domestic servants for SS families, and a select group in a kommando called the *Obere Nähstube* – Upper Tailoring Studio.

Near the neat brick arch of Birkenau's main entrance was a wooden building – Block 3. It was a sewing factory; nothing like as elite as the Upper Tailoring Studio. French communist dressmaker Marilou Colombain was escorted here for a month's work placement with the Auschwitz II sewing kommando in 1943. Her escort across Birkenau's expanse was a bright, energetic prisoner from Belgium named Mala Zimetbaum. Mala worked as a *Lauferin*, or courier. It was a job that gave Mala a certain amount of trust as she moved around the sprawling camp complex on errands for the SS. All the dressmakers came to know the irrepressible Mala.[17]

In the sewing factory Marilou stitched German uniforms. It was a stuffy hut, the air thick with textile fibres and fluff. There were two shifts of about thirty women, one working days, the other nights. They repaired German military kit, darned SS socks, stitched crosses on inmate clothes to mark them out and made camp underclothing. Some of the underwear was re-cycled. One Jewish girl was issued pants of a finely woven cloth with dark-coloured border stripes. Despite the bonus of getting underwear – rare for Jews – she was utterly revulsed: they were made of a *talles*, a Jewish prayer shawl. It was yet one more way the Nazis used clothing to degrade.[18]

One of the sewing factory kapos was a Slovakian seamstress called Božka, saved from the gas chamber because of her skills. She did her best to support other women in the kommando and let them do their own secret darns and patches when needed.[19] SS man Friedrich Münkel was in charge of the industrial dressmaking and tailoring workshops in Birkenau. He never beat inmates himself and occasionally handed out cigarettes.[20] According to one of the workers on the night shift, even the SS women guarding the kommandos were more stupid than cruel.[21] Best of all, the sewing kommando was indoors – no blistering sun or freezing snow – and they worked sitting down. At times the kapos permitted singing.

And yet the factory sewing kommando was still only a pause in the journey towards death. Twelve-hour shifts were exhausting, particularly squinting at close work in dim light. Starving women slumped over their sewing machines. The singers lost their breath when struck by typhus. If daily quotas were not met, more brutal SS supervisors could erupt in a violent frenzy, beating the sewers. During the night shift, the room was lit by fires from the crematoria chimneys. Trucks rumbled past taking corpses to the ovens. Lines of living people marched under the entrance arch, going to the gas.

Several of us SS women had short whips made in the camp work-shops with one of which I several times struck prisoners

– Irma Grese[22]

'We'll all end up being gassed,' said one of Hunya's companions, echoing Irene's pessimism about leaving through the chimney.

Hunya, an optimist, had been talking about what she was going to do after Auschwitz. The pessimists had no time for such fantasies. 'Let's make a bet then,' said Hunya. 'When we're finally in the queue for the gas you can slap *me*, but if we get out of here alive I'll slap *you*.'[23]

Hunya's defiance often got her into trouble, even accidentally, such as when she was hit across the face for being too tired to take her hands out of her pockets in front of a guard. Luckily, there were those who admired her for it, so she was not without allies. These allies got her assigned to an indoor kommando. It was not exactly dressmaking, but it was at least making use of textile skills: it was the weaving squad, called the *Weberei*.

After being greeted by SS woman Weniger, who 'welcomed' workers to the hut each shift by beating them over the head with a rubber truncheon, Hunya found a space to sit in a tidy room. About a hundred women tore rags into ribbons about three centimetres wide. Scissors were scarce, so teeth were used on tough pieces. Some lengths were plaited into ropes about five centimetres thick and a metre long, supposedly for throwing hand grenades. Some rags and clippings were woven into tank mats and caulking for submarines.

Hunya plaited whips, fingers working to the distant tunes of the Birkenau women's orchestra, forced to serenade new arrivals. These whips, made of linen or cellophane, were freely used by camp guards. By 1944 there were 3,000 workers in the weaving kommando. When no longer functional, individuals were easily removed to the gas chambers and replaced from Birkenau's pool of prisoners.[24]

Bribery and connections to prominent prisoners – those tasked with making up worker quotas for the Nazis – were one way to get on a list for so-called privileged work. Even Bracha, ever a go-getter, did not yet have the influence or contacts to get picked for either the sewing squad or the weaving kommando, let alone the Upper Tailoring Studio.

Each morning when they were chosen, the women wondered what that day's work would be. One day Bracha was selected for a mysterious task in Block 10.

It was clean in the building. There were pleasant nurses and doctors in white coats. Women lay in real beds – one each. Some even had a room to themselves. There were medical procedures to endure; nothing troubling at first. Then someone with a conscience took Bracha aside and said, 'If you stay here you'll be warm, but you'll never have children.'

Block 10 was the infamous medical experiment block, where women were sterilised by the most horrific and unscientific methods. Luckily, Bracha never got called back. She wondered if, despite her optimism, everything was about *luck*, good or bad. Which sort of luck did she have? Could she make her own?

Then, some nine months after arriving at Auschwitz, her luck changed for the better. She was picked for the Kanada Kommando.

'What's *Kanada*?' she asked.

A pell mell of all colours could be seen on the ramp. There were
smart Frenchwomen in fur coats and silk stockings, helpless old men,
children, their heads in curls, old grannies, men in their prime, some
wearing fashionable suits, others in workmen's clothes
– SS Rottenführer Pery Broad, *KL Auschwitz As Seen By the SS*

What was Kanada?

Kanada was a wonderland of treasures, endlessly renewed.

The biggest black market in Europe.

A morgue of lost hopes.

Camp mythology claimed that the name 'Kanada' was chosen for the multiple plunder storage sites because they represented a land of plenty, as the country Canada was rumoured to be.

In Kanada, Bracha found something close to her optimistic dream of coffee and pastries: olives and lemonade.

Back in early April 1942, when she scrambled down from a cattle wagon at the Auschwitz camp siding, Bracha had been assured that her suitcase would be well taken care of. That was, in essence, no lie. The deportees' luggage was of more value than the people who had first packed and carried it, and the SS took great care to profit from it. A bulging complex of warehouses and workers was organised in Auschwitz with the sole purpose of sorting and redistributing the contents of this luggage, as well as the items carried by hand to the undressing rooms of the gas chambers, and the still-warm clothes from those who went naked to their deaths.

Kanada contained the entire portable wealth of those bewildered crowds emerging from trains day after day, night after night.

The luggage processing system was carefully structured. A telephone call from a mainline station alerted the camp to a new transport's arrival. Prisoners on the *Ausfräumungskommando* – 'clean-up squad' – were hustled from their barracks by an

SS man on a motorbike, and marched to the railway station. There was a two- to three-hour turnaround slot for each train of between twenty to sixty freight cars. Each wagon contained about one hundred people. The arrival process was perfected over time: overwhelm, bewilder, organise, select. Where the first transports of Jews to Auschwitz had been female-only, then workers only, it did not take long before entire families, entire villages, were being deported.

Males and females separated, no time for goodbye. An SS doctor assessed each person in columns lined alongside the train – flicking a finger for them to go to the left or to the right. Unable to walk? No problem. Sick, disabled or elderly arrivals were helped up portable wooden steps and onto the back of trucks, for a nice ride into camp. The rest marched.

The only known photographs recording the arrival of transports are collected in an album from May 1944, at the height of the extermination of Jews from Hungary. The scenes are unchoreographed, but still censored: there are no snapshots of dogs straining at their chains, or SS men beating bewildered civilians, or children screaming for their lost loved ones, or corpses dragged from the trains.

A sequence of images titled *Frauen bei der Ankunft* – Women on Arrival – shows Carpathian Jews marked with yellow stars. Their clothes are a contrast to the striped suits of the clean-up kommando. They are a reminder of the real world: print skirts, knitted shawls, buttoned shoes . . . aprons, sailor collars, cardigans, tailored coats . . . boots, bonnets, wrinkled socks . . .

The album photos are an extraordinarily poignant view of individuals – mostly nameless and helpless – being transformed into *häftlings*: inmates. One other aspect of the censorship: there are no photographs in the album showing the fearful frenzy of the undressing rooms, or the panic and claustrophobia of the gas chambers. Usually only ten or twenty per cent of each transport were spared for labour. Some of these would end up in a Kanada kommando.[25]

During the whole selection process, men of the clean-up kommando were tossing luggage from the trains and gathering it into huge piles. Luggage took longer to process than people. Meanwhile, the locomotive engine driver would loiter nearby, finding something mechanical to tinker with until there was a chance to pilfer something for himself. No question the men on the railways understood the nature of their cargo's final destination. SS men stood around with weapons ready, already counting down the minutes until they would get their bonus ration of vodka: one fifth of a litre for every transport.

Moritz Mädler luggage advertisement, in the German Die Dame *magazine, 1939. Arrivals at Auschwitz brought every conceivable kind of luggage with them.*

Bags, boxes, crates, trunks, cases . . . wheelchairs, walking sticks, prams . . . All were loaded onto carts and lorries by the clean-up squad, who then washed all effluvia from the freight cars so the train could be shunted back onto the main line, pistons working and steam billowing, to collect fresh victims.

After all the activity, there was only litter to be swept up. Fluttering newspapers, empty food cans, and dropped toys.[26] A bonfire was made of miscellaneous debris: prayer books, rags and family photos.

At its height, the clean-up squad consisted of two to three hundred prisoners. Among them was a young Slovakian called Walter Rosenberg, although history remembers him by his adopted name Rudolf Vrba. Vrba provided muscle: he lugged the booty to Kanada I, near the main camp. It was dumped in a huge yard surrounded by buildings and barbed wire, with watchtowers at each corner, part of an SS armaments enterprise called D.A.W.[27] Vrba called it the 'warehouse of the body snatchers'.

Once opened, the contents of cases, bags and bundles were roughly categorised and divided onto blankets, which men dragged to the nearby barrack buildings for the next stage of sorting. When Vrba got promoted from ramp work to porter in Kanada, he was entranced by the sight of Slovakian girls at work there. Seeing them was a 'little ray of sunshine in my life,' he said.[28] The women in this section of Kanada were known as *Rotkäppchen* – Red Caps – because they wore red headkerchiefs.

This was the kommando Bracha first joined, marching nearly two miles out and two miles back from her Birkenau barrack. Her sister Katka would follow, as well as Irene, Marta Fuchs, Herta Fuchs and many other Slovakian Jews. Bracha and her sister worked on different shifts, so she would return to barracks in the morning to look for Katka, who then left for the day shift. The kommando had to work day and night, because the transports kept coming, and the luggage kept piling up.[29]

Rotkäppchen is also the German word for Little Red Riding Hood, and there was something reminiscent of fairy tales in the Red Cap work: Kanada was like an ogre's hoard in a storybook; a treasure trove of small treats that were magical enough to inmates who acquired them. Scharführer Richard Wiegleb, a big blond man in his mid-thirties, was in charge of Kanada in the main camp. He was a real-life ogre. He readily dealt twenty-five lashes to any prisoner caught stealing. Even so, it was possible to squirrel away bits of food from the luggage of new arrivals, before the bulk of it was sent to the *Fressbarracke* – the 'Gobble Block' for the benefit of the SS, near the main camp kitchen.

Rudolf Vrba, dodging Wiegleb's rubber truncheon, managed to smuggle the Red Cap women lemons, chocolate and sardines, hidden in blanket bundles. Irene was one of those lucky enough to receive bread and chocolate from Vrba, whom she came to know well. One time she unfolded the blanket bundle and found Vrba had hidden a bottle of eau de cologne inside – luxury! She rubbed herself with it in lieu of washing. The Red Caps were later able to repay Vrba's generosity by hiding him on top of a plunder mountain when he was ill with typhus – and therefore in danger of being gassed – and by bringing him pills and lemonade until he was fit to work again.

Bracha had reason to fear Scharführer Wiegleb in Kanada. She saw how he took a perverse delight in making the men do punishing fitness routines in the Kanada yard, forcing them to do push-ups and squats until they collapsed. One time, crossing the yard from the outside toilet, Wiegleb whacked her on the head for no reason with the rubber end of his whip, leaving her dazed, pained and furious. Bracha had to squash down the outrage and take comfort in what perks she could. Sorting through clothes in the Kanada barrack in early 1943, she felt in the pocket of one garment and found what she took to be plums. She popped them in her mouth and got a shock – her first startling taste of olives, brought to the camp by transports from Greece.

Like any fairy tale, there was romance in Kanada, particularly as inmates working there improved in strength and health. At twenty-one, Bracha still thought herself too young for a boyfriend. Other women chose a *kochany*, as their lovers were called in camp slang. There were playful assignations, and some more serious relationships. Vrba even acted as go-between for a kapo named Bruno and a beautiful Viennese girl called Hermione, who was kapo of the Slovak women in the kommando. Bruno wooed Hermione with eau de cologne, soap and French perfumes. She enjoyed her pick of fabulous clothes, dressing in expensive blouses and skirts, matched with gleaming black boots.

Off-setting the romance was the ever-present threat of sexual violence. Vrba respected the female prisoners, saying 'somehow the bitterness of the place was melted a little by this feminine warmth.' Other men – guards and kapos, gorged on pilfered food and booze – saw the women as bait, harassing them in the open washrooms, and hunting them among mountains of clothes, cases and eiderdowns. Rape was one more horror of camp life.

The Nazis had turned those clothes into mountains and they rode around them on bicycles, holding a whip, a barking dog in front of them   – Marceline Loridan-Ivens[30]

Bracha's job was sorting through the bundles dragged in by porters like Rudi Vrba. Irene, too, had the task of clambering up onto the mounds of goods to pull out different clothing categories such as lingerie, decent clothing, ratty garments. If careful, inmates were able to acquire underwear for themselves, and change it as needed. Irene really appreciated this boost to her self-esteem.

There were times when Bracha managed to smuggle out cigarettes, which she shared with friends who used them for barter. Kanada created a crazy economy, where diamonds could be swapped for fresh water and silk stockings exchanged for quinine tablets.

Keeping items or 'organising' them for other prisoners was not considered theft among the inmates. Sharing with friends helped generosity flourish in defiance of the scarcity and barbarity the SS encouraged. Everyday objects found in pockets and purses were items of treasure to inmates. Handkerchiefs, soap and toothpaste were especially prized. Medicines were more precious than gold.

Watches for sale in the Bon Marché *shopping catalogue,*
winter 1939/40

One day Bracha came across an old pocket watch, and she was too tempted to resist. Having one's own watch was a way of regaining a sense of time-keeping, independently of the shouts that signified roll call, reveille, or meal times.

However, Kanada kommando workers were regularly searched

as they left the site, and Bracha's new acquisition was discovered by a German kapo, who hit her so hard as punishment she got a black eye.[31] She was lucky not to be sent back to outside work, or even to her death. Kanada workers could not necessarily bribe themselves off lists for the gas.

It being such a risky business, women needed nerve and ingenuity to smuggle goods out. They pinned things inside sleeves, headkerchiefs, or within their 'pinkly' bags. They even clamped tins of food between their legs while marching past the SS scrutineers. Spot-check internal searches were carried out, catching those who hid things inside their own bodies.

However, an excellent way to get past the checks was simply to wear pilfered garments. Hunya Volkmann benefited this way. Since having her decent boots stolen, she had been hobbling to work at the weaving shed in ill-fitting wooden clogs, called clappers, which left her feet swollen, torn and infected. One of the Kanada workers – a lovely chatty girl called Kato Engel – decided to help her out, since they were both from the same home town of Kežmarok. Kato walked barefoot to Kanada so that she could walk back to barracks in a pair of shoes for Hunya. Hunya called Kato an angel, the gift meant so much to her.

As for the hundreds of thousands of shoes in Auschwitz now without owners, those that could be salvaged went to cobbler's workshops to be reconditioned, then they were made available to civilians in the Reich, who still had the freedom to walk in the streets of their home towns, to visit friends, perhaps to go to a café for coffee and pastries. One slave labourer in the Salamander shoe factory in Berlin spent her war repairing shoes without owners, somehow understanding that the tonnes of footwear being delivered without tags or instructions represented an 'endless world of pain'.[32]

One day, as Bracha handled a ladies' cardigan, she noticed

that the five buttons were particularly bulky. Curiosity got the better of her. Looking behind the button fronts she saw that each contained a tiny jewelled watch: a cache of portable wealth for the one-time owner. She did not dare keep any of the watches this time.

There was actually a team of specialists whose job it was to search the house-high piles of clothes and shoes for hidden treasures such as diamonds, gold and cash. They might be wadded inside shoulder pads, slipped into seams, layered within corsetry or weighting down hems. Wherever they were found, valuables went into the *Schatzkiste* – a booty box supervised by the SS. Full trunks were then dragged to the cellars of the nearby SS admin building, the Stabsgebäude. Here a team of people counted out the immense wealth, which was sent to Berlin.

An SS officer named Bruno Melmer oversaw deposits of loot from all the extermination camps. Non-cash items were handed to the Reichsbank, with the full compliance of the bank president Walter Funk, or sold in the Municipal Pawnshop in Berlin.[33] Commandant Höss was well aware of the dark commercial heart of Auschwitz. At his post-war trial, he admitted that gold taken from the teeth of corpses was melted down and sent to Berlin.[34]

Where possible, workers in the Kanada kommando buried valuables, to stop them benefiting the Nazis. Bank notes also made excellent toilet paper. It was sometimes possible – with luck and skill – to smuggle valuables out of Kanada. Unbeknown to the SS, one of the kapos at Kanada – Bernard Świerczyna – was part of the Auschwitz underground, as were several of the privileged Kanada kommando. Kanada valuables would play their part in funding escape attempts and the extraordinary camp uprising in autumn 1944.

The SS did not only covet the obvious treasures. Textiles

had great value too, to reclothe German citizens, to save factory space for armaments, and to boost morale on the home front. Bracha's sister Katka was one of the workers making up new bundles of clothes from the sorted piles, graded according to type and quality. Katka was set to coat bundles – quite appropriate given her coat-tailoring skills, passed on from her talented father Salomon. The selected garments were first fumigated with Zyklon B, then put into packs of ten. The most wearable items were to be sent back to Germany on daily freight trains, along with signed inventories.

Höss noted there could be up to twenty trains of goods a day leaving Auschwitz. He did not concede that these were stolen goods. On the contrary, he had received an order stating that concentration camp administrations were the legal owners of possessions formerly belonging to deceased inmates.[35] Sometimes clothing was sent on to other concentration camps via the Office for Processing Second-hand Goods.

Wiegleb organised logistics for the transportation of bundled garments. It might be top-quality men's shirts on Monday, furs on Tuesday, children's underwear the next day, and so on.[36] As with the gross appropriators of Jewish property back in their home towns, Nazi scavengers were now profiteering from the last remnants of their belongings – the very clothes off their backs.

Unwearable items were categorised *Klamotten* – rags. Defiant Kanada workers, keeping a careful eye out for the SS, did their own secret ripping and wrecking, to deprive the Nazis of at least some of their booty.[37] Nothing was wasted, not even rags. They were torn into strips for the weaving workshop; Hunya's fingers became raw from the feel of them as she wove whips. Or they were sent to a textile factory in Memel to be pulped and made into paper. Or transferred to the concentration camp at Płaszów near Kraków, to be made into rugs by other Jewish inmates.

One rug-maker at Płaszów did wonder what had happened to all the people who had once worn the clothes she was turning into floor coverings.[38] Workers at a slave labour factory in Grünberg, Germany had no illusions about the old clothes that were shredded and re-woven in the big spinning halls. They knew the daily deliveries of old clothes came from Auschwitz, and they knew this would be their final destination once they were too sick or broken to work any longer.[39]

Whether shoes that still held the shape of the wearer's foot, or made-to-measure suits, or baby layettes embroidered with names and motifs, every single item sorted in Kanada was evidence of mass murder. Bracha, Irene, Katka and the others had to live with this knowledge. When a new Kanada complex opened in Birkenau in 1943, the workers became direct witnesses to the processing at the gas chambers.

Some of the Kanada barracks in Birkenau, looking unusually orderly. Thousands of inmates laboured here to sort barrowfuls and truckloads of expropriated goods.

Initially the new Kanada site in Birkenau – called Kanada II – was one huge warehouse between crematoria III and IV, labelled area B-IIg. It expanded to five barracks, and then a staggering total of thirty barracks, each 55 metres long, laid out on either side of a boulevard wide enough for convoys of lorries. Fresh green lawns were planted outside this new emporium of plunder, with well-tended flower beds.

Young female inmates sunbathed here during short summer lunch breaks, wearing clean, white blouses and smart slacks. Captured by an SS photographer in 1944 as they sorted through bundles and cases, they look healthy – normal even. 'Smile,' the photographer told them, and they had to oblige. It was all part of the Nazi illusion, designed to fool new arrivals or Red Cross inspectors: to give the impression nothing bad was happening here.[40]

These able-bodied women were the *Weißkäppchen* squad – the White Caps. They dealt with clothing and hand luggage brought directly from the gas chamber undressing rooms. From the grass outside the huts, they could clearly see lines of people destined for the gas. Bracha was transferred to the Birkenau Kanada for a few months. She could only watch as almost her entire class of friends from the Jewish Orthodox elementary school in Bratislava were lined up – girls who had shared the same crazes for bobbed hair and volant collars.

The White Cap workers could observe each time an SS man crawled along the roof of the crematoria to shake a canister of crystals into an opening – Zyklon B. By this time Bracha had seen so many deaths from illness and violence that she no longer registered corpses. She kept on sorting clothes.

It was Bracha's sister Katka who found the coat. Katka, the coat-making specialist.

So precious to the bearer, so worthless to the Nazis, photographs,
letters and other personal memorabilia were burned as junk.
This Berkovič family photograph from 1937 shows Bracha's parents
(seated, far left and right) her uncles (back row) and her
grandparents (seated, centre.) All save one were murdered.

She knew it at once – her own familiar coat, left behind during
the round-up for transportation. She took it and wore it once
more, first painting a red stripe down the back to make it
acceptable as prisoner gear. Also on the pile to be sorted was
a coat belonging to Bracha; a memento of the time before
Auschwitz.

Katka knew exactly what finding the coats meant: their
mother and father were dead. Preparing for their own deportation, Karolína and Salomon most likely packed their daughters'
coats thinking to deliver them on arrival. Instead, they had been
dragged off to Lublin in June 1942 and murdered soon afterwards – probably in Majdanek extermination centre – after
which their belongings were transported to Auschwitz for
sorting.

There was no time for Katka to process the tragic implications of finding the coats. The mounds of clothes were growing higher day by day. Later there might be the space to mourn, wondering what the last minutes of life had been like for their beloved parents. Deaf-mute Salomon trapped in a silent world of anguish without words and no wife to guide or comfort him; Karolína, undressing with trembling hands, afraid to die without seeing her girls again. They became smoke, ashes and memories – out through a crematorium chimney.

Herta Fuchs, Marta's cousin, spotted a dress and shoes that belonged to her sister Alice while walking near the gas chamber, mute testimony to the loss of yet another dear life.

Irene's friend Renée Ungar learned her family had been deported to Auschwitz in June 1942. She found their clothes in Kanada and so said a final farewell to them.

Irene herself edged closer to despair when she uncovered clothes of her sister Frieda, murdered in July 1942. Frieda had been married with a small child. Mothers with children were inevitably selected for death on arrival.[41]

Was it possible to carry on? To follow Bracha's quest for optimism?

Irene had at least been reunited with her other married sister Jolli, when Jolli was admitted to the camp, and she was still with her younger sister Edith, so perhaps there was something to live for despite the horrors.

Then Jolli got sick. Edith fell ill.

Typhus.

Lice thrived in Birkenau barracks, even more than back at the Auschwitz main camp. Irene was repulsed by the straw bags they slept on. They were almost moving with colonies of lice that quickly invaded hair, skin folds and clothes. Her first summer in Auschwitz saw the eruption of a typhus epidemic, killing hundreds of people daily. Women coming back to barracks, filthy from outdoor kommandos, struggled to find the energy to fight for a share of the drizzling tap water only made accessible for short periods each day.

Prisoners were screamed at for being dirty . . . and screamed at for trying to wash. Kapos with clubs and dogs with a taste for human flesh added to the chaos. On one occasion, Herta Fuchs tried to get water to launder her trousers. A German guard spotted her, gave her twenty-five lashes on her bared bottom and kicked her out of the washroom. What chance did the women have to keep lice-free?

Weak from fever and malnutrition, their immune systems simply could not cope. Irene was horrified to spot a girl she recognised drinking from a dirty puddle, she was so crazed with typhus thirst. It was Rona Böszi, the Berlin refugee who had shared clandestine sewing lessons with Irene back in Bratislava. That was the last time Irene saw Rona.

Early December 1942 saw the first of several *Entlausung* efforts – Great Delousings. Terrified that the disease would infect SS personnel, SS doctors ordered drastic disinfections. Birkenau went into lockdown; there was to be no work, and no entry to the barracks. Straw sacks were burned and buildings fumigated.

Women and girls were forced to strip outside, dumping their clothes in buckets. These were deloused by laundresses wearing gas masks, then spread up on roofs to dry, or along fields of wire washing lines, if drying was possible in sub-zero temperatures. Bodies were dunked *en masse* in cold water, shaved, and hair stubble slathered with stinging disinfectant. At the same time, 2,000 female prisoners were selected for the gas chamber.

Hunya experienced one of the later delousings. Naked, shorn and degraded, she stumbled around the so-called drying ground, one of 30,000. She was numb with shock, barely feeling the sun's warmth. While some women snatched at clothes that looked to be an improvement on what they had worn before,

Hunya – like most of the others – was desperate for the familiarity of her own sorry garments. When she finally spotted her own clothes, she actually burst into tears it was such a relief.

During winter delousings, there were more clothes strung on the lines than people to collect them: cold had killed off the weakest as they waited to re-clothe themselves.

A few days later lice reappeared. Irene's sisters Jolli and Edith were admitted to the *Revier*, a block set aside for desperately sick prisoners, optimistically called a hospital. Here inmate-medical staff begged patients not to complain about lice, or the SS would empty the whole building and send them all to be fatally fumigated with Zyklon B. Irene told her sisters she would bring them something from Kanada every evening – a morsel of bread, whatever she could. One day she came off shift to see Jolli dead in bed next to Edith.[42]

Bracha's sister Katka was in the Revier at the same time as Edith, getting help for the wound on her leg, which would not heal. Irene came to hold a candle while a friend who was a medical student – Manci Schwalbová, brought to Auschwitz on the second transport from Slovakia – did her best to heal the wound. Every evening Manci lanced Katka's infected leg, but every day the swelling and pain returned. There were few medications and only paper bandages. They all did what they could for each other; loyalty counted for a lot, even in the absence of proper medical help.

One night Bracha woke in the barracks to find Katka sneaking into the bunk.

'What are you doing here?' she asked, relieved to see her sister, but confused. 'You should be in hospital.'

'I had a bad feeling,' Katka replied. 'I snuck out of the window.'

'Is Edith with you?'

'She wanted to stay and rest . . .'

The next day the sick of the Revier were carried out of the hospital and set on the ground. Time for a selection. Irene stood at roll call with the other 'fit for work' prisoners, watching a large contingent of soldiers with dogs drive into the camp. SS Rapportführerin Elisabeth Dreschler presided at the camp exit as work kommandos marched past. A point of the finger – left, right. Irene was selected to pass.

Selection is such an innocent word out of context. In happier times, one might select the right thread to sew a fabric, or a hat to match an outfit, or a cake from a café menu. In a Nazi concentration camp, *selection* was a word weighted with fear. It signified teetering on the edge of death, usually to fall. There were selections of new arrivals on the ramp, sent left or right, to die or live a little longer. Selections where prisoners stood naked under the scrutiny of SS doctors: one hint of sickness or injury and they were to shed clothes and go to be showered in poison. Selections at the Revier too, to make a clean sweep.

Commandant Höss was under orders from Himmler to make room in Auschwitz for all the Jews being transported out of Germany, so that the Fatherland could be declared officially Jew-free. Höss objected, saying there was no room. *Make room*, said Himmler.

Sometimes selections were carried out that lasted many hours in extreme weather conditions. Healthy, able-bodied girls and women would be picked out and brought to the crematoria to die. Sometimes selections took the guise of physical fitness tests. Tired, starved prisoners were told to sprint down the camp's main street, under a barrage of SS women with sticks. Those who stopped or gave up were dragged to the roadside. Perhaps they did not realise they were literally running for their lives; maybe they were too exhausted to care.[43]

One sadistic test was to select for death all those who could not make the leap across a drainage ditch that ran along the main street in Birkenau, the *Lagerstrasse*. Called the *Köningsgraben*, this ditch was a notorious site for SS beatings and murders. Katka, with her weak heart and swollen, infected leg, simply could not manage the jump. Luckily, she had Bracha and another girl lifting her across with them.

'Hey! Why are you jumping so close together?' shouted a guard.

Quick-witted as ever, Bracha replied, 'Oh, we just wanted to keep a neat line . . .'

The guard let them pass.

Sometimes selections were more focused: the prisoner hospital blocks were cleared of patients. SS doctor Johan Kremer described in his private diary how, on 5 September 1942, women selected from the prisoners' infirmary in Birkenau were stripped naked in the open, then shoved into trucks and driven to Block 25 – the death block. 'They begged the SS men to be allowed to live, they wept,' he said at his post-war trial.

In his diary for that day in Auschwitz, Dr Kremer also noted that he had enjoyed an excellent Sunday dinner of tomato soup, chicken with potatoes and red cabbage, and 'magnificent ice cream'.[44]

One terrible autumn day, when the sick of the Revier had been brought outdoors and Irene had passed as fit for work, she came back from her kommando in the evening to find the Revier was deserted. Outside there was an immense pile of discarded shoes, eighteen-year-old Edith's included. Irene knew what those empty shoes meant. Her little sister was dead. She threw herself to the ground screaming with grief, totally broken.

I did not want to live anymore – Irene Reichenberg

Irene lay in the top barrack bunk, prickled by lice from the straw sack mattress. She did not want to climb down. She would not go to work. She was crying when Bracha came in from her shift.

'Someone stole my blanket,' Irene wept. She hadn't the will to fight for it.

Bracha had enough will for the both of them, insisting, 'You can't stay here! You have to get up – to *work*.'

There was another friend from back home in the barrack. She murmured to Irene, 'Why not go to the wire?'

Barbed-wire fences separated different areas of the camp complex. They were dotted with sentry towers and patrolled by guards with dogs. The fences were high voltage, maintained by an inmate-electrician called Henryk Porębski. It was his task to make regular checks along the miles of wire. To *go to the wire* did not mean to escape, it meant suicide.

Despairing prisoners crossed a Death Zone in front of the electrified fence. If sentries did not shoot them first, they reached out for a fatal electric shock. Their corpses then hung on the wire for a while like grotesque ornaments; a warning to others, or a temptation. Before prisoners from a special kommando detached the bodies with hooked sticks, officers of the Political Section's investigation services – the *Erkennungsdienst* – came to photograph them from all angles. At night, inmate-policewomen wearing blue work outfits patrolled, chasing off those intent on self-destruction. Even this measure of self-determination was to be denied the wretches trapped in Auschwitz.

Irene had seen how people snagged themselves on the wire and how they smoked.

'I'm *not* going to the wire,' she said.

Every day the friend from Slovakia came back to the barrack and said, 'Let's go to the wire . . .'

'If you go you'll die!' Bracha argued, 'And you'll only be doing the fascists a favour. You have to survive, not die. You have to live!' Bracha was determined to survive Auschwitz. To have coffee and cake in Bratislava. To tell her story.

Irene wavered, but despair was hard to resist. *Nobody can survive this,* she thought. *Why should I?*

She was not alone in succumbing to hopelessness. It was a common phenomenon in the camps, the body and mind slowly shutting down in protest at the physical and emotional trauma. Eventually total apathy would set in. Unable to wash, feed or rouse themselves, these broken people became shuffling skeletons – as good as dead before the SS finished them off.

It got worse before it got better. A few days later, Irene was hit with a high fever. Now she was ill too. It seemed the perfect excuse to give up and go out through the chimneys.

Bracha was having none of it. 'You're not staying here, you're coming with me!' she announced, and she dragged Irene to work. Shortly after they left the barrack block, trucks collected all those who had stayed behind. The trucks drove on to the crematoria.

Day after day Bracha forced Irene to Kanada. Irene had another friend there, a kapo. She begged this kapo for some quinine, saying it was to lower her temperature because she was so sick. Bracha also hunted for medicine in the suitcases and bags of Kanada; that evening Irene held a palmful of pills. She had no clue what sort of pills they were but thanked Bracha for the gift. Later, when Bracha was asleep, Irene made the decision to swallow all the pills, not caring if she overdosed and never woke up again. It would be a release from her suffering.

Irene did not wake up the next morning.

She was unconscious for three days and nights, during which time Bracha nursed her as best she could. And then – a miracle. Irene opened her eyes. She was dizzy, she stumbled, but the fever had broken.[45]

Her despair was still solid. Being healthy did not change her circumstances; it did not bring her sisters back. Irene made a final plan. She would get transferred to Block 25, the infamous death block where victims were held until their turn in the gas chambers.

Block 25 was run by a Slovakian girl called Cylka. She had arrived at Auschwitz aged barely sixteen, still wearing a school-girl's apron. Hideously corrupted by the SS, Cylka set aside her former life with her former clothes. She looked like an angel, but was almost universally feared by the other prisoners. She swapped the rags of a regular inmate for a raincoat, a colourful headscarf and waterproof boots.

When asked by another Birkenau inmate how she could be so brutal to the poor women waiting for death in Block 25, Cylka replied, 'You probably know that I put my own mother in the cart that took her to the gas. You should understand that there remains for me nothing so terrible that I could not do it. The world is a terrible place. This is how I take my revenge on it.'[46]

Irene had decided that Cylka was to be her jailor in the antechamber to death.

'What do you want?' asked a woman leaning on the wall of Block 25.

'To go in there,' Irene said.

'You need de-listing from your barrack first, then bring your card here and we'll take you.'

Back Irene went, defeated by the perversity of camp bureau-cracy, which meant she could not be murdered until her paperwork was in order.

'I'm not giving you your card,' Irene's barrack block leader said firmly. She was a Slovakian from Žilina. In her thirties, she seemed like an old woman to Irene, who was still only twenty. 'You'll get nothing from me. You'll see, one day you'll stroll along the Corso in Bratislava.' Her words echoed Bracha's promise of future coffee and pastries.

If not despair, then what about optimism?

It would be a network of love and loyalty that helped keep Irene from suicide. For Irene, Bracha, Katka and Hunya, luck turned in their favour when clever fashion cutter Marta Fuchs appeared in Kanada I one day, with a Scharführer as escort. Marta was calm, she was confident, she was choosing fabrics from the stockpile.

Marta had a new client.

7

I Want to Live Here Till I Die

Hier will ich leben und sterben – I want to live here till I die
                                                    – Hedwig Höss[1]

Marta Fuchs, brilliant dressmaker from Bratislava, sat on a swing in the commandant's garden.

Around her, roses climbed up wooden trellises. Bees hummed around the bright clumps of bedding plants, making honey in the garden's hive. Young trees spread their leaves. They had not yet grown high enough to hide the view of barrack roofs beyond the high garden wall. Hedwig Höss's artist brother Fritz loved to come out early to paint flowers in the morning light.

The same sky spread over Marta on the swing and Marta's friends back in the camp. If they looked up, they would see the same clouds and the same sun, yet they were two utterly different worlds.

Hedwig called her garden *paradise*.

Crazy paving paths invited you to wander under shady pergolas, around an ornamental pond, alongside a superb glasshouse and down to a cool stone pavilion with two plush green sofas, a rug on the parquet floor and a cosy stove when needed.[2] Relaxing on much-appreciated days off, the camp commandant joined his family for al fresco meals around an elegant picnic table with matching benches, covered with a lovely blue cloth.

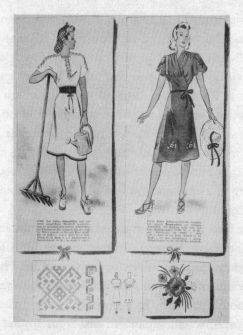

*Early 1940s gardening outfits from the German
dressmaking magazine* Mode und Wäsche.

When they picked fruit from the garden, Hedwig was said to remind the children to 'wash the strawberries well, because of the ash'.[3] Auschwitz 1 crematorium was just over the wall, after all.

Not so many years before, young Hedwig and Rudolf had dreamed of family life in the country, through the enterprises of the Artaman organisation. Heinrich Himmler had shared their Artaman farming fantasy. Now the married couple presided over a realisation of the dream, with vegetable plots in their villa's garden, and, more significantly, the establishment of vast agricultural sub-camps in the Auschwitz zone of interest, including the appropriated village of Rajsko.

It was a dream made possible by slave labour. Hedwig's

paradise and Rudolf's agricultural domain were essentially slave plantations. The 'blood-and-soil honest toil' ethos promoted by Artaman ideology was carried out by enslaved workers. A hideous biological symbiosis also linked masters and victims: vegetables at Rajsko were fertilised with human ash still sharp with pieces of bone that were not entirely burnt up.[4]

The Höss villa pleasure garden, running alongside Auschwitz main camp, was designed, built and tended by prisoners. Between 1941 and 1942, the early years of Höss occupancy, a kommando of 150 inmates reworked the garden into the paradise so adored by Hedwig.

Hedwig and Rudolf were not the only SS family to covet a green sanctuary. Properties requisitioned from local Poles were all to be made more idyllic for the SS who had moved in. Lidia Vargo of the *Grassabstechen* kommando – the mowing squad – noted that Jews had 'no right to see green grass' as she was forced to cut squares of turf from around the camp perimeter and transfer them in wheelbarrows to make SS lawns. Lotte Frankl of the *Gartenbau* kommando – the horticulture squad – was compelled to sing German marching songs as she dug over ground for SS gardens, wearing clogs without socks.[5]

Charlotte Delbo, transported to Auschwitz with seamstresses Marilou Colombain and Alida Delasalle, described running with aprons full of soil to make SS gardens.[6] Human excrement from the *Scheißkommando* was used to fertilise vegetable patches. Italian prisoner Primo Levi said human ashes were used to cover pathways around the SS village.

Stanisław Dubiel, prisoner number 6059, joined the Höss villa gardening team in April 1942, at the same time as Marta Fuchs arrived in Auschwitz. With him was Romanian inmate Franz Danimann, number 32635, who befriended Marta while tending the Höss fruit and vegetables. Danimann was a veteran of Nazi prisons, thanks to his long-term communist activities in Austria. Dubiel replaced another gardener: Bronisław Jarón, a Polish biologist and university professor, who had been executed. Hedwig never seemed satisfied with Dubiel's efforts. She was always sending to Rajsko for more pots, more seeds, more plants, as if it were her own personal garden centre. All for free, of course.

Hedwig even had coke fuel diverted from camp supplies to heat her greenhouse in winter. Her hothouse plants were snug while not so many metres away, prisoners massaged frostbitten feet and huddled in their chilly barracks. This was the same glasshouse used to grow the bouquets sent to Adolf Hitler and Eva Braun at Berchtesgaden every Christmas.[7]

As in any plantation, the slave 'owners' assumed that the servile appearance of their workers meant a servile spirit. On the contrary. Both prisoners and local Polish servants used their relative freedoms to nurture active links in the Auschwitz underground network. Marta's gardener friend Franz Danimann was a key member of the secret organisation *Kampfgruppe Auschwitz* – the Auschwitz Fighting Group.[8] When prisoners needed to gain favour with SS doctor Eduard Wirths (a favourite of the commandant but also tolerably supportive of prisoners who worked in medical roles) another of Marta's friends, inmate Hermann Langbein – secretary to Dr Wirths and member of Kampfgruppe Auschwitz – arranged for pink roses to be stolen from Hedwig's glasshouse and sent to Frau Wirths for her birthday. Unfortunately, Hedwig was invited to the birthday party. The atmosphere when she recognised her flowers was described as 'awkward all round'.[9]

Hoeing, planting and mowing, Dubiel became part of the garden scenery, easily able to eavesdrop on conversations and later share information on the underground network. During Heinrich Himmler's second visit to Auschwitz in 1943, Dubiel overheard Höss declare he was convinced he was serving his Fatherland well through his actions in the camp.[10]

It was obvious that however disagreeable Höss might find his work, he acted from compliance not coercion. His participation in genocide might be considered 'following orders', but Höss was unwavering in his support of the regime that issued, enabled and condoned these orders. Obeying commands to slaughter tens of thousands of innocent people was logistically difficult, but there is no surviving evidence that it violated his core beliefs in a Europe where 'subhumans' were replaced by worthy Germans.

Dressmaker Marta Fuchs was on the swing in the garden Dubiel and Danimann tended. She had been deported, degraded and dressed in prison gear, but not defeated. Hedwig acquired Marta to support her privileged lifestyle. Marta would use the position to save lives.

> *Today I deeply regret that I didn't spend more time with my family*
> – Rudolf Höss[11]

'You can swing if you like,' the little Höss girls told Marta. 'We'll watch to make sure you don't run away.'[12]

Eight-year-old Brigitte – born Inge-Brigitte and nicknamed 'Püppi' – saw nothing strange in having prisoners in the house and garden. 'They were always happy and wanted to play with us,' she said many decades later.[13] Heidetraut – 'Kindi' – was sixteen months older. The two sisters were often dressed alike. There was a big brother Klaus, aged twelve in 1942, and Hans-Jürgen, a round little five-year-old who liked his sweets. We can speculate who stitched the children's clothes.

For the Höss children, the garden was a playground. In summer they splashed in the small swimming pool with its very own slide. They played with the family Dalmatians on the lawn and pottered in the sandpit. In winter they set off on sleigh rides and came home to cuddles and hot cocoa. Prisoners made toys for them: a giant wooden aeroplane for Klaus with a motorised propeller, and a working model car for Hans-Jürgen to drive around in, like SS officers in cars from the Auschwitz motor pool.

Marta was originally brought to the household as a general domestic servant, to help with housework and the children, who liked to spend time with their visitors from the world beyond the high brick walls. In turn the inmates loved to see happy children and sometimes affectionate relationships developed. On one touching occasion, a well-loved prisoner-gardener came to say goodbye to the children. Hedwig did not explain to them that he had been taken away and shot against the 'Wall of Death' in nearby Block 11 of the camp.[14]

Hans-Jürgen, Kindi and Püppi liked Marta – she was friendly by nature – and they did not mind her having a go on the garden swing. Marta knew she had to be more wary of Klaus, the oldest. Klaus was a member of the Hitler Youth, and a bully. Leo Heger, Höss's chauffeur, said Klaus shot his catapult at inmates. Danuta Rzempeil, a teenage Polish girl from town drafted in to clean the children's shoes and help in the kitchen, remembered Klaus as a spiteful boy who liked to hit and whip prisoners.[15] He had been gifted a miniature SS uniform by 'Uncle Heini' – Heinrich Himmler himself – and was known to tell tales on prisoners he thought should be punished.

Hedwig also made similar reports to her husband when he came in from work. Shedding his uniform, Rudolf shed his role as commandant of an extermination centre. Püppi later described him as 'the nicest man in the world'.[16]

Of course, the children knew nothing of the true horror of their father's work. They were too young to bear responsibility; they were innocent. As were all the babies and children murdered in the camp under Höss's command, including young relatives of Bracha, Irene and their friends.

One day Hedwig let it be known that she urgently needed someone to refashion a collection of fur pieces into a coat.

'I can do that!' Marta said.

The up-cycling project was a success. Marta became a full-time seamstress in the Höss villa. Her new workroom was not a fancy salon. Hedwig had the house's attic spaces converted into separate garret rooms. Here Aryan German women doing their national *Arbeitsdienst* – work duty – were quartered, including the children's governess Elfryda, and also their Polish servant Aniela Bednarska.

Although Elfryda apparently enjoyed seeing prisoners beaten, Aniela furtively passed messages from prisoners and also smuggled food from the well-stocked Höss pantry. Aniela did concede that Rudolf was loyal to the domestics and the gardeners, even taking baskets of food and bottles of beer to the men outdoors on special occasions. The two German servants were eventually dismissed by Hedwig for being 'too lazy'. They were replaced with two Jehovah's Witnesses incarcerated in Auschwitz on account of their faith.

Hedwig said Jehovah's Witnesses made the best servants because they never stole anything. There was also the small matter of not needing to pay them wages, although officially SS families were supposed to remit 25RM to the camp administration in return for having female inmates in domestic service.

A stylish wrought iron gate opened to connect the Höss garden to the house. Steps led up to the back door, and so into the kitchen, where Hedwig did much of the everyday cooking herself. Marta, an art lover, would have been interested in the paintings hung around the house. Some were arranged by renowned Polish artist-turned-inmate Mieczysław Kościelniak, all plundered; others were originals by Hedwig's brother Fritz

Hensel – mostly landscapes of the Auschwitz area and the River Sola, across the road from the house.

A large oil painting of flowers dominated the main bedroom. Hedwig's clothes hung in a four-bay wardrobe with glazed doors reflecting twin beds. Hedwig's lingerie drawers contained underwear taken from the luggage of murdered deportees. She even appropriated underwear issued to her servants, giving them old cast-offs instead.[17]

A Polish prisoner called Wilhelm Kmak was often in the Höss house as a decorator, painting over the children's scuffs and scribbles. He asked the household dressmakers not to discourage the children from drawing on the walls, because it was his only contact with the civilian world.[18]

Höss's study was very private, supplied with books, cigarettes and vodka. Among the books was one about the birds of Auschwitz written during Höss's residence. Inspired by a friendship with his children's teacher Käthe Thomsen and her bird-loving SS husband Reinhardt – also an agronomist at Auschwitz – Höss gave orders that no birds in the camp area were to be shot. Prisoners were fair game.

Magpies made their nests in tall poplar trees around the camp: very appropriate, for a place owned by people who liked to steal whatever took their fancy.

The walnut furniture of the study and the adjacent dining room were all made by prisoners in camp workshops, as was the brightly painted furniture of the children's nursery upstairs. In fact, the Höss family were so familiar with their procurer at the workshops, a one-time professional criminal called Erich Grönke, that little Hans-Jürgen said he could not sleep unless Grönke came to say goodnight.

Grönke was manager of the *Bekleidungswerk Stätten-Lederfabrik* – a camp clothing workshop, based in a former tannery. He made daily visits to the Höss villa, providing leather-covered chairs, briefcases, handbags, suitcases and shoes; also sparkling chandeliers, and toys for the children.[19] Hedwig signed chits for delivery of ready-made plunder including tablecloths, towels, little dresses and a used grey wool Bavarian waistcoat. The waistcoat was for Hans-Jürgen.[20]

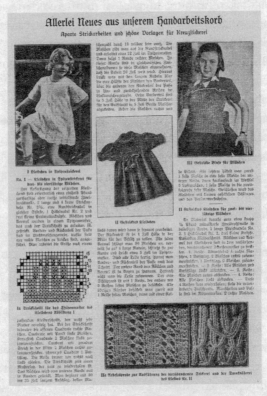

German knitting patterns for children's wear. Hedwig was persuaded by her Jewish hairdresser Manci that she should acquire an inmate to knit for the children, and so inmate Ella Braun got a protected position.

The clothes Hedwig acquired from Auschwitz plunder were then delivered to the attic sewing room for alterations. Family tradition has it that she had the buttons removed from these clothes and replaced, because of a distaste for fingering fastenings that Jewish hands had touched.[21]

Marta was not the first or only seamstress to work for Hedwig. She would, however, be the most influential and the one who lasted longest.

One of Hedwig's close friends was Mia Weiseborn. Mia was married to a camp guard. She was a very talented seamstress and produced some exquisite goldwork embroidery for Hedwig: the Höss family heraldry on purple silk. For everyday sewing, Hedwig hired a local Polish seamstress, 32-year-old Janina Szczurek. Janina had no choice but to present herself at the house on Legiónow Street. Being understandably afraid of the Nazi occupiers, Janina took one of her apprentices for support, a woman named Bronka Urbańczyk.

Girls' school outfits, featured in a 1944 edition of the German sewing magazine Mode Für Alles – *'Fashion For All'*

Hedwig was not a generous employer. Janina quit work because she got only three marks for wages and one bowl of stew during the day. Anxious not to lose her help, Hedwig offered ten marks and Janina returned. Janina linked with Agniela Bednarska, the housekeeper, to help smuggle medicine and messages where needed. She also used the excuse of needing sewing machine repairs to talk to male prisoners and share news of the war's progress.

In turn, Agniela passed packets of food to Janina, hidden inside bunches of flowers from the magical Höss garden, which Hedwig graciously permitted Janina to have.[22]

One day the Höss children came running to Janina, asking her to sew props for a game they were playing. She dutifully obliged. The commandant returned home to find Klaus wearing a newly stitched kapo armband, while the younger children were dashing about the garden as prisoners, each with a coloured triangle sewn to their clothes. Rudolf tore off the fabric emblems and any such games were forbidden. When Janina finally left the Höss villa, she was presumably glad to be free of such drama. Hedwig saved paying dressmaking wages by acquiring Jewish slave labour instead.

Hedwig was by no means the only one to take advantage of the labour pool in the concentration camp. Although there are no extant records of all inmate-servants, one Auschwitz admin-istration document lists the SS families who used Jehovah's Witnesses in their homes. About 90 such women were lodged in the Stabsgebäude with the specialist dressmaking and laundry kommandos. In May 1943, there was a request for more Jehovah's Witness prisoners to be brought to Auschwitz to help families with multiple children.[23]

Every SS family was tainted from hypocritical use of pris-oner labour. Dr Hans Münch from the Hygiene Institute in Auschwitz perhaps expressed it best. He said everyone had

Dreck am Stecken – dirt on their walking stick. He elaborated: 'It was a foregone conclusion that everybody who could had a tailor sitting in some corner to sew uniforms or other things.'[24]

There are many examples that illustrate SS complicity. An SS man in the ammunition factory asked an inmate to sew a teddy bear for his son, complete with Tyrolean hat and matching trousers.[25] An SS woman demanded a dainty home-sewn doll as a Christmas gift, with golden curls taken from a store of human hair. The seamstress in question bravely said she would use embroidery silk instead.[26]

SS auxiliary Irma Grese took her privilege to extremes, having her own pet dressmaker scurry to do her bidding in camp. Grese, only nineteen when she arrived at Auschwitz after training in Ravensbrück, was exceptionally beautiful, and called a 'blonde angel' by prisoners, who could not help contrast their own wretched appearance with Grese's tailored suits and impeccable hair.

The inmate-seamstress – Madame Grete – was rightly terrified of Grese, who was a pure sadist, and who would fly at her in a fury if her impossible demands were not met. Madame Grete had once directed her own fashion salon in Vienna, now she sewed for crusts of bread. She reported that Grese's closets were crammed with couture clothes from Paris, Vienna, Prague and Bucharest, all impregnated with the aroma of plundered perfumes.[27]

Hedwig Höss, as the commandant's wife, had even greater opportunities for exploitation. Hedwig had grown accustomed to the confident superiority of National Socialism. It suited her to make the most of it.

*Only a tiny number of SS members did not enrich themselves in
the places of destruction*   – Hermann Langbein[28]

Höss family portrait, 1943

A family portrait was taken to celebrate the birth of baby
Annegrete Höss in November 1943. Annegrete's birth certificate
has 'Auschwitz' as Place of Birth. In the photograph, Rudolf
and Klaus are in SS uniforms. Püppi and Kindi have identical
smocked dresses with puffed sleeves. Hedwig wears a stylish
afternoon dress with white polka-dots and piping. Viewed through
the filter of Nazi ideology, they are the Aryan family incarnate.

The camera used to take the picture was a gift from 'Uncle
Heini', Heinrich Himmler. The uniforms were made by slave
labour. The civilian clothes were most likely made from stolen
cloth, or altered from the belongings of murdered deportees.

Marta sewed clothes for Hedwig that perfectly suited the image of a perfect German family. As they played at home or in the garden, the Höss girls looked sweet with plaited hair and matching cotton frocks. The boys had shirts and shorts. Naturally everything was washed before being worn, unlike prisoner garments.

The children had no clue about the provenance of their clothes. Hedwig knew perfectly well. She sent her servants on errands to Grönke's tailoring workshop, and she sent Marta 'shopping' in the great warehouses of Kanada.

It was here that Bracha first spotted Marta.

Bracha and Katka had become select sewers for the SS in Kanada. Bracha, along with two sisters from southern Slovakia, had been drafted by the boss Scharführer Wiegleb. They sat and stitched in Kanada I, up on an indoor balcony that was lined with broad shelves loaded with textiles, clothing and sewing notions, as well as the sewing machine Bracha used. All were taken from the plunder piles; some from deportees' luggage, and some brought in from Aryanised Jewish shops.

In came Marta Fuchs. She spoke Hungarian – many Slovakians slipped easily from one language to another – telling Bracha what she needed from the shelves. Up Bracha jumped to find what was wanted, pulling out fabrics.

'Is this what you mean?'

'Maybe . . . or a different colour,' said Marta, and so the consultation continued.

Such was the abundance of goods there was no need for stock control, and of course, never any need for payment.

The SS helped themselves to anything and everything in the plunder warehouses of Auschwitz. In one section goods were laid out like display counters in a department store – perfumes, lingerie, handkerchiefs and hairbrushes. The appropriation was by no means solely a female vice. On the contrary, male SS officers stole quantities of money, fountain pens and watches. SS doctor Johan Kremer regularly sent parcels of goodies to friends back in Germany.

'Prisoners let me have various things from among these objects, such as soap, toothpaste, thread, darning thread, needles, etc.,' he explained at his post-war trial, adding that they were 'necessary for everyday use'.[29] The prisoners themselves were not permitted to keep such 'necessary' objects, not even their own belongings, carried into camp on arrival.

Local Polish servants forced to work in SS households reported seeing Jewish belongings in everyday use, from linens to jewellery, and that steamer trunks of valuables were sent back to Germany. Hedwig Höss kept her relatives in the Fatherland supplied via parcels from Auschwitz.

The looting was brazen, and yet entirely *illegal* according to the declaration signed by all staff at Auschwitz: 'I am acquainted with the fact, and I was thus instructed today, that I shall suffer the death penalty if I lay hands on Jewish property.'[30]

Civilian nurse Maria Stromberger, who would become one of Marta Fuchs' allies in the Auschwitz underground, refused to sign the declaration, stating indignantly, 'I'm no thief!'[31] Even Himmler, who knew full well how swollen Nazi coffers were with Jewish valuables, spoke out against theft at the same time as he congratulated his men for staying 'decent' while they slaughtered tens of thousands of Jews in killing sprees across Eastern Europe and occupied Russian lands:

'We had the moral right, we had the duty towards our people to destroy the people that wanted to destroy us. But we do not have the right to enrich ourselves by so much as a fur, as a watch, by one Mark or a cigarette or anything else.'[32]

Of course, the reason the lower SS were told not to steal was because it would be an unwelcome drain on centralised State resources. The bigwigs in Berlin wanted more profit for themselves.

SS theft became so extreme that an investigating commission eventually arrived at Auschwitz. Legal officer Robert Mulka ordered searches of the female SS and found jewellery and lingerie taken from Kanada. Sentences ranged from two to three years in prison. In contrast, unauthorised killings and sadistic torture were not investigated: they were all in a day's work at Auschwitz.

In several instances plunder was the undoing of SS men long after Auschwitz was liberated.

One of those who went on trial was SS Untersturmführer Maximilian Grabner, sadist and murderer. Kapos from Grönke's workshops brought Grabner looted commodities, which he posted back to his family in Vienna. (He also had his orderly, Corporal Pyschny, shoot foxes so his wife could have a new fox fur coat.) After the war, a former Auschwitz inmate heard of a family called Grabner in Vienna who had frequently received boxes from Upper Silesia – the Auschwitz region. Police were alerted and the wanted war criminal was arrested, then executed in December 1947. The parcels had led to his downfall and death.[33]

Greed also led to the arrest of SS Scharführer Hans Anhalt, who posted himself multiple parcels of valuables from Kanada. Post-war he took them to pawnshops to cash in. Suspicions were not aroused until 1964, when his house was searched and the remaining Kanada loot was discovered, including classy leather bags and gloves. Anhalt was sentenced to life imprisonment.[34]

One of the last SS men from Auschwitz to go to trial was Oskar Gröning, who counted and sorted valuables taken from new arrivals at the camp. In 2015 he was found guilty of facilitating mass murder. He testified that theft was 'absolutely common practice in Auschwitz'.[35]

The SS pledge of obedience unto death to the Führer and

Reich was a convenient excuse for those wanting to be exonerated of crimes post-war, using the *I was only following orders* argument. Clearly the SS in Auschwitz chose which orders they were happy to follow, and which orders could be disregarded.

Only the wives of high-ranking Nazis had been invited. Many of them were absolutely hideous, others were very elegant; our fashion was supposed to make them cultivated
> – Gerd Staebe, Berlin fashion designer, presenting to SS wives at the Goering residence[36]

A leading SS judge noted that SS leaders at Auschwitz were not searched for stolen goods; it was the small fry who were hauled up for infringements. Rudolf Höss spoke out against black-market dealing, yet did not question the provenance of his well-furnished house and well-stocked garden. He was undoubtedly complicit in acquiring goods, and in protecting SS staff who procured them, including the man who picked up nice 'Aryanised' fabrics for him while on buying trips for the camp administration.[37] Rank has its privileges.

In the Third Reich, differences in rank had to be emphasised to maintain the power structure. Hedwig Höss was hostess to influential and illustrious guests such as SS general Oswald Pohl, chief of SS industrial enterprises, who dined on generous portions of baked pork, real coffee and refreshing beer during a ceremonial dinner at her Auschwitz house in September 1942.[38] Hedwig not only had Marta making clothes to suit her personal taste, she also needed a wardrobe that reflected her status as the commandant's wife. Hedwig did not shine with the brilliance of jewelled Emmy Goering, or have the extreme grooming of Magda Goebbels, but she welcomed high-ranking dignitaries and important industrialists, along with their wives.

Men dominated the political and military spheres of the Third

Reich. Hedwig's role, in keeping with Nazi ideology, was domestic. Behind the scenes, in a wrap-around apron, she compelled inmates to fill her pantry with food from the camp black market – sugar, cocoa, cinnamon, margarine – paying them in cigarettes for this extreme risk. At the dining table, in elegant evening wear, she treated guests to exquisite feasts. There was no hint of wartime rationing or food coupons. Hedwig's own brother Fritz commented on the hospitality: 'I felt comfortable in Auschwitz, it was all in abundance available.'[39]

Not so far away, Bracha, Irene, Katka and Hunya drank turnip soup and gnawed on hard bread. Rudolf Höss was correct when he described Auschwitz-Birkenau as 'another planet' while giving Fritz a tour of the camp.[40]

On the occasion of Himmler's second visit in January 1943, Hedwig served such a fine breakfast he was late arriving to a demonstration of the gas chamber operation. The chosen victims endured the wait locked inside the cement hall with its fake shower heads. After a tour of the camp in bitterly cold weather, Himmler could warm up at the villa, which had been fitted with modern central heating. When Adolf Eichmann visited, he described Hedwig's domain as 'homey and nice'.[41]

The villa guest-book filled with compliments: 'Thanks to Mother Höss' – 'Wishing you health, happiness and contentment' – 'I spent many hours of relaxation with old friends'.[42]

A Nazi wife existed to produce children, and to support her husband. Hedwig succeeded with honours, inviting old friends to stay as well as comrades from the camp, so Rudolf could relax after a hard day facilitating genocide. There were picnics and horse rides along the nearby river bank, and even excursions to a nearby SS resort called Solahütte, where officers and female auxiliaries relaxed on a sun deck, sang to accordion accompaniment, took meadowland walks and picked fresh blueberries.[43]

SS personnel could enjoy the diversion of theatre perform-ances, live opera and raucous sing-a-longs, as well as film showings, a casino and a library. There were numerous restaur-ants in the nearby town, such as the Ratshof or Gasthofzur Burg.

As the most important people in Auschwitz, Hedwig and Rudolf had front row seats for all staged entertainments, and they dressed accordingly. Music was a highlight of camp life for the SS. On Sundays an orchestra of male prisoners played in the square between the Höss villa and the crematorium building.

In Birkenau there was a women's orchestra entirely comprised of prisoners. They played Viennese waltzes and Liszt's *Hungarian Rhapsody* at a special summer concert. One senior SS wife attended with her family, wearing a dirndl skirt of generous proportions. Her son had a sign around his neck declaring that he was the son of SS Lagerführer Schwarzhuber, to ensure he was not mistaken for a Jewish child and gassed.[44]

For evening concerts, the orchestra soloist was given a red, low-cut evening gown from Kanada. The main orchestra were dressed identically, with outfits sewn in a Birkenau workshop. Hungarian seamstress Ilona Hochfelder remembered stitching white and red blouses for the orchestra, to be worn with black or navy skirts. Her reward was a cube of sugar and an apple. Ilona's previous dressmaking job had been for the illustrious house of Chanel in Paris. Ilona was so moved to hear the music, she went to speak with the conductor.[45]

Hunya Volkmann had no such rapturous memories of the orchestra, much as she had adored concerts back in Leipzig. In Auschwitz and Birkenau, musicians were forced to play jolly tunes for prisoners marching to and from work. Hunya found it a terrifying discordant ritual, and visualised the musicians 'like ghosts from another world'.[46]

★

Another role Hedwig had to take on was that of mother-figure for the female camp guards. Their average age was twenty-six; some were mere teenagers. They underwent dehumanising training but they were still very human, with their own individual spectrum of indulged vices and supressed virtues. They came to Hedwig to pour out their troubles; about how they suffered because of the brutal work they had to do. The only 'consolation' on offer from Hedwig was that when the war was over, their troubles would be over too: the Jews would all be dead.[47]

When Hedwig and Rudolf were dressed for an excursion out of Auschwitz, they could call on SS Lagerfüherin Maria Mandl to babysit. Mandl, a committed, violent Jew-hater, was patron of the women's orchestra, and she also loved children. The Höss family photograph album shows her in a jazzy bathing suit at the swimming pier on the River Sola, ready to take a dip with the Höss girls. Nurse Maria Stromberger described Mandl as 'the devil incarnate'.[48]

One evening Hedwig and Rudolf went for a night at the casino in the officers' mess. In a variation of the anecdote Polish seamstress Janina Szczurek told about the children playing prisoner, Hedwig's embroiderer friend Mia Weiseborn sewed brassards and insignia so that everyone could play at kapos beating a prisoner. In this instance the target was real-life inmate Sophie Stipel, the cook. In this 'game', Sophie Stipel was tied to a chair and hit with soap-weighted towels. Hedwig and Rudolf were apparently unimpressed when they came home to such a scene.[49]

After my wife found out what I was doing we seldom desired sexual intercourse
                                        – Rudolf Höss[50]

Home was a haven for SS men severely mentally destabilised by their relentless murderous actions. Frau Moll came to tell

Hedwig that her husband Otto often cried out in his sleep – the conversation was overheard by a seamstress in the house. Did Frau Moll know that among many other atrocities, Otto had personally thrown living babies into boiling human fat? Marianne Boger, married to one of the most brutal torturers in the camp, said her husband often came home exhausted at meal times, and that she worried about his nerves.[51]

Lingerie and nightgowns played their part in soothing menfolk, for marital sex was recognised as a relaxing influence on SS men. SS doctor Hans Delmotte had serious qualms about mass executions, so his wife Klara – a striking woman who wore black and white to complement her Great Dane dog – was brought to Auschwitz as a calming sexual outlet.[52]

Emotionally reclusive, and often burdened with administrative pressures, Rudolf Höss allegedly found his sexual outlet with a non-Jewish prisoner who had been responsible for sorting valuables at Kanada – 'Diamond' Nora Hodys. She was introduced to Höss through Hedwig's love of fine furnishings: Hodys was brought to the villa to mend a tapestry carpet, and then extended her needlework skills to produce two new tapestries, as well as silk pillows, a bedside rug and bed covers. She also supplied Höss with jewellery from the plunder warehouse.

In August 1942, Hodys was invited to celebrate her fortieth birthday in the Höss garden. She has been identified in a surviving family photo, with little Hans-Jürgen on her lap and Püppi nearby. Her hair is in lush sausage curls, held in place with a colourful scarf. Her front-buttoned dress is neat and modest. Although the commandant was highly critical of low-quality guards who had sexual liaisons with prisoners, this did not stop him advancing on Hodys.

It was the gardener, Stanisław Dubiel, who spotted them embracing. He also claimed to overhear Hedwig rowing with her husband about 'that woman'. Hedwig had Hodys dismissed as soon as Rudolf was away from home. According to Hodys, the commandant visited her for non-negotiable sex while she was in prison in the camp; she claimed to have been forced to abort a baby soon afterwards. Mentioning her name was forbidden in the Höss family. In later years, Hedwig defaced a printed account of the Hodys affair with the words: 'This made up romance which no one knows the truth about.'[53]

As for Hedwig's own sex life in Auschwitz, despite rumours of a clinch in the gazebo with a canteen manager from a shoe factory in nearby Chełmek, she maintained the image of a perfect Nazi wife and mother. Rudolf claimed that sex between them was infrequent once she found out the true nature of Auschwitz – that it was an extermination camp. It begs the questions, how much did SS wives know about the escalating genocide, and, more significantly, how much did they care?

Höss had promised Himmler that the extermination programme would be kept a secret Reich matter. Himmler himself declared it to be 'an unwritten and never-to-be-written page of glory in our history'.[54] As Himmler toured killing sites across Eastern Europe, he regularly wrote to his wife Marga and his daughter Gudrun, giving updates about his health and his heavy workload, and taking every opportunity to post packages of treats. He sent brandy and books, soap and shampoo . . . chocolates, cookies, condensed milk . . . fabrics, embroideries, frocks and furs.

Although Marga Himmler was committed to Artaman and Nazi ideologies, calling Jews 'rabble' and wishing they would be 'put behind bars and made to work until they die', her husband wrote nothing about the exterminations he ordered and witnessed. Marga, despite having prisoners from Dachau labouring on her land, was to be protected from sordid realities.[55]

Hedwig, however, became curious during a social event with Fritz Bracht, who was Gauleiter of Upper Silesia, a territory that included Auschwitz. He and his family lived in nearby Katowice. Bracht had played host to Heinrich Himmler during Himmler's July 1942 tour of the Auschwitz zone of interest. By Himmler's special request, Hedwig Höss was also invited. During formal dinners, the custom was for ladies to 'retire' from the dining room so the men could discuss political and business matters. On one occasion, Bracht spoke too freely about the true nature of the death camp in front of Hedwig. She later asked her husband if the Gauleiter's comments were true; Rudolf conceded that they were.[56]

Hedwig was no stranger to Nazi hate speech. She had willingly absorbed the racist tenets of the Artaman society. She had raised her children on the periphery of Dachau and Sachsenhausen 're-education' camps. She was living in a house seized from its rightful owner, wearing clothes taken from the dead, and served by enslaved labourers stolen away from their own lives and families. Was it really such a revelation to know that the poison of anti-Jewish propaganda had gradually been escalated into the poison of Zyklon B crystals dropped into a sealed chamber?

If Marta, sewing in the attic of the Höss house, could look out over the camp and see how her fellow prisoners were treated, how could Hedwig be so blind? If local Polish people understood the significance of smoke from pyres and flames from chimneys and people who arrived but then vanished, how could Hedwig be so ignorant? Perhaps Hedwig saw only what she wanted to see – her beautiful garden, her paintings, her tapestries and dresses.

Other SS wives found comfort in avoiding all acknowledgement of the crimes being committed by their husbands. Maids cleaned shit from SS boots when husbands came home from work, and laundered blood from uniforms. And the smell from

the camp? 'Just the stink of garlic from the sausage fac...'
said Elfriede Kitt, married to a camp physician who conducted
hideous experiments on prisoners. Frau Kitt worked with her
husband as an assistant. Off-duty she indulged in fabrics and
perfumes purloined from the camp.[57]

Dr Josef Mengele's new wife Irene was more direct about
questioning her husband.

'Where does the stink come from?'

'Don't ask me,' he replied.

She obligingly avoided the topic, yet knew about her
husband's medical work, and his role in selecting people for
death. She was even treated for diphtheria at the SS hospital
opposite the crematorium.[58]

'I've heard that you people are gassing women and children
here. I hope you don't have anything to do with that,' said
Frieda Klehr to her husband.

'I don't kill, I heal,' he reassured her.[59]

Dr Klehr personally murdered many thousands of prisoners
with phenol injections to the heart, dressed in a white lab coat,
or in pink rubber apron and rubber gloves. From 1943 he was
in charge of the disinfection kommando, using Zyklon B to
delouse clothes and barracks, and to gas prisoners.

Good-looking Eryka Fischer luxuriated in velvet sheets and
monogrammed lingerie. Her husband was Dr Horst Fischer,
responsible for selections at the Birkenau camp. Frau Fischer let
her Polish maid play dress-up in glamorous clothes. During Frau
Fischer's stay in the SS hospital, the 'Gypsy camp' in Birkenau
was liquidated. Her husband was frank about the action, saying
the gypsies had 'gone up in smoke'.[60]

Even if they knew of the mass exterminations of Jews, Poles,
POWs, Roma, Sinti, homosexuals and many others, could the
SS wives be classed as complicit? Were they bystanders, or
so intimate with the perpetrators they could be said to be

same guilt? Although Nazi women were

luded from a pro-active political or military

ime, they supported the men who made and

policies. Crucially, these actions were not crim-

Third Reich. It is perhaps more pertinent to

cons. ., did the women *care* about the fate of those their

menfolk persecuted?

Frau Faust, director of the Red Cross in Auschwitz, screamed and called the police when a Jewish inmate begged her for bread.

Frau Wiegleb, wife of the Scharführer for whom Bracha sewed in Kanada, gave inmates cake when they came to work in her house or garden.

Frau Palitzsch, married to the man the camp resistance labelled 'the biggest bastard in Auschwitz', was a gentle soul according to her Polish maid. When Frau Palitzsch complained about an inmate's shoddy work at her home, the inmate was tortured.[61]

Greta Schild, wife of an Auschwitz guard, gave her Polish maid money, sweets and an apron at Christmas. When Greta's mother visited to help look after a new baby, she stood at a window looking out at prisoners labouring in the gravel pits outside and wept, saying over and over, 'It shouldn't be like this.'[62]

Well-groomed Käthe Rohde lavished treats and fabric on her Polish maid. She loved parties and pretty things. Items that came from Kanada were carefully washed with a solution of potassium permanganate. She was overjoyed to hear about mass transportations of Jews arriving from Hungary in summer 1944, because they would bring 'whole mountains of treasure'.[63]

And then there was Hedwig.

*My grandmother was a malicious and greedy woman, who shame-
lessly exploited her position as wife of the Commander*

– Rainer Höss[64]

Hedwig was said to be loyal to the inmates who worked in her house and garden. She gave them food, cigarettes and flower bouquets. She and her husband interceded to stop transfers, punishments and even executions. Marta's own life was spared thanks to Hedwig and Rudolf. Three times the Höss gardener Stanisław Dubiel had his life saved, yet he heard Hedwig refer to her husband as *Sonderbeauftragter für die Judenvernichtung in Europa* – Special Plenipotentiary for Exterminating Jews in Europe. Hedwig also declared that 'at the right moment, the turn of even the English Jews would come.'[65]

Perhaps it was a matter of convenience for the commandant and his wife to save their own personal slave workers, while hundreds of transports of Jews arrived at Auschwitz to be killed immediately, or worked to death after unimaginable suffering.

While working as a dressmaker for Hedwig Höss, Marta had to balance a dual role of service and subterfuge. On the one hand, her work was valued and she was a familiar face in the house; on the other hand, she knew from bitter experience how prisoners suffered in the camps, and she was determined to use her own protected position to help others. Marta was able to arrange for a second Jewish seamstress to join her in the attic salon, and therefore lift another woman out of the hell of Birkenau.[66]

One day Hedwig climbed the stairs to the attic and sat watching the two women sew. She suddenly spoke.

'You work quickly and well. How is that possible? After all, Jews are parasites and con artists, and the Jews used to do nothing but sit around in cafés. Where did you learn to work like this?'[67]

Hedwig's admiration was saturated with antisemitism. Did she see Marta as a Jew or as a human being?

Hedwig was not the only one to admire Marta's sewing skills. The other SS wives became envious of the personal service Marta provided. They too wanted to take advantage of Jewish talent to refresh their wardrobes. Why should Frau Höss have all the benefits? Hedwig saw an opportunity to expand the attic sewing workshop. She conceived of a new establishment: a select fashion salon in the concentration camp, catering to a Nazi elite.

Whether bystanders, sympathisers or collaborators, SS wives of Auschwitz were to become Marta's future clients at this salon. Upon their fashion whims the fate of many others would depend. The Auschwitz system of exploitation was designed to pauperise and destroy inmates; Marta would use it to try to save them.

8

Out of Ten Thousand Women

*Out of the ten thousand women in Birkenau, there were def-
initely at least five hundred good seamstresses, but if they didn't
have any contacts, they didn't have any luck* – Bracha Berkovič

'Your number's up' – an expression easily used in everyday
conversation.

For a prisoner in the concentration camp system, being
singled out by number could be the final step before the end.
One day in early summer 1943, Irene Reichenberg's number
was called – 2786.

Standing out from the crowd usually meant trouble at the
best of times, far better not to draw the attention of the SS
guards, yet Irene heard her number and stepped forward,
expecting the worst. What did she care about her fate? She was
still mourning the deaths of her three sisters, Frieda, Jolli and
Edith; still courting the idea of death as an escape.

Irene was sent to the Birkenau administration offices, situated
alongside the now-infamous brick entrance to the camp. Here
she was stripped, assessed by doctors and asked, 'What is your
profession?'

'Dressmaker,' she replied.

This simple answer saved her life, and her sanity.

Irene had been chosen to join a select group of seamstresses
in the new fashion salon established in Auschwitz by Hedwig
Höss. It was called the *Obere Nähstube*, or Upper Tailoring

Studio. Irene had been picked not because she was the most skilled, or most experienced in her field, but because she was related by marriage to the salon's superb new kapo, Marta Fuchs. (Irene's brother Laci had married Marta's sister Turulka.) Marta told the SS woman in charge of the salon – SS Rapportführerin Ruppert – that there were too many orders for clothes and not enough workers.

Autumn suit fashions in Mode Für Alle, *1944*

'Have you got anyone in mind?' Ruppert wanted to know.

'Yes. Reichenberg, Irene, number 2786.'

Once safely at the workshop, Irene began to pester Marta: 'Listen, I have a good friend – Berkovič, Bracha, number 4245. She's wonderful – could you request her too?'

Marta did not take much persuading. Two months after Irene arrived, Bracha was welcomed to the salon. She promptly announced, 'I have a sister . . .'

Two weeks later Katka Berkovič, number 4246, was summoned to sew as the new specialist in coats and suits.

By autumn 1943, the Upper Tailoring Studio had grown from two women to fifteen, and it would not stop there.

Where the SS selected people for death, in picking out her helpers Marta was selecting them for a better chance at life. Inevitably her first choices were for women she knew. This was how privilege worked in the camps. Networks of connection, or 'protection', were crucial. The example of Marta gathering dressmakers in Auschwitz demonstrates how close the bonds of family and nationality were for Jewish inmates, as well as for other groups who were imprisoned. When families were wrenched apart, the anguish could naturally lead to despair, as it had for Irene. Some form of connection and collaboration was essential for mental survival, and this emotional strength in turn gave people more physical resilience.

Commandant Höss sneered at evidence of Jewish family ties, stating, 'They cling to each other like leeches.' Next he contradicted himself by deploring what he saw as Jewish lack of solidarity. 'In their situation,' he wrote, 'you would assume that they would protect each other. But no, it was just the opposite.'[1]

Despite frequent boasts that he understood prisoner mentality, Höss not only shrugged off his own responsibility for creating conditions of either solidarity or infighting, he also avoided any expression of compassion for the complex human experiences endured by inmates in Auschwitz. Acknowledging normal instincts of love, loyalty or self-preservation would have meant acknowledging that the prisoners were fully human.

This was something Höss put great effort into resisting: if the prisoners were human, his treatment of them could only be considered inhuman. It was more comfortable for Höss to create a protective barrier of prejudice than to think of himself – ostensibly a loving family man reading bedtime fairy tales to his children at home – as a monster.

Höss was aware of the system of favouritism among privileged prisoners, but he chose to ignore the fact that he and his regime were responsible for the antagonistic environment in which too many people fought for too meagre resources. He criticised women who competed for good jobs in the camps:

'The safer the position, the more desirable it was, and the more it was fought over. There was no consideration for others. This was a fight in which everything was at stake. No means were spared, no matter how depraved, in order to free up such a position or to hold on to it. For the most part, the unscrupulous were the winners.'[2]

Auschwitz did have a large numbers of prisoners who were genuine criminals – murderers and rapists included – as opposed to civilians who had been arrested because of their race, religion, politics, sexuality or culture. Survivalists of any background certainly fought their way to positions of relative status and power. Veterans of the system, who had survived for months and years against the odds, were respected and often feared.

Arrivals at Auschwitz in the early years were tattooed with the lowest batches of numbers. Those who endured the longest were known as Low Numbers. As 'old-timers' in the Auschwitz system, it was inevitable that Low Number Slovakian Jews – those who came on the first female transports into the camp – would know how to turn situations to their advantage whenever possible. Having gained coveted jobs, some of them used their positions to support a favoured few, engineering a hardcore, semi-criminal clique, but others created more nurturing groups, motivated by a spirit of co-operation and generosity that Höss either did not see, or could not acknowledge.

Höss observed Auschwitz inmates as if they were a different species, caged in a savage zoo, not human beings his own organisation had reduced to raw survival tactics. His cool condemnation, 'There was no consideration for others,' is particularly chilling in view of his own detached authority over mass murder. It is also demonstrably false when applied to kapo Marta Fuchs.

In short, Marta used her privilege to help others. The new dressmaking studio was to be a haven to rescue as many women as possible from Birkenau.

Much as the traditional female skill of sewing was to be a salvation, the gendered world of secretarial work would also enable prisoners to support one another, since within the SS administration system it was female Jewish inmates who did the typing, filing and record-keeping regarding work deployments. They were based at the SS admin building, the Stabsgebäude.

Katya Singer was a Czech Jew in the Auschwitz administration who worked on the prisoner tally log book – the *Lagerbuch* – for two years. She definitely used her connections to get favours. When an SS officer asked her why she was pestering him to help particular prisoners, she told him bluntly, 'These are my people.'[3]

Secretarial staff in the Stabsgebäude would also learn to use the complex filing system for camp resistance. The *Lagerbuch* that Katya maintained became an essential tool for analysing worker statistics. The *Arbeitsdienst* (work registry) logged how many prisoners were available in certain professions. The *Arbeitseinsatz* (work deployment department) aimed to supply prisoner labour where it was needed.

Bureau DII of the Economic Headquarters was notified once a month how many prisoners were available in certain professions. Kapos from different work kommandos would put a request to admin each week, stating the numbers and skills of labourers required. Inmate-clerks recommended suitable workers. They could reward friends with better work kommandos, or take revenge on prisoners they did not like by arranging for them to be sent to a tough squad.

So it was that Marta could check the meticulous card index to see which of her friends were in the camp, and which numbers might be called.

For their part, prisoners mired in the nightmare of Birkenau also did their best to make connections. It was not simply a question of wanting a few improvements, it was a matter of life or death. Renée Ungar, rabbi's daughter and Irene's friend from Bratislava, had a temporary office job until October 1942, when she was thrown back into the general labour pool. Weakened by typhoid fever and malaria, Renée knew she was not likely to last long. Day and night she thought about how she could save herself. She spread the word that she could do secretarial or seamstress work, and, when it seemed she could not hold on any longer, she was accepted to Marta's kommando at the Upper Tailoring Studio.

Renée was very frank about her luck. She knew there were haute couture dressmakers from France trapped in Birkenau, while she was not even a professional seamstress yet. Marta reassured her: she could work and learn. Even when she had reached relative safety, Renée could not forget other girls dying by the thousands, including many of her friends.

Rudolf Vrba, the Slovakian who had been so kind to Irene back in Kanada, recognised that the privilege of Low Number Slovakian woman came at a price. He commented, 'If today they enjoy certain privileges, they have previously undergone frightful sufferings.'[4]

Of the first transports of Jews to arrive in Auschwitz in 1942, over ninety per cent were dead within the first four months. Of the 10,000 Jewish women deported from Slovakia, only about two hundred would ever return home.[5]

We'll find out if you can sew. If it turns out you lied, you will be sent to Block 10! — SS Lagerführerin Maria Mandl[6]

Hunya Volkmann, despite her innate dignity and resilience, was also close to despair when her number – 46351 – was called. She did not have the advantage of being a Low Number. Ground down by hard labour in the weaving shed, fogged by fever, and weakened by highly painful infected abscesses, Hunya had no choice but to have her number put on the hospital sick list. She was revolted by the conditions in the prisoner Revier. The beds were thick with faeces. There was no bedding, and no chance of washing. Lice crawled over her naked body. Bed mates quickly became corpses.

Hunya was saved by friendship and loyalty – something the Nazis could not stamp out despite all their abuses. In the Revier she was cared for by a friend formerly from the Leipzig Jewish hospital, Otti Itzikson. While there was not much that could be done medically, Otti arranged for Hunya to be hidden in a non-Jewish part of the hut on the day that all Jewish patients were selected for death. Number 46351 was not thrown onto the wagon of living dead destined for the gas.

After four weeks of clinging to life, Hunya was released. She stumbled back to her barracks, where her friends greeted her with unbelievable news: she had been summoned to a job at the Stabsgebäude – a legendary placement. However, she had missed her chance by being in the Revier. No one sick was allowed near the SS.

'Don't worry,' friends reassured her. 'You'll be asked again, for sure.'

The key to the request for Hunya's transfer was actually Kanada. Some young women from her home town of Kežmarok were sorting documents from plundered baggage in Kanada when they came across Hunya's passport. Quickly they alerted one of Hunya's cousins, a woman named Mariska, who worked as secretary to a high-ranking SS officer in the Stabsgebäude. Marishka consulted with Marta Fuchs, and the summons went out.[7]

Hunya hardly dared hope for a second chance. When it came, she was still nervous, because she was sent to Block 10. All horror stories spread around the camp about Block 10 were true. It was a place of medical torture, where SS doctors headed by Josef Mengele experimented on live human subjects.

Hunya waited to have a medical assessment, along with several other candidates for the dressmaking position. Anyone working in close proximity with the SS had to be declared fit and free of infection. Hunya's wounds were healing, but she was still feverish from her illness; there was a strong chance she would not pass. Once again luck and human decency played a part: a nurse in Block 10 knew Hunya's family and quickly shook down the thermometer before the doctor had chance to read the high temperature.

Again Hunya was deloused. Even so, the SS doctor was reluctant to go near her. From his seat he ordered her to turn this way and that, and wrote his verdict without even looking at her. To him, she was merely one more body. To her, this would be a decision of life-changing implications.

Then came the agony of waiting for results. Finally Hunya heard her name. She had passed.

Simultaneously excited and anxious, Hunya ran to her next appointment, a work audition. Other hopefuls were already sewing. One by one inmates were called before the examiners. Only two women were picked from the group. One of them was Hunya: number 46351 was now officially transferred to the Stabsgebäude.

We completely left hell – Katka Berkovič[8]

It was bliss to be marched for about two kilometres out of Birkenau's polluted air, over the railway sidings, through the outskirts of the town and along the link roads to the main Auschwitz site. Hunya's destination – the Stabsgebäude at 8 Maksymiliana Kolbego Street – was bigger than most camp buildings, with five floors in total and a pleasantly symmetrical gabled roof. When the Germans initially appropriated land and property for the new concentration camp complex, this handsome building was seized from the Polish Tobacco Monopoly Company. Dating back to the Great War, it was now repurposed as the heart of Auschwitz bureaucracy.

Himmler intended the Auschwitz zone of interest to be a centre of agriculture and industry, all supporting the war effort, as well as contributing to SS power. The multitude of enterprises required thousands of staff and appropriate administration. The Stabsgebäude was the hub of this complex – 'swarming with female Jewish prisoners,' sneered Höss, even as he took advantage of their unpaid labour. The Stabsgebäude also housed female SS guards, inmate-servants to SS families (mainly Jehovah's Witnesses) and various kommandos for laundry and mending. In addition, there were ammunition stores, a beauty parlour and hair salon for guards, basement dormitories for three hundred inmate-workers, and Hedwig Höss's fashion salon.

Hedwig's comfortable villa was a mere ten-minute walk around the perimeter walls of Auschwitz main camp. Not too far to come for a fitting. Marta was very familiar with the route, as she still had to return to the villa to work there in addition to her duties as kapo in the Upper Tailoring Studio.

Arriving at the Stabsgebäude, Hunya barely had time to register a manicured garden, an electrified fence and sentry towers. She was not to know she had crossed the yard where the first roll call in the history of Auschwitz camp had been held, or that the first ever prisoners in Auschwitz had been housed in that very building. She had no way of foreseeing that decades in the future, the building would be re-purposed as an airy vocational school for local Polish students. All she could think when she arrived was that she must be dreaming.

Hunya's escort led the two new seamstresses to a basement door and shouted, 'Here's the latest shipment!'

There were sounds of laundry slapping, and food odours from a kitchen. Simple details, reminiscent of ordinary life.

A pretty young girl ran up, looked Hunya over, and frowned. Then she brightened and exclaimed, 'It *is* you!'

Conscious of her sack dress and stockings tied with string, of her gaunt features, greying hair and scrawny body, Hunya answered wryly, 'What did you expect? That I'd look like I did back in Kežmarok?'

They had known each other before the war, but Hunya had been so transformed by Birkenau she was almost unrecognisable. The girl apologised over and over for the mistake and invited Hunya to wash before meeting other Slovakian inmates, down on the lowest basement level of the Stabsgebäude, in the *Flickstube* – the mending room.

It was completely surreal for Hunya to shed Birkenau misery and be welcomed into such warm, happy company. Everyone was delighted to see her. The reunion got a bit rowdy, drawing the attention of the block leader, the inmate responsible for general order, cleanliness and food distribution.

In the Stabsgebäude the block leader was Maria Maul, a Christian political prisoner from Germany. Thanks to her fervent communism, Maria had been in and out of prisons and camps since the Nazis came to power in 1933.[9] She was respected for being fair and reasonable. Even so, she demanded to know what the racket was.

'It's Hunya,' the young women replied happily. 'We haven't seen her for years!'

Hunya felt a hand on her shoulder and turned to see Marta Fuchs, the Upper Tailoring Studio kapo. Marta smiled and introduced herself.

'Do you want to come up to the dressmaking studio?'

To be asked her preference after months of orders and violence was astonishing. Hunya felt some of her self-respect returning.

'Actually,' she said, 'since it's late now, I think I'll start work tomorrow morning.'

A simple act of agency such as this was powerfully restorative to someone whose independence had been so radically stripped away.

Only when Marta had gone did the other women tell Hunya to watch her tone: any other kapo would have punished her severely for a response.

The SS demanded cleanliness from the prisoners who came into contact with them and the faultless appearance of their clothes!

– Erika Kounio[10]

Life in the Stabsgebäude was heaven compared to the rest of the camp complex, but there were still bars on the dormitory windows. A prominent sign in the Stabsgebäude summed up the ambiguous status of the inmates working there:

EINE LAUS DEIN TOD
A Louse Is Your Death

On the one hand, the SS fear of typhus and other diseases meant prisoners had access to running water, working showers and flushing toilets in the admin block. On the other hand, any symptom of contagion from the prisoners could mean ejection from the Stabsgebäude, to almost certain death in Birkenau. Conditions in the Stabsgebäude were too good to be lost.

Because there were not enough beds for everyone in the huge basement dormitory, the women slept in shifts. They had a bed to themselves at least. As the day shift got up to work, the night shift crawled into the warm bunks; Hunya was to share with a laundress who was exhausted by night-long washing of SS dirty linen. By normal standards the two-storey wooden bunks were crude and the bedding was meagre – only one sheet stretched over the straw-filled mattress, with a single blanket cover. By Auschwitz standards it was five star luxury. Eventually Hunya would organise a quilt for her bunk.

In those first few days at the Stabsgebäude, Hunya luxuriated in the novelty of having time to wash and dress each morning. Reveille was 5 a.m., and roll call was held at 7 a.m. in the wide corridor of the basement, not out in sun, rain storms or snow. It was also over quickly, so they could all get to work. Hunya delighted in the sight of women running along the corridor with the tips of their headscarves bobbing 'like a flock of little geese coming out of the water and shaking their tails'.[11]

There was the possibility of surreptitiously using facilities in the lower-basement laundry kommando, the *Wäscherei*, to wash uniforms. Stabsgebäude clerical staff wore striped dresses and white headscarves; the seamstresses had grey cotton dresses, white aprons and brown overalls. SS laundry was all done by hand until the installation of machines in the camp extension in 1944, with a team of 100 women working day and night shifts. There were tubs with cold water for soaking dirty clothes, and tubs for boiling them; washboards for scrubbing and mangles for smoothing. Clothes were dried up in the attic.

In the *Bügelstube*, the ironing room, forty women sweated over their work, also on day and night shifts. Commandant

Höss liked his shirts to be presented as fresh and crisp as if brand-new from a shop. One of Hunya's dorm-mates, Sophie Löwenstein from Munich, had the dubious honour of washing the underwear of Dr Mengele, Oberaufseherin Irma Grese and Lagerkommando Josef Kramer – sadists all of them.[12]

The food was the same inadequate fare served to all prisoners. It was a menu of ersatz tea and coffee, turnip soup with the occasional bonus of potato peelings, bread with margarine and sausage. It came from the main camp kitchen, just over the road, and the cooks sometimes added extra portions of fat to smear on the bread. Birkenau slops had left Hunya's stomach too sensitive to manage the half-decent fodder of the Stabsgebäude. In common with all the women, she suffered symptoms of long-term malnutrition.

However, she did not have to fight for each meal, which was a significant improvement on the meal-time savagery in Birkenau. Food was served in real crockery and eaten in the basement corridor, or on their bunk beds. The Upper Tailoring Studio even had a hot plate for warming lunchtime soup. SS women sometimes brought the seamstresses lumps of sugar or bars of chocolate, given out of gratitude, or guilt perhaps.

Better still, four times a year Stabsgebäude inmates were allocated a parcel from the postal store. These parcels were originally meant for other Auschwitz prisoners, but the SS never delivered them. Most of the food would be spoiled by the time they were redistributed, since the best items were pilfered by the SS, but occasionally the women got lucky. They shared whatever they acquired.

Remarkably, the Stabsgebäude women were occasionally able to send and receive mail, or to arrange communications through covert channels. Surviving postcard messages are evidence that they got parcels from friends back home. One of Marta's closest friends in the Stabsgebäude, bright little Ella Neugebauer, wrote to 5 Liptovská Street in Bratislava to thank Dezider Neumann for sending two cheeses, chocolate, bacon, sausage, tomatoes, preserves, cream and almonds: a feast![13]

Marta herself wrote to her family in hiding, expressing gratitude for food parcels – especially bacon and lemons – as well as sending 'millions of kisses' to her loved ones.[14] The stamp on the postcard featured Adolf Hitler's profile, of course.

Detail of postcard from Marta Fuchs, 3 March 1944

The most obvious difference between Stabsgebäude workers and Birkenau inmates was something Hunya experienced first-hand – their appearance. The transition from low-status clothes to better outfits made a powerful impression on all the women lucky enough to be selected. However, it also disturbed the well-established Nazi theatrics of guards who looked powerful and prisoners who looked like vermin. To maintain the distinction between 'superhumans' and 'subhumans', Stabsgebäude workers still had their hair cropped short. SS women had four beauticians on hand to amplify their own privilege, as well as a hairdressing salon.

Having clean, decent clothes helped restore a feeling of being human. In the Stabsgebäude there was far more tolerance of inmates who had 'non-uniform' garments. One of Bracha's friends in the admin block, Greek deportee Erika Kounio, organised a pink blouse from Kanada. She wore it under her striped prison dress. It felt like pure luxury, and she even dared permit a hint of pink at the neckline. By the summer of 1944, the SS had so far normalised their interactions with Stabsgebäude staff that they decreed the inmates would be issued with fashionable dresses. Naturally, there would be no financial outlay for such extravagance: the new clothes came from Kanada.

That season polka-dot dresses were in fashion – this can be seen in photographs of Jewish people being 'processed' on arrival in Birkenau in the summer of 1944 – so there was an abundance to choose from among the garments tipped from deportee luggage, or stripped from deportee bodies. Blue-grey uniforms were swapped for blue frocks with white spots. Even while she revelled in the soft elegance of her new frock, Erika Kounio wondered what had happened to the unfortunate woman who had first worn it. She told herself to harden her heart and wear it, and to remember everything that she heard or saw in the Stabsgebäude.[15]

In addition to the personalisation and dignity offered by clean, decent clothes, there was also the factor that SS staff worked alongside some highly qualified and intelligent prisoners in the Stabsgebäude. Inevitably they would be forced to concede some acknowledgement of their humanity. For example, French inmates who carried out scientific work at the nearby agricultural laboratories were treated almost as colleagues by the director of Auschwitz farms, SS Obersturmbannführer Dr Joachim Caesar.

Rudolf Höss deplored all such liberality. 'It was hard to distinguish the civilian employees from the prisoners,' he complained. Worse, in his opinion the more human the female inmate looked, the more danger there was of liaisons between SS guards and their Jewish workers: 'When an SS soldier stubbornly blocked their path, they simply worked on him with their beautiful eyes until they got what they wanted.'[16]

Höss wanted to maintain the distinction between SS and slave workers. Hedwig and the other SS wives wanted to maintain their distinction as well-dressed elite women. Marta's team at the Stabsgebäude fashion salon would have their work cut out for them.

We did meaningful work – Irene Reichenberg[17]

To Hunya, the first few weeks in the Stabsgebäude were like a holiday, even when she began work the day after her arrival. This first day of work fell on a Sabbath, but the Nazis deliberately ignored the religious observances of their slave labourers. There were to be no elements of Jewish life permitted; work took precedence over everything.

According to Rudolf Höss, work made a prisoner's life more tolerable, because it was a distraction from the 'unpleasantness of everyday prison life'. Höss was responsible for the infamous *Arbeit Macht Frei* sign arching over the gateway into the Auschwitz main camp. It had originated in the first Nazi concentration camp, Dachau. Höss took its meaning – *Work sets you free* – quite seriously. Having been a prisoner himself during the 1920s, as a result of his participation in a violent murder, he had experienced the loss of self-esteem and motivation that enforced idleness could cause. During his incarceration, he was given work as a tailor.

In his memoir Höss preached at length about the value of work, asserting that work could literally lead to freedom. True, in the early concentration camps some prisoners were released at the whim of the Gestapo or the SS, but there was no verifiable link between their work and their liberation. During wartime, most camp prisoners were worked relentlessly to support war industries. Their only freedom would be the release of death. However, one of Höss's insights would resonate with the workers of the Upper Tailoring Studio. He observed that if a prisoner 'finds a job in his trade or suitable work which suits his abilities, he can achieve a state of mind which cannot be shaken, even by very unpleasant circumstances.'[18]

Unlike inmate-secretaries in the Political Section in Auschwitz, who had to take shorthand notes of proceedings during interrogations and torture, the fashion salon was a good kommando. Hunya called it 'paradise' compared to hard labour in Birkenau. She was not alone in feeling protected there. Ironically, in the outside world dressmakers had very low status in the male-dominated fashion industry. Now they were elevated to privileged workers.

On her first day at work, Marta introduced Hunya to the other twenty girls. All these veterans – including Irene, Renée, Katka and Bracha – were instantly friendly and welcoming. Most of the dressmakers were Jewish women.

There was Mimi Höfflich and her sister from Levoča in Slovakia. Mimi had curls of golden hair slipping out from under her headscarf. She specialised in shirts and underwear.

There was Manci Birnbaum from northern Slovakia, a very good seamstress, with a sister, Heda, who worked in Kanada tallying valuables plundered from Jewish luggage. Manci was the woman who'd had to parade naked in front of Heinrich Himmler during his inspection of the Auschwitz main camp in July 1942.

In her mid-thirties, Olga Kovácz from Hungary seemed positively matronly to the younger women. She was a slow, steady, reliable person. She had watched her sister being marched away to a gas chamber; she had no doubt Auschwitz was hell.

Slovakians Lulu Grünberg and Baba Teichner were always together, as close as sisters. Lulu was engaged to Baba's brother. Lulu was the dainty, feminine one with mischievous eyes and a constant craving for the indulgence of *strapačky* potato dumplings with stewed sauerkraut. She coined the phrase, 'Just let me have strapačky before I die!' and her friends loved teasing her about it. Baba was sturdier, even though her nickname meant 'doll'. Baba had been deported on the very first transport of Jews from Slovakia.

Young Šari, from Slovakia, transferred from factory work at nearby I.G. Farben, was always complaining – not always without reason.[19]

A beautiful woman called Katka from Košice was not at all good at sewing, but had protection nevertheless, possibly because of her good looks. She was nicknamed Blonde Kato to avoid confusion with Bracha's sister Katka.

Perhaps the least talented of the team was also the youngest: fourteen-year-old Rózsika Weiss. Her pet name was *Tschibi*, a Hungarian diminutive of *csirke*, or Little Hen. Rózsika's aunt Berta had helped Marta establish the Upper Tailoring Studio, but had died not long afterwards. Marta promised to take care of the Little Hen. She adopted her as an apprentice, to pick up pins and perform other easy tasks. Rózsika could not have survived long on her own: she was one more life saved.

Herta Fuchs from Trnava in Slovakia was not a top notch dressmaker either, but she was Marta's cousin, and a bonus in the workroom because she was always smiling and pleasant.

Other seamstresses included two Polish girls called Ester and Cili; also Ella Braun, Alice Strauss, Lenci Warman and Hélène Kaufman, and possibly a German woman named Ruth. Details about their lives and fates are still tantalisingly incomplete.

Then there were the non-Jewish communist prisoners, Frenchwomen Alida Delasalle and Marilou Colombain. Alida, being older, was something of a mother-figure to the young girls. She rallied round her compatriot when Marilou was despondent.

Alida Delasalle, photographed after her January 1943 arrival and processing. Pol.F. signifies Political prisoner, French. The image was taken at the camp Erkennungsdienst identification department. Later in 1943 photography was stopped; there were too many inmates to process. Many plates were destroyed during the evacuation of the camp; about thirty thousand survived.

The two most senior inmate-staff in the salon were undoubtedly the most talented, and they were both cutters. There was Borishka Zobel from Poprad in northern Slovakia, incredibly gifted and very intelligent. And of course, Borishka's close friend, the kapo Marta Fuchs.

Marta was only twenty-five years old in 1943, yet she was already immensely respected as a dressmaker and a kapo. She was no delicate flower, but her resolution and energy were absolutely founded in compassion, which made her both fair and generous.

> *The sewing room produced not only beautiful everyday wardrobes, but also elegant evening gowns, the kind of which the SS ladies would probably not have imagined in their wildest dreams*
>
> – Hunya Volkmann[20]

Whatever their initial level of sewing skills – experts or apprentices – under Marta's guidance the women of the Upper Tailoring Studio gained a reputation as elite professionals. Their professional achievements are all the more remarkable considering the environment they worked in.

The workshop was on the upper basement level of the Stabsgebäude. When Hedwig Höss and other high-ranking SS clients arrived they were greeted by the sight of neat, clean seamstresses seated around a long work table, doing hand work by the light of two windows and electric lamps. As if getting an innocent fashion fix in a normal salon, they began a consultation with Marta.

Ordinarily clients commissioning new clothes in the 1930s and 1940s would pick outfits from a fashion house catwalk, or browse designs shown in fashion magazines such as *Die Dame* (The Lady) or *Deutsches Moden Zeitung* (German Fashion Times).

For home dressmakers, popular 'housewife' magazines would offer free paper patterns with each purchase. Several ingenious systems of pattern-drafting were available to home sewers, including *Union Schnitt* (Golden Rule) tailoring patterns, which needed precise mathematical abilities. As the war progressed, paper supplies became drastically limited across the Reich, leaving the dressmaker to decipher a single sheet of tissue-fine paper overlaid with multiple patterns on both sides.

In March 1943, *Die Dame* magazine folded, unable to sustain production. Along with *Der Bazar* (Bazaar), it had been Germany's longest-running fashion magazine. Its collapse highlighted precisely how much war had impacted the fashion industry.

The fashion studio in Auschwitz had no issues with sustainability. There were plenty of magazines for potential clients to flick through, featuring daytime dresses and coats, evening wear, sleepwear, lingerie and children's clothes. There was also a folder of selected designs. Those with a good eye – Hunya included – could recreate a garment simply from looking at it, or even from seeing a picture of it. Marta was a talented artist and could sketch a pattern onto paper, freehand if required. Both Marta and Borishka created the two-dimensional paper patterns or card templates that would then be used to cut fabric pieces to be stitched into three-dimensional garments. Next, the client chose fabrics and trimmings and Marta went 'shopping'.

On her acquisition expeditions to Kanada, Marta was escorted by the SS woman in charge of the fashion salon, Rapportführerin Elisabeth Ruppert. Described as sallow and quiet, Ruppert was a surprisingly nice guard during her time in the fashion workshop. Her behaviour in the Stabsgebäude is an important reminder that the SS should not be characterised as a homogenous mass of evil automata. They were human beings, with human vices and virtues. As such, they were responsible for their behaviour within the concentration camp system, good and bad.

Elegant dresses featured in dressmaking magazine Les Patrons
Universels, *1943*

Although Ruppert generally followed SS regulations, it was in her interest to treat the dressmakers well, because they sewed for her on the side, all for free. Ruppert's room was just along from the salon. She brought her mending to the seamstresses and gave them no trouble. There were mutterings from other SS women that Ruppert was too nice, that her position was too cushy, and so she was eventually transferred to Birkenau.

The Stabsgebäude women begged her not to leave, because she seemed to have a good heart. Once in Birkenau, Ruppert's behaviour deteriorated to match the environment. She is remembered as bullying and brutal by Hungarian survivors of sector B-11b. Ruppert was replaced in the Upper Tailoring Studio by a Polish Volksdeutche woman, heavy-set and slow. The dressmakers did not sew for her.

Unlike domestic sewers, the dressmakers of the Upper Tailoring Studio were under no pressure to conform to austerity measures that affected war-weary civilians worldwide. There would be no re-purposing of old sacks or socks or parachutes to create new garments; no reusing of tacking threads as spools ran low. Kanada's bounty supplied fabric yardage and every kind of dressmaking notion required – buttons, embroidery silks, scissors, zips, press-studs, shoulder pads and tape measures. Every single object had once belonged to another tailor or dressmaker.

Even the sewing machines – made by companies such as Singer, Pfaff and Frister & Rossmann – had been confiscated. There was so much workshop content in Auschwitz, it was actually insured by a consortium of German insurance companies, including Allianz and Viktoria, who apparently had no qualms about indirectly supporting concentration camp exploitation and forced labour.[21]

The fact that the Upper Tailoring Studio was superbly outfitted with modern equipment was corroborated by another Jewish dressmaker, Rezina Apfelbaum.

Rezina Apfelbaum, pre-war, in a dress of her own making

Rezina arrived in Auschwitz from northern Transylvania at the end of May 1944. She was tattooed with the number A18151 and put to hard labour. Rezina had a somewhat covert view of the Upper Tailoring Studio. She was actually smuggled into the Stabsgebäude at night by a German guard. This officer – name unknown – had selected a beautiful, blonde Hungarian prisoner called Lilly to be his mistress. Lilly's feelings for the officer are not recorded; she had no choice in this selection. She did what she had to do to survive.

The SS man wanted his 'girlfriend' to be well-dressed, so after a long day of labouring outdoors, Rezina then had to spend her nights sewing tailor-made clothes for Lilly. She cut and stitched a complete wardrobe, from blouses and dresses to long heavy coats, all in secret in the studio. In return, the officer took her to the SS kitchen and gave her extra food.

Rezina then distributed this bounty among the twelve relatives who shared the same wooden bed in her Birkenau barrack block, including her two sisters, her mother and aunts. Her actions kept them all from starvation. Once again sewing saved lives. Rezina's actions were particularly poignant, as she'd had to fight to train as a professional dressmaker, since her family did not consider it a respectable enough trade for a girl of her background.[22]

Was Marta Fuchs aware of the night-time intruder? If she was, she never spoke of it. Her professional concerns were with daytime commissions, and the orders kept coming in. The dressmaking process moved from design, to pattern-cutting, fabric selection, a *toile* – or practice piece – in calico, then the finished article, followed by fittings and any alterations.

Nightgown and lingerie designs from Les Patrons Universels, *1943.*

Popular designs for the war years were day dresses that swished just below the knee, short-sleeved knitwear with lacy patterning, lingerie cut on the bias so it skimmed the body's curves, and elegant two-piece suits known as 'costumes'. Nightgowns and evening gowns were long. For evening, the SS women had no need to worry about keeping warm while wearing flimsy fabrics with low décolletages: they had requisitioned fur stoles and coats.

In addition to custom-made clothes, Hunya, Irene, Bracha and the others were put to altering high-quality clothes that had been picked out from the general piles of goods in Kanada, making them a good fit for their new wearers. There is no record now of which international haute couture labels were seen in the Kanada warehouses. Chanel, Lanvin, Worth, Molyneux . . . all were coveted names in the pre-war fashion world, along with a multitude of prestigious labels from every country invaded by the Nazis.

In the 1930s and 1940s, it was quite commonplace for even middle-class clients to have ready-to-wear clothes altered to fit by in-house seamstresses or tailors. It was not at all common for ordinary women to have access to high-end fashion, choosing what they wanted on a whim, like the SS women at Auschwitz.

Between them, Marta and Borishka were responsible for choosing which seamstress would work on which project. The core work for each seamstress was to produce a minimum of two custom-made dresses a week. Much of the work was done by hand, particularly the 'finishing'. Instead of coarse burlap, frayed at the edges, crusted with filth and moving with lice, the dressmakers felt the sensation of silks, satins, soft cottons and crisp linens. In basting, hemming and seaming, they were creating functional garments that were also attractive. The new clothes, with embroidery, smocking, piping and braiding, were designed to enhance, not to degrade or brutalise. It was an extraordinary flowering of beauty in a camp that was otherwise sloshing in shit.

Most remarkable of all, in her capacity as kapo Marta Fuchs received dressmaking commissions from far beyond the camp wire – from the heart of the Third Reich itself. Hunya was aware of a secret book in which orders were detailed containing 'the first names in Nazi Germany'.[23] It is open to speculation whose names were in that order book, and whether they knew their commissions were being made up in Auschwitz by Jewish inmates. No fashion order book exists in the extensive Auschwitz-Birkenau State Museum archives now. In all probability it was destroyed during the chaotic January 1945 purge of incriminating documents at Auschwitz, designed to erase evidence of all camp bureaucracy.

Whoever the illustrious Berlin clients were, they often had a six-month wait for their orders, as the Auschwitz SS women got priority: their orders were to be filled immediately. Hedwig Höss took precedence.

Bracha watched Hedwig walk through the workshop to her fitting. In the eyes of a dressmaker, Hedwig looked ordinary. Her figure was rounded by motherhood and approaching middle age. Remarkably, Bracha felt no hatred for the woman, or for any of the SS wives, supposing they were as much caught up in wartime circumstances as she was. Bracha's main pre-occupation was to work and stay safe.

Marta supervised all fittings, under the watchful eye of the SS guard. Rózsika 'Little Hen' was there to assist; there might be a few alterations before the garment was complete. On Saturdays, at noon exactly, SS big shots arrived to collect their wives' orders. These were men whose names were synonymous with violence, tyranny and mass murder.

After the initial euphoria of feeling safe in the Stabsgebäude, Hunya recognised that the younger women in particular were feeling the strain of carrying out so much work under intense pressure. The job was something they were trained for, yet the anxiety of sewing for SS women and SS wives was ever-present. They could never forget they were dressing the enemy.

The interaction between dressmaker and client is peculiarly intimate. The seamstress takes a tape measure to a semi-naked body; she is aware of all the physical defects. She perhaps senses her client's insecurities, and has to pander to their vanity. A dress fitting would ordinarily be quite a chatty, friendly affair, as client and seamstress discuss the garment. For the Auschwitz dressmakers, these conversations were fraught with layers of tension. The SS had gone to great lengths to distance themselves physically and symbolically from 'subhumans', as the inmates were called.

Yet here were Jewish prisoners laying hands on elite Nazi women, pinning hems, checking darts and smoothing seams. At any moment the client might resent familiarity from an inmate, resulting in punishment or dismissal from the coveted job. The interactions also meant the SS were forced to concede that the inmates were human beings – something that went contrary to all training and indoctrination.

One such precarious interchange took place as Elisabeth Ruppert, the suited, booted SS guard, strode between the rows of women working. Hunya was bent over her needle and thimble in apparent submission, but she had come a long way from the days of being stripped, beaten and humiliated in Birkenau.

Ruppert stopped to admire Hunya's sewing skills, declaring, 'When the war's over, I am going to open a large dressmaking studio with you in Berlin. I never knew that Jewesses could work, let alone so beautifully!'

'Not on your life!' muttered Hunya, speaking Hungarian.

'What did you say?' snapped the SS woman.

'How nice that will be,' came the more dutiful reply, in German.[24]

When the war's over . . . It was easy for a guard to daydream about a fantasy fashion shop staffed by obedient Jews. For the inmates, there was a very strong possibility they would not live to see the end of the war. However light the atmosphere in the sewing studio, beyond this haven the camps continued their grisly process of turning healthy people into fearful skeletons; of converting living people into smoke and ash and bone fragments.

Bracha's sister Katka was under no illusions about the precarious nature of their work in the fashion salon. She knew one of the SS women who had paid a bribe to get priority with a commission. It was the same guard who had walloped her so hard during the horrible undressing process on arrival at Auschwitz that her earring broke when she tried to remove it.

Now there was a change in dynamics, because the guard needed Katka's special skills: she wanted a new tailor-made coat. Even so, Katka understood the client–worker dynamic clearly, stating, 'We were not human beings to them. We were dogs, they were the masters.'[25]

Although it was all done for free, the work carried out in the Upper Tailoring Studio was of the very best quality; Marta's quality-control scrutiny saw to that. Even Hunya, with long years of experience, improved her skills. Occasionally, when the dressmakers worked well beyond their quota, their SS clients rewarded them with a scattering of extra food, a piece of bread or a slice of sausage. Beyond that and basic accommodation, their only payment was the right to life for another day.

We became an extended, closely knit family, united in sorrow and
  joy by fate   *– Hunya Volkmann*[26]

'I believe things are too good for you!' shouted an SS guard one day, rushing into the workroom on hearing the sound of unrestrained laughter.[27]

As the dressmakers worked hard to fulfil their quotas, ten to twelve hours daily, they also formed incredibly strong, supportive bonds. During the day there were lively conversations recalling home life and loved ones. In the evening, the dressmakers grouped around the bunk beds, enjoying – in whispers – time with other friends from the Stabsgebäude.

Camaraderie, shelter and meaningful work helped restore Irene's self-belief. Thanks to the semi-civilised conditions in the Upper Tailoring Studio, she no longer felt reduced to the lowly status of a number without a name. She still mourned her sisters Frieda, Jolli and Edith, but she now had a new family of friends. There would be no more suicide attempts, no 'going to the wire'. She had moved from despair to resilience.

Resilience led to defiance. The dressmakers were no longer cowed, nameless victims. They felt human.

One day Hedwig Höss came for a fitting at the workshop, bringing her youngest son, Hans-Jürgen. It seemed the little six-year-old liked visiting the salon. No doubt the women enjoyed having a child to play with while his mother was occupied. Perhaps he reminded them of murdered siblings, or babies they one day hoped to have.

That day the tension became too much for seamstress Lulu Grünberg, the young Slovakian Jew with mischievous eyes. While Hedwig was in the fitting room with Marta, Lulu suddenly leapt to her feet, wrapped a tape measure round the boy's neck and whispered to him in Hungarian, 'Soon you are all going to hang, your father, your mother and all the others!'

When Hedwig came back for another fitting the next day, she remarked, 'I don't know what happened to the boy. Today he absolutely didn't want to come with me!'[28]

Lulu risked severe reprisals for her daring. Somehow she got away with it, and it would not be the last time she defied her situation.

Marta Fuchs felt the same defiance, and she also drew from a deep well of compassion. It was a potent combination, and one that would draw her into the dangerous world of underground resistance in Auschwitz.

Solidarity and Support

Our daily life was focused on solidarity and support for those who suffered more than us   — Alida Delasalle[1]

Marta Fuchs had a plan.

Needles in, needles out, the women of the Upper Tailoring Studio sewed.

Marta had a visitor, another prisoner. The dressmakers did not know his name or see his number. She spoke with him in low tones, and then he was gone, on to his next point of contact.

Needles in, needles out, the weeks and months passed.

Across the Auschwitz zone of interest, prisoners and civilians created clandestine networks intended to defy the SS regime. Secrecy was essential for most acts of resistance, so information on resistance movements is inevitably sketchy. Record-keeping was close to impossible, survival rates were precarious, and those in the underground were often reluctant to discuss their work even after the war. Marta took many secrets to the grave.

However, under her aegis, the Auschwitz dressmaking salon became a refuge, saving seamstresses and non-sewers alike. Marta's wider involvement in resistance runs like silvery threads through the murky weave of Auschwitz life.

Resistance of any kind took courage in the concentration camp universe. Death was a common punishment if caught. Resistance also took many forms. It ranged from spontaneous acts of revolt to quiet gestures of generosity and solidarity. It is fascinating to note how clothing so often played a role in resistance, as life-saving warmth, a heart-warming gift, a hiding place or a disguise.

A girl in a swimming costume appeared at the Birkenau Revier one day, trembling with fear. According to her panicked account, she had been on a transport of Jews from Paris. The women wore bathing suits because of the unbearable heat. One of them – a dancer – was ordered to undress. She refused. She grabbed an SS man's revolver, shot him dead first, then herself. Unbelievably, the witness was smuggled out of the dressing room by a German soldier. Manci Schwalbová, Bracha's medical friend at the Revier, calmly donated her only sweater to warm the girl.[2]

Organised resistance faced many obstacles, not least the chaotic whims of their captors. One day Bracha and the other dressmakers took the stairs up from their dormitory to the workshop, only to encounter a stranger, a young Jewish woman.

'How did you get here?' they asked her.

'On the back of a Scharführer's motorcycle,' she replied. 'Naked.'

The woman told her story. She had just arrived on a transport to Auschwitz. She had been selected for death and stripped for the gas chamber. In a flash of defiance, she spoke – in German – to the SS Scharführer in charge.

'Look, I'm strong and young and it would be a waste for you to kill me like this. Help me get away.'

He eyed her voluptuous figure and replied, 'OK, come with me.'

She got on the back of the motorbike and off they rode from Birkenau along the main road to the Stabsgebäude. Block leader Maria Maul was woken up and told there was a new arrival. She passed the nude woman on to Marta Fuchs in the fashion studio and Marta organised clothing. The young woman survived the war as an admin worker, sharing a dorm with the dressmakers.[3]

Who knows what motivated the SS man to save her, when hundreds of thousands of others equally innocent were murdered? A naked woman on a motorbike was one surreal incident out of many in the death camp: Auschwitz was a grotesque world where lives could be rescued, ruined or ended on a whim.

Before her transfer from Birkenau, Bracha saw a truck of Jewish women being driven to the gas chamber. One of them, who happened to be best friends with the wife of Czechoslovakia's founder and first president, was screaming, 'I don't want to die! I don't want to die!' There was nothing Bracha, or any of the other selected victims, could do.[4]

SS power seemed complete and yet, against the odds, the Auschwitz complex of camps also had dedicated, defiant networks of resistance, spanning all faiths, political backgrounds and nationalities.

Each dressmaker found her own way to resist both SS oppressors and the general grinding down of their humanity. They were lucky to have more opportunities than most inmates to nurtured self-respect and identity, and this was contagious. Small acts could have positive repercussions.

One day in 1944, Hunya Volkmann was among camp veterans watching a group of new arrivals at the Stabsgebäude. One of the newcomers jostled Hunya and roughly demanded her spoon. Naturally courteous, Hunya gave it up, even though a bowl and spoon were basic treasures in camp life, and a prerequisite for receiving food. The woman abruptly apologised, saying she had not expected to be treated like a normal person after her experiences in Birkenau. Hunya had humanised the encounter and made a profound difference to the hostile woman. She eventually became close friends with her.[5]

The dressmakers were part of a hub of international friendships centred in the Stabsgebäude that defied racism, antisemitism and any political divisions. The hub comprised Jews and Gentiles, believers and atheists, artisans and intellectuals. Because of their relative privilege, women in the basement dormitories could huddle into evening study groups. They pooled their knowledge and shared a love of the arts. Irene and Renée decided to learn French. Others took German lessons, or picked up Russian language and culture from talented inmate Raya Kagan. Many young women found they had a thirst for learning that went far beyond their education back home.

Those who enjoyed secretive doses of literature and sciences were mocked by sceptics and told they were living on the moon, in a fantasy land that had nothing to do with reality. Perhaps that was the attraction. At least the study groups proved their minds could not be contained by barbed wire.

Anna Binder, one of Marta's close friends, thrived on the scientific and philosophical discussions. She also liked crafting wickedly satirical poems, which led to a three-week incarceration in the punishment bunker when she was caught. One SS woman said, 'Binder is insolent even if she is silent.'[6]

Resistance for Orthodox Jews in the Stabsgebäude meant crafting an illicit prayer book and calendar, smuggling in provisions to celebrate Pesach seder, and candles for Hanukkah. They could not observe Sabbath, but some women did insist on observing dates for fasting, where possible. Other women lost their faith before deportation, or during their camp existence. Bracha never prayed in Auschwitz.

The Nazis, in contrast, were supremely enthusiastic about Christmas celebrations. One December the women of the Stabsgebäude organised a Christmas show in the laundry drying room with singing, dancing and satirical sketches. The music of the concert was a bittersweet experience for Hunya, who could not help remembering concerts of the past, in Leipzig, with dear friends and her husband Nathan.

Commandant Höss gave permission for the show and insisted that SS families should be invited to front row seats at repeat performances, no doubt wearing clothes stitched by Marta's team of seamstresses.

In our Sewing Commando we pilfered everything we could to transmit it to those who needed it most   – Alida Delasalle[7]

Camaraderie made cultural resistance possible. The bonds between some female inmates were a powerful contrast to the 'survival of the fittest' dogma enforced by SS in the concentration camp. As kapo of the dressmaking workshop, Marta's confidence and compassion set the tone for those around her, encouraging natural instincts towards mutual aid. Somehow Marta heard about the time Irene had received a whole egg to herself as a childhood birthday present, back at Židovská Street in Bratislava. Against the odds, Marta 'organised' a chicken egg to gift to Irene as a birthday celebration in the camp. The egg's nutrition was matched by the loving thoughtfulness behind the present, and the symbolic link to happier times.[8]

Prisoners in the Stabsgebäude had opportunities to share fruit and vegetables, smuggled back from Rajsko's fields hidden in large knickers. They raided wastepaper baskets for pencil stubs, forbidden to inmates. They pounced on books – also forbidden – wherever they could be found, lending them out like an informal library, or reading them aloud to friends. Even the smallest objects were treated like treasure, to be hidden in mattresses, or carried in 'pinkly' bags under clothing: combs, cracked mirrors and sewing kits.

The dressmakers also chose to use their skills to sew for

friends, even when exhausted by long shifts sewing for the SS. One day Hunya was approached by Lina, inmate-secretary to a senior SS officer. Lina thrust a piece of white cloth at her and asked her to make a pair of pyjamas – another forbidden luxury. Hunya was happy to oblige. She chose not to comment on the fact that the fabric was clearly bedding taken from a Stabsgebäude store. A week later she was called before the block leader and interrogated.

'Did you sew pyjamas for one of the girls? What was the fabric you used? Was it a pillowcase shape?'

Hunya remained calm. 'No, definitely not. It was a simple piece of fabric . . . I did not ask where it came from.'

Somehow she got away with it. Lina was harshly punished. The fate of the bed linen pyjamas is unknown.[9]

The network of friends was never more needed than when one of the dressmakers fell ill. Alida the French corsetière was hospitalised five times, suffering dysentery, typhus, blood poisoning and a cardiac crisis after a beating, among other ailments. When Irene had surgery on an infected eye, the wound became flooded with pus that had to be drained daily. Her immune system was simply too weak to fight infection and she was off sick for nine weeks. Bracha's chronic vitamin deficiency was so severe she was transferred to the main camp surgery. Katka needed frequent dressings for her injured leg. Even Marta got dangerously ill with typhus.

Always, it was human decency and loyal friendships that restored them. A lemon smuggled to Marta. Apples gifted by SS nurses sympathetic to Katka's plight. Irene's nightgown and bandages boil-washed nightly by the laundry kommando. Milk arranged by Alida's French compatriots.

Bracha was so soothed by the loving kindness of her surgical care that she actually slept well while ill, and dreamed of the beautiful Christmas tree she had seen as a child in the tuberculosis hospital.

Hunya hovered on the threshold of death for nine weeks after passing out from vitamin deficiencies. Like the other prisoners, her immune system was too battered to put up much of a fight. What saved Hunya was not only the physical care of inmate-nurses, or black-market food smuggled to the hospital, or the fact that she had a clean nightgown. It was the fact that all of these attentions were offered with love and solidarity. Human kindness boosted her recovery every bit as much as the improved diet and bed rest.

All helpers risked a beating or death for their acts of kindness.

Hunya, Bracha, Irene, Alida and other dressmakers were lucky to be supported during their time in the Revier, or in the small recovery room for sick inmates at the Stabsgebäude. Despite the desperate efforts of humane inmate-medical staff, Auschwitz hospital blocks were understandably feared by most prisoners, as places of hideous human vivisection by SS doctors, or as antechambers to the gas.

However, camp hospitals could also be hubs of organised resistance activity. Many doctors and nurses were dedicated members of the underground, despite the dangers. Some of this work was medical in nature, such as the personal help to prisoners. Food and medicines were even smuggled into the camp from sympathetic Polish people in the Auschwitz area.[10]

Inmate Janina 'Janka' Kościuszkowa was doctor in the small nine-bed medical room at the Stabsgebäude, intended for prisoners with minor ailments. A sturdy woman with a generous figure as well as a generous heart, Dr Kościuszkowa treated women with smuggled medicine and deliberately falsified diagnoses so infectious patients would not simply be dumped back in Birkenau and left to die. When her resistance was discovered, she was the one sent to Birkenau. The grateful seamstresses of the Stabsgebäude sent her the gift of a large pair of knickers, sewn from a blanket.

The doctor who had saved so many lives said these knickers saved her: 'For I felt I was dying of cold, and when I put on those bloomers I came back to life. I felt that I was a doctor again and not a fagged out prisoner.'[11]

While in hospital, Hunya was personally aided by a remarkable nurse named Maria Stromberger. Nurse Maria, as she was called by her friends, was a professional nurse and devout Catholic. She was not a prisoner. Hearing rumours about atrocities in the East, she volunteered to work at Auschwitz. On her arrival in October 1942, aged forty-four, she was told, 'The front is child's play compared to Auschwitz.' She was sent to nurse in the SS hospital with full knowledge of the 'cleansing of the Jews' that was taking place.[12] At this time the SS hospital was in the same building as the *Politische Abteilung* – the Political Section. She often heard screams of torment during interrogations of prisoners. The sound was nicknamed the Auschwitz Siren.

Nurse Maria was one of Marta Fuchs's contacts in the camp underground. She saw it as her humanitarian mission to help inmates wherever possible, including Jews. Her visits to the Stabsgebäude were timed to avoid SS intrusion so she could talk freely with Marta, passing on contraband as well as news. At times this included luxuries such as medicine, chocolate, fruit and champagne, taken from SS stores.[13] It was from Nurse Maria that Marta learned of the Allied D-Day landings in Normandy, June 1944 – hopeful news that she could happily share with the others.

Sewers working on the night shift in the Mending Room below the Upper Tailoring Studio were occasionally able to

tune the room's radio to BBC news when their placid SS guard
fell asleep. Other updates were gleaned from newspapers smuggled from admin offices back to the dorms. This was a risky
operation. One underground operator in the Stabsgebäude was
horrified to be stopped and searched by an SS woman, in the
full knowledge she had incriminating newspapers hidden under
her dress. Luckily, the search got no further than her pockets,
because these were full of sodden, used handkerchiefs, due to
her having a bad head cold.[14]

> *I received your card from April 28th with infinite joy in which you*
> *tell us in detail about all my loved ones. I have no words for my*
> *gratitude to you (. . .) I kiss you a thousand times and my thoughts*
> *are always with you*
>
> – Marta Fuchs, postcard message, 5 June 1943[15]

Remembering that there was a world beyond the wire gave
inmates a sense of connection, particularly when they received
news of Nazi defeats. Bracha's natural optimism was boosted
by reports that the war was not going well for the Germans.
She was always hoping that one day she would be free.

Meanwhile, there was the miracle of communication with
family and friends back home. Some of this was facilitated by
SS staff, and not only brave Nurse Maria.

In camp, Bracha happened to meet a young man she had
known in Bratislava before the war. He had been in the Slovak
army and then forcibly drafted to military service for the
Germans. Their childhood bond overcame distinctions of guard
and prisoner. He agreed to post a message to her grandparents
living in Hungary. Next, while on leave, he took a note to Ernst
Reif, a Jewish friend Bracha had known while in the Ha-Shomer
youth group in Bratislava. It was dated 'Birkenau June 1943'.

Bracha wrote that she was healthy and working with Katka: 'I have now been here fourteen months but my mind dwells always and eternally on my home . . . I would like to be in the past again . . .'[16]

Since Ernst Reif was in hiding, his sister wrote a reply, sending it with a hastily assembled care package of salami, chocolate and other treats. The Slovakian guard brought it back into camp, to Bracha's great delight.

This guard was not the only one to help inmates. One of Irene's friends in the admin block used some 'organised' fabric to make a shirt. She sewed a letter into the collar describing what was happening in Auschwitz and it was smuggled out by an SS man from Bratislava.[17] Lilli Kopecky and Ella Neugebauer, among others, were also able to get letters and even photographs from their families thanks to a Slovakian SS man called Rudasch. He warned Bratislavan Jews still at liberty about gas chambers and selections, but they chose not to believe him. The truth was too terrifying to accept.[18]

Remarkably, for a short period of time Jewish prisoners in Auschwitz were expressly permitted to write home. They were even issued with official postcards for this purpose.

Marta Fuchs and the fashion salon dressmakers took up the offer.

Marta made enquiries about her sister Turulka's husband Laci Reichenberg – Irene's brother. Both were resisting the Nazis with partisans. Seamstress Manci Birnbaum wrote to Edit Schwartz on Židovská Street in Bratislava: 'You cannot imagine what an unspeakably great joy it is when the post is distributed and we get mail from you . . .' She said nothing of her suffering in the camp.[19]

How could a few pencil lines on a postcard explain a place like Auschwitz, where naked women were delivered on motorbikes and they sewed fashions for SS wives? Even if the truth had been permitted in messages from the camp, an infinite number of postcards would be needed to describe each person's anguish and the enormity of Nazi crimes.

Allowing limited correspondence was by no means an act of Nazi benevolence. The postcards would be monitored to help identify Jews still in hiding. Although the return address was *Arbeitslager Birkenau* all replies were to be sent to Berlin, where they would be analysed. In addition, only positive news would pass the censors, to encourage the Jewish recipients to believe that deportees were thriving in a perfectly ordinary work camp.

Knowing the true murderous purpose of the Auschwitz-Birkenau complex, writers did their best to send coded warnings. On New Year's Day 1943, Marta wrote to loved ones suggesting they invite 'Mrs Vigyáz' over: 'She should always be with you, she is very useful in the household.' *Vigyáz* is Hungarian for 'caution' or 'warning'.[20]

These pencil-written postcards from Auschwitz somehow had to transmit news of family deaths. To pass the censors subterfuge was required. When Irene sent a postcard to her father, she wrote that her three sisters were with her mother, travelling through a town called *Plynčeky*. Her mother had died in 1938; *plyn* means 'gas' in Slovak. The message got through, and was understood. Shmuel Reichenberg the shoemaker now knew his daughters Frieda, Edith and Jolli were dead, but at least Irene was still alive and in Marta's care.

On the front of one of Marta's postcards from the camp, across from the stamp showing Adolf Hitler and under the 6 April 1944 postmark 'Berlin', Marta's cousin Herta has scribbled a message:

'Many warm greetings and kisses from Herta! Are you not in contact with our relatives?'

Not one of Herta's family survived the war.

Postcard from Marta Fuchs, sent 3 March 1944,
stamped 6 April, with Herta's pencil note

Messages received in camp have not survived. They could not be cherished as mementoes of loved ones; all incriminating paper had to be torn up and flushed away or burned.

Hunya could not correspond with her parents, who had escaped to Palestine. She was not to know that every Monday and Thursday they maintained a fast and gave special prayers for 'their daughter in trouble'.[21]

We were convinced we would never get out of that hell, and we wanted the world to know everything some day – Věra Foltýnová[22]

After the war, SS nurse Maria Stromberger testified that she felt her help had been minute, but in fact this help meant the whole world to those on the receiving end. Twice she was denounced for her resistance involvement. The second time brought her to the attention of camp commandant Rudolf Höss. Both times she claimed utter innocence. Both times she was freed with a warning and she did not reveal the names of her co-conspirators, including Marta Fuchs.

It did not hurt Stromberger's case that she was the nurse who helped Hedwig Höss during the difficult birth of her last child Annegrete, in September 1943. After the birth, Hedwig could recover in maternity clothes sewn in the dressmaking salon. There would be no hardship sourcing a baby layette when she had her own coterie of personal seamstresses, and access to Kanada warehouses bulging with plunder.

Marta's contact Nurse Maria – codename 'S' – had freedom of movement outside the camp complex, which made her a hugely valuable asset to the underground. At great personal risk, she smuggled messages and personal packages out of the camp. Sensitive information was hidden inside a clothes brush with a secret cavity. Her starched white uniform was some protection as she waited in Polish railway stations and on Polish street corners to whisper passwords to contacts on the outside.

Among other information, Nurse Maria acted as clandestine courier of photographic plates – she did not know their subject – and hospital medical records. She was part of a very spirited network of people risking their lives to get evidence of Auschwitz atrocities to the Polish resistance, that went far beyond the careful notices of individual deaths on the dressmakers' postcards home.

Inmate-secretaries lodged at the Stabsgebäude and working in the SS Central Construction Office made clandestine copies of blueprints for the Birkenau gas chambers and crematoria. These were hidden in jars buried in the cement of the block washroom and eventually smuggled out to the Polish Home Army, stitched inside a belt.[23]

Even more damning evidence was captured for posterity: a

camera and film were smuggled into Birkenau to photograph the work of the Sonderkommando – Special Squads – whose job it was to process the bodies of those murdered. Inmate Alberto Errara took hurried snapshots at the western entrance of Crematorium V. Errara himself was later tortured and killed after a failed escape attempt, but in September 1944 the camera film was successfully passed to Polish photographer Pelagia Bednarska in Kraków, via resistance worker Teresa Łasocka, who was also one of Maria Stromberger's contacts.[24]

Of all the images taken under the most fraught circumstances, Bednarska was only able to salvage three. They are the only known photographs of the actual extermination process in Auschwitz. They show women in the woods near Crematorium V, undressing before their murder, and naked bodies being burned in pits since the ovens were working at capacity.[25]

Needles in, needles out, the dressmakers of Auschwitz continued to sew for SS wives of the SS husbands who organised and oversaw such horrors as those captured in the three clandestine photos. Marta was still tasked with 'shopping' in Kanada for the clothes that the Nazis' victims had stepped out of with such fear and confusion.

The Kanada warehouses were not only repositories of the dead, they were also a vital centre for underground resistance. Marta's acquisition trips on behalf of Hedwig Höss were the perfect cover for sharing news and making plans.

One of the kapos of Kanada was a courageous man from Kraków called Bernard Świerczyna, resistance codename *Benek*. He had been a prisoner in Auschwitz since July 1940 – a real Low Number – and his position in the plunder warehouses certainly helped him survive so long. With his protection, workers in the clothing stores were able to knit ear-muffs, sweaters and gloves to be smuggled out to the Polish Home

Army units operating in harsh conditions outside the camp. It was extraordinarily empowering for the knitters to be able to help others, even while incarcerated.[26]

In addition to assisting the covert distribution of information, clothes, food and medicine, Świerczyna knew that Kanada could provide the ultimate resources: bribes, papers, and disguises for escape. Marta had access to the same resources.[27]

Escapes were not merely a matter of saving one's own life. There was an urgent need to break the code of secrecy about the Final Solution, and the true nature of Auschwitz. Postcards sent personal warnings. Couriers passed on shocking evidence of atrocities. Still the Jewish deportations continued and still the world seemed indifferent.

In 1944 the situation became even more urgent. The German Wehrmacht occupied Hungary, their own ally. The takeover was swiftly followed by actions against Jewish people, both Hungarian citizens and those who had fled to Hungary for refuge from persecution elsewhere in the Reich. Bracha's beloved grandparents were now at risk, as were Marta's Hungarian friends and family. The operation to deport Jews from Hungary to their deaths was named after Rudolf Höss. During one of his logistical trips to Hungary in May 1944, Höss sent Hedwig some crates of wine, to enjoy on his return – a reward for all his hard work arranging for the annihilation of 10,000 people a day.

Prisoners in Birkenau were all too aware of the preparations being made for scaled-up genocide: they were building a new rail spur from the main train line into the camp, a short walk from the crematoria. Members of the Auschwitz underground knew that for utmost credibility, inmates themselves must escape and bear witness: Jewish civilians should not be decoyed on to transports believing they were heading to life in a labour camp.

Escape was difficult but not impossible. There were over eight hundred escape attempts from the Auschwitz zone of interest. Successful escapes were far fewer. Of these, a small percentage were female.[28] Marta intended to be one of them.

To break out of the camp, she would need a lot of planning, support and luck to make it through the intense security. During the day there was an extended sentry chain of armed SS guarding outside work kommandos. At night, all prisoners were illuminated by arc lamps shining onto high voltage barbed-wire fences. There were sentries with machine guns in watchtowers and regular patrols. The Birkenau camp was also protected by a wide, deep water-filled trench. The SS could call upon three thousand guards and two thousand dogs when needed.

Even before breaking out, a potential escapee might be betrayed by another inmate. The camp system was rife with informers, motivated by spite, desire for rewards, or even out of fear of the mass reprisals that usually followed when the siren sounded to signal an escape. Marta was well-liked and respected, but this would count for nothing if someone outside her group saw an advantage in betraying her.

If these obstacles could be overcome and she made it clear of the camp, she would be wandering in Nazi-occupied territory. Strangers she approached might offer sympathetic support, but hostility and betrayal were not uncommon thanks to Nazi reprisals. The risks were particularly high for Jewish inmates, who faced being caught in regular round-ups and Jew hunts. The rewards for SS personnel who foiled escapes were significant: vodka galore and a nice holiday at the jolly SS recreation centre in Solahütte.

Marta knew the penalty for being caught. She was friends with inmate-secretaries who had to type up notes after interrogation-torture sessions. She had stood shoulder to shoulder with other women from the Stabsgebäude when forced to watch the executions of those who failed to get away entirely.

At one hanging of three men and one woman, Marta's

co-worker Hunya was tormented by how powerless the witnesses were, and how tragic the four victims. But as the four walked to the gallows their backs straightened and their chins lifted. Hunya interpreted their defiant expressions: 'We have failed, you will succeed. Dare to try!'[29]

Achtung! Lebensgefahr! Attention! Danger of Death! – signs along the fences around the Auschwitz zone of interest

Appearance was a major factor in escape attempts. An emaciated, mottled figure with shaved head and tattooed arm was distinctive as an Auschwitz inmate. The right clothes were crucial to pass as 'human' rather than 'subhuman', according to the Nazi categorisation. Auschwitz authorities were well aware that striped or marked prison clothes singled escapees out. They made repeated, specific attempts to forbid civilians passing garments to inmates, and to warn SS personnel not to leave uniform items unattended.

Some escapees chose to acquire the power of German uniforms, breaking into SS stores to get the goods they needed. Two men made it out of camp this way in a stolen truck. Two others wearing SS uniforms got as far as Prague by train. Four men coolly drove out of Auschwitz in a classy civilian car, accepting salutes as they went. Cyla Cybulska, admin worker in the Political Section, escaped when her lover, inmate Jerzy Bielecki, donned an SS officer's uniform and marched her out of the building as if she were on her way to an interrogation.[30]

In April 1944, two men initiated their own escape from Auschwitz, to try to halt deportations from Hungary. If they failed, Marta Fuchs was set to follow their lead and get out herself.

It was one of Irene's old acquaintances from Kanada who

made this bold attempt, the most famous escape from Auschwitz: Walter Rosenberg, prisoner number 44070, known as Rudolf Vrba after he was out of the camp.

Vrba's first flight had been to escape deportation from Slovakia. His resourceful mother Helena sewed a ten-pound note into the fly of his trousers, to pay for his fare to England and safety. This was spring 1942, at the same time as Irene, Bracha, Marta and the other Slovakian dressmakers were being broken into camp life. Vrba carried extra clothes for the journey by simply wearing them. This was his downfall. He was stopped and arrested because it looked highly suspicious to be wearing two pairs of socks in hot weather. Other escapes were thwarted and Auschwitz became his end destination.

Vrba had learned the hard way that 'a man on the run needs clothes'.[31] His outfit for the April 1944 escape came from Kanada. He and his companion Alfred 'Fred' Wetzler – inmate 29162 and one-time underground ID forger with Irene's brother-in-law Leo Kohút – had warm overcoats, woollen riding breeches, heavy boots and smart Dutch suits. Vrba had the additional morale boost of a white sweater and leather belt, gifted by a prisoner he admired greatly, unfortunately executed after a failed escape attempt.

Wetzler and Vrba hid under piles of lumber on a construction site in Birkenau until the three-day search cordon was cancelled. They crawled out to freedom on the evening of 10 April. By 25 April they arrived in Žilina, Slovakia, having narrowly escaped being shot and captured while on the run. Vrba's boots were so worn from the scramble, he had been donated a pair of old slippers by one of the generous Poles who sheltered the two men along their route.

Vrba and Wetzler were interrogated separately by Jewish authorities. They were able to give clear, concise information about the operation of mass murder, and the imminent threat to Hungarian Jews. It helped that Vrba looked quite distinguished in his tailored jacket from Amsterdam. The original owner, who had worn it from Holland to Auschwitz, would have no clue as to its small part in world affairs – if this poor man were even still alive.

From Žilina, typed copies of the Vrba–Wetzler report were sent around the world.[32] The outside world now had proof of industrial-scale murder. Whether the world would or could act on the knowledge remained to be seen. Allied response to the reports was inadequate, on the whole. British Prime Minister Winston Churchill conceded that the persecution of Jews in Hungary 'is probably the biggest and most horrible crime ever committed in the whole history of the world.'[33]

There was a lacklustre letter from Pope Pius to Admiral Horthy, regent in Hungary, as well as diplomatic pressure from other nations to stop deportations, which were arriving day and night into Auschwitz. By the time Horthy eventually agreed to end the transports, over 400,000 Jews from Hungary had already been deported. Of these, at least eighty per cent went straight to the gas chambers.

Vrba and Wetzler succeeded in setting off a cascade of international communications about Auschwitz. No one could deny there was mounting evidence of mass murder. Jews remaining in Hungary at least had a chance of surviving once deportations halted.

While smoke swirled above the high crematoria chimneys, the dressmakers still had to sew. Did they know about the relentless extermination in Birkenau?

'We knew everything,' said Bracha's sister Katka.[34]

Seamstress Renée Ungar commented, 'The summer months of 1944 were full of blood.'[35]

When Marta went to get stock at Kanada for her clients' commissions, she found sodden mountains of rotting clothes:

there was more plunder from Hungary than could humanly be sorted.

Resistance is always worthwhile, while passivity means death
                                                    – Herta Mehl[36]

On 22 May 1944, the female inmates of the Stabsgebäude were transferred from the old Polish Tobacco Monopoly buildings to brand-new blocks not far from the main camp workshops, built with prisoner labour. For many of the dressmakers, the move was their first time outside in months – a chance to see sky again. They were housed in a block marked '6' of this camp extension. There were twenty buildings, in four rows of five blocks each.

While the laundry, ironing and mending kommandos shifted to repurposed stables nearby, set around a cobblestone yard, the elite dressmakers continued to sew for SS clients in the Stabsgebäude Upper Tailoring Studio. They were busier than ever. Marta brought in new sewers to replace Frenchwomen Alida Delasalle and Marilou Colombain, who were transferred to Ravensbrück women's concentration camp in August 1944.

Although ugly on the outside, the new living quarters were supremely luxurious by Auschwitz standards. There was a dining hall with tables and chairs, and even a raised platform for a piano, pleasing for music lovers such as Marta and Hunya. There were woven mats on the floor, tiled shower rooms, and eiderdowns on the bunks. Such symbols of civilisation were decidedly not for the inmate's benefit: the camp extension was designed as a showcase for inspections by the International Red Cross, to 'prove' Auschwitz was no horror camp.

The windows were not barred, but a wire fence still kept inmates contained. The big square outside the blocks was the scene of executions: a sobering reminder of the penalties for transgression, and of the fate of most escape attempts. Marta would be only too well aware that she might be brought to the same place for execution if she escaped but was captured.

One misty evening in September, the dressmakers stood in lines to watch their friend Mala Zimetbaum being marched to a swinging noose. Mala, normally in a smart, sporty white-collared outfit, was a familiar sight in the camp complex. She had a sunny nature, and was a genuinely nice person. Even SS woman Maria Mandl trusted her. As *Lauferka* – SS messenger, courier and escort – Mala had freedom to roam, and she used this freedom to pass news and contraband for the underground.

In Auschwitz she met a Polish inmate, Edek Galiński, and the two fell deeply in love. In June 1944, Edek got out of the camp wearing an SS uniform, and Mala escaped with him. Some accounts say she was disguised in men's overalls; some that she wore an SS raincoat.

All Mala's friends burned with the hope that the two lovers could reach safety.

Two weeks later, news was spread from women dealing with laundry from the infamous Block 11 punishment building in the main camp: Mala and Edek had been captured. One of Hunya's friends at the Political Section, inmate Raya Kagan, acted as unwilling interpreter at their torture, which was extreme and long-lasting.[37]

Mala's spirit never broke.

Edek was hanged first. When Mala's turn came for the gallows, she was no longer smart and sporty, but bruised and in tatters. Defiant to the end, she slashed her own wrists with a razor passed on by the resistance. With bloodied hands she fought a nearby SS officer. She was beaten, dumped in a wheelbarrow, and had her corpse displayed as a warning to others.

Far from being cowed at Mala's execution, the Stabsgebäude

women were more determined than ever to resist their persecution and survive to the bitter end so that they could bear witness. Bracha was struck by Mala's last message to them – 'Run away, you may be luckier than me and get away . . .'[38]

That September, when bombs started falling, it seemed there might be a chance.

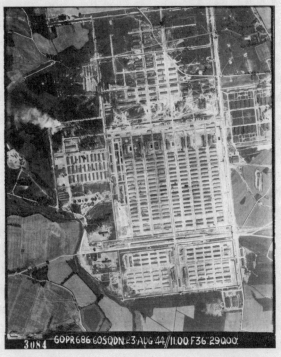

Photograph taken 11 a.m. on 23 August 1944, discovered in the Aerial Reconnaissance Archives at Keele University, showing the thirty Kanada huts of Birkenau and crematoria IV and V

Allied planes had been flying reconnaissance missions over the Auschwitz area since May that year, photographing the I.G. Farben industrial plant at nearby Auschwitz-Monowitz. The Allies aimed to obliterate German armaments production, but they chose not to target the gas chambers specifically, or the railway lines that led to them. As the cameras rolled for shots of Monowitz, the recon planes unwittingly captured images of Auschwitz-Birkenau.

From above, the camp complex is in miniature, with rows of buildings and dotted trees like a toy diorama. Photographs from 31 May 1944 clearly show columns of people marching to undressing rooms. One shot from 11 a.m. on 23 August shows the thirty huts of Kanada II in Birkenau, next to Crematoria IV. Choking plumes of white smoke from body burning pits are also unmissable.

Allied air crews flying over the camp made their way back to base and safety; those still in the camp had no such freedom. The dressmakers kept their eyes on pin tucks, pleats and button holes; needles in, needles out. Then the sirens sounded.

The missions on 13 September were not reconnaissance flights. Now the aerial cameras caught pictures of bombs being sprinkled, falling indiscriminately around the intended target of I.G. Farben. A total of one thousand bombs would be dropped from an altitude of 23,000 feet. When the air raid siren went off, the dressmakers in the fashion salon dropped their sewing and ran – completely exposed – across to the camp extension, to shelter in the basement of their block.

It was chaos, with women crying, kapos shouting, and friends calling out to each other. Hunya had the habit of keeping calm in emergencies, practised from her Leipzig days. Other girls and women gravitated towards her, an island of serenity within surging panic. A blast deafened them and sent them reeling. A direct hit on Block 6. The walls shook and the air filled with suffocating dust.

'Get out!' was everyone's first thought now, from fear of being buried alive.

Those who scrambled out found the wires around the block

were cut. Men and women prisoners were suddenly free to mingle, and even to escape the boundaries.

Bracha stood looking at the broken fence, but did not start running. 'Where would we go?' she asked.[39]

Somehow it was the downcast and downtrodden who rebelled
— Israel Gutman[40]

A total of forty prisoners were killed in nearby workshops during the 13 September raid. One of Marta's seamstresses was injured by the bomb that fell on Block 6. This was cheeky Lulu Grünberg, and Lulu went to hospital to recuperate. Her friends somehow got together the ingredients to make *strapačky* potato dumplings for her, which she had continually craved — 'Just let me have strapačky before I die!' she would joke. Luckily, Lulu recovered and was more determined than ever to get out from under Nazi control.

Fifteen SS men were killed in a residential block during the same raid and twenty-eight more were seriously injured. There were also more minor incidents from other bomb blasts, such as the pot of jam that exploded all over Oberaufseherin Irma Grese's curtains. What cheered the prisoners most was the sight of seeing SS look suddenly vulnerable. Their uniforms and whips were no protection against bombs; they were not so superhuman when death rained down.

This knowledge bred defiance and even covert acts of sabotage from Stabsgebäude inmates, such as clogging the toilet system with bits of thread and torn fabrics, since it would take a lifetime to sit and sew all the orders required of them: a little bit of the work could go down the drains.[41]

It was worth the five hours standing at attention for evening roll call while a block inspector screamed, 'So this is how you react to my efforts to improve your lives? That's it! No more help, not even a little bit!' The block toilets were overflowing thanks to the sabotage. 'Tell me! Who has *dared* to do this . . .?'

The women said nothing. They shivered on the outside, but smiled on the inside.

There was only one fatality among the Stabsgebäude women due to a bomb falling on Block 6 on 13 September. The victim was an inmate from the Political Section called Hedi Winter, who was well known as being a snitch to her sister, kapo Edith Winter. Hedi was killed when the bomb blew shards of glass from her spectacles into her brain.

The camp was unfortunately riddled with spies and informers, which made resistance work doubly dangerous. Marta only shared her resistance activities with contacts she could trust completely, such as her communist friend Anna Binder. Marta's trust was well placed. Others were not so lucky. Tragically, it was an informer posing as a devoted boyfriend that led to the arrest and torture of four female prisoners, who contributed to the most extraordinary act of insurrection in Auschwitz.

Marta, Hunya, Bracha and the others knew many of the women who worked at the nearby Weischellmetal Union Werke ammunitions factory, called the Union kommando. In the summer of 1944, the women handling gunpowder and fuses were decked out in navy blue and white polka-dot dresses, with white kerchiefs and white aprons – a fine sight. Unknown to all but co-conspirators, a group of them had been smuggling tiny amounts of powder from the factory. They would hide paper packets of it in their clothes, their hair, tied under armpits, or inserted into soup bowls with false bases. The youngest were teenagers, only sixteen.

The lynchpin of the smuggling operation was fiery Róza Robota, a young Jewish inmate from Poland, working in the Kanada kommando. Like Bracha, Róza had been a member of the HaShomer youth group. Now she used her base in Kanada to link with the camp resistance. Loot from Kanada was crucial as bribes for obtaining illegal supplies, or for persuading corrupt SS to turn a blind eye to resistance activities.

For Róza, death was an acceptable price to pay, to avenge the murder of her entire family by the Nazis. She first ran her own underground cell, then was recruited by men linked with the Sonderkommando – those tasked with disposing of the corpses. The Sonderkommando were periodically murdered and replaced; slowly, secretly, they began to plan a revolt. They needed explosives to succeed, which is where the workers from the ammunitions factory came in.

Róza told them, 'I will try and do something.'[42]

She recruited an equally dedicated core of resisters. Ala Gertner – a stylish Pole who dared to add a home-made ribbon or belt or hat to her prison clothes – knew Rósa in Kanada before being transferred to the Union kommando, where she recruited others: Regina Safirsztayn's family had all been wiped out by the Nazis too; sisters Ester and Hana Wajsblum had been deported from the Warsaw ghetto.

The revolt was doomed to failure. What could even six hundred desperate Sonderkommando men do against SS with machine guns? Even so, the sound of explosions on 7 October 1944 set off a tsunami of excitement among inmates, and panic for the Nazis, similar to when Allied bombs fell. Crematorium IV next to Kanada II was destroyed. Inmates scattered into the fields and barns of Rajsko's agricultural lands; some attempted to hide in the piles of clothes in Kanada, helped by women working there. Although all were caught and killed, their dramatic rebellion was an inspiring testament to Jewish courage and fighting spirit.

Inmate-secretaries at the Political Section dutifully typed up transcripts of interrogations following the betrayal of Róza Robota and the Union kommando conspirators by camp snitches. Commandant Höss complained that his siesta was disturbed by noises of nearby torture.[43] Róza was spotted waiting for yet another bout of questioning. She was on a chair in a corridor of the Political Section, wearing only coarse cotton pants and a bra that did not hide bloody wounds and bruises. Despite being beaten until she was as limp as a pile of rags, Róza managed to smuggle out a note to say she had no regrets: '*Chazak ve Amatz*,' she wrote – Be strong and of good will.[44]

Four of the powder-smugglers were led to the gallows outside the camp extension – Ala, Róza, Ester and Regina. All Stabsgebäude workers were summoned to watch the hangings. The first to die were Ala and Regina, on the evening of 5 January 1945. It had been Ala's sweetheart who betrayed them. The following morning Róza and Ester shared the same fate. They turned like puppets on strings.

'We did not want to watch,' said dressmaker Katka Berkovič, standing with her sister Bracha and the other dressmakers in the square of the camp extension.[45] Even so, they bore witness. Hunya felt the tension as hundreds of hearts beat with pride to see the four women remain so calm and so dignified to the end.

Bombs kept falling until early January 1945.

It was a cold, harsh winter. Hunya found her hands were almost too frozen to sew. Needles in, needles out, heads raised: the sound of Russian artillery, only forty miles away at Kraków.

Marta took Katka aside, asking her and Bracha to take care of 'Little Hen' Rózsika, the youngest girl working in the fashion salon. Marta's escape plan was ready to go into action.[46]

The Air Smells Like Burning Paper

The air smells like burning paper rather than burning flesh
– Rena Kornreich[1]

The dressmakers sewed, but the rest of the Stabsgebäude was in turmoil.

Admin workers hurried down the building corridors with armfuls of ledgers and boxes of files. Lists, indexes, registers . . . any scrap of evidence about executions was to be destroyed, by order of Rudolf Höss. Höss, in turn, was under orders from Himmler to ensure there was no incriminating evidence of the scale of mass murder. All the records so methodically created – names, numbers, dates, deaths – they were all to go up in flames, like the corpses of those they recorded.

The volume of papers soon smothered office fireplaces, so bonfires were built outside the admin block. There were many such fires around the whole camp complex, for work records, hospital records, plunder records. If they were burned, it was as if the crimes had never been committed. Somewhere in the chaos, the secret order book of the Upper Tailoring Studio was lost. Burned or buried in archives, it has not been seen since; the identities of the clients it recorded are not now known. Marta never told.

Bureaucracy attempted to function even amid the confusion. On 8 January 1945, the SS Central Administration at the

Stabsgebäude was informed that there were serious deficiencies in the management of camp clothing, following an inspection of clothing supplies and distribution the previous November.[2]

Documents about prisoners still living (against the odds) were loaded into trucks and sent west, away from the rumble of Russian guns. What would be the fate of the prisoners themselves?

On Wednesday 17 January 1945, the dressmakers were informed without drama that this would be their last day of work. No other information. It was a heady moment. They set aside their sewing – the fashions that would no longer be finished and fitted – to discuss possibilities.

There had been rumours of plans to bomb the entire camp, or machine-gun the remaining prisoners, or both. There had also been ever-increasing transports heading west. It was glorious to think there would be no more drudgery for their SS clients. However, leaving the dressmaking salon meant leaving a kommando that had saved their lives thus far. What next?

The consensus was, whatever the outcome of the next few days, it was best to be dressed warmly. This was despite an official order specifically stating that possession of several pieces of clothing was strictly forbidden, beyond the single set of garments issued.[3] Marta's connections with Kanada meant they could all organise underwear, good shoes and coats. The SS issued additional striped prison jackets.

Marta also had a small, well-packed rucksack. The previous November her contact in the SS hospital – nurse Maria Stromberger – had smuggled in grape sugar, a form of glucose. Bracha and Katka had saved theirs, threading it in lumps on a string like a necklace, so they could break off a bead and suck on it to get a boost in emergencies. Hunya had been ill in hospital only two weeks before, and she had a stash of vitamin pills, worth their weight in gold. Where possible, the women each got a blanket.

The inmates of Auschwitz-Birkenau were not the only ones prepping for departure. There was an orgy of plunder by the SS in the Kanada barracks. Over the Christmas and New Year period, SS families had been frantically packing their ill-gotten belongings into trunks to send back to Germany. Hedwig Höss left Auschwitz late in 1944, joining her husband in his new posting at Ravensbrück concentration camp.[4] Her wardrobes and drawers were emptied, her house stripped of furniture and her garden paradise left muffled under thick snow.

With no one to stoke them, the fires of the glasshouse ovens went cold.

Hedwig did not leave empty handed. One SS man complained that it had taken two whole freight cars to transport the Höss belongings west. The Höss gardener, Stanisław Dubiel, claimed it was four. Hedwig travelled with bespoke fashions from the dressmaking salon folded neatly into high-class leather luggage. She would have a very different journey from those who had stitched the clothes and provided the suitcases.

And then the most amazing thing happened – Hunya Volkmann[5]

It was snowing heavily on Thursday 18 January 1945, when the dressmakers were woken and told to muster. They were leaving on foot for an unknown destination and temperatures were down to minus 20°C. SS guards were torn between punishing prisoners for having forbidden items of civilian clothing, or acting magnanimous because there was a chance that prisoners might one day be in a position to bear witness against them to the advancing Russians.

One guard asked Bracha, 'When the Russians come, what are you going to tell them? Was I good to you?'

Bracha answered carefully: 'I will say you were not among the bad ones.'[6]

Tens of thousands of prisoners were gathered in pre-dawn darkness. Suddenly men and women could mingle after months or years of separation. Everywhere there were searches for husbands, wives, friends, relatives; sometimes even joyful reunions.

Hunya could not believe her luck when she came across her dear friend Ruth Ringer among the weak, dazed women from Birkenau. Ruth had been Hunya's companion during the last months in Leipzig, and on the transport to Auschwitz. It was Ruth whose husband had advised she should stick with Hunya to survive. Separated on their first day in camp, the two women determined to stay together now.

Amid the chaos, friends and loved ones desperately memorised rendezvous information, fired with the hope that they could reunite once the war was over. If they survived the coming march.

'Should we stay behind and hide?' Irene and Renée wondered. 'You never know what they'll do to us – kill us, shoot us, burn us, so that no witnesses will survive.' They decided it was safer to stay with the rest of the dressmaking kommando and leave the camp.[7]

By eleven in the morning they heard the sound of bawled orders. In groups of five hundred, prisoners were leaving the main camp. With more than 30,000 people to shift, including incomers from Birkenau, the exodus took hours. Somewhere there were boilers for tea and supplies of bread, but only the strongest inmates could reach them.

Marta took the initiative. With calm authority she cleared a way, returning with as much bread as she could carry. It was twilight by the time Marta's kommando approached the camp exit. Hunya could not believe they were actually leaving. The moments marching out of the gate were indescribably blissful, even if they were moving at gunpoint into the unknown.

When Bracha and Katka walked out together, along with Irene and Renée, they had endured one thousand days in Auschwitz. The pessimists had been wrong: they were not leaving the camp out of the crematoria chimneys. They were hardly marching towards coffee and cake on the Bratislava Corso either. The important thing was to stick together and keep going.

Those too ill to be evacuated were left behind, along with those who had hidden thinking they would stand a better chance of survival in camp than marching towards the unknown. Some of those who remained were shot by trigger-happy SS still doing sporadic patrols of the camp grounds. Some died of malnutrition, exposure and illnesses. The lucky ones, the hardy ones, scuttled about the half-abandoned camps in search of food and clothing. Various stores had already been broken open, with clothes spilling out.

In the last days of the camp's operation, train after train of loot had been sent west, leaving Kanada kommando workers wandering around empty halls and huts. The thirty Kanada barracks in Birkenau were too gorged with plunder to be completely cleared in time. Some were set on fire and they burned for days.

Among an estimated 7,500 inmates still in the camp was Rezina Apfelbaum, the seamstress from Transylvania who had been smuggled into the fashion salon to sew on the sly for an SS guard, who wanted fashions for his mistress Lilly. Rezina's relatives – those she had saved by this illicit sewing – were too weak to walk and had remained huddled in the barracks. She was there with them when the barrack door was locked and they were told they were to be set on fire like the clothing stores.

Sometime afterwards, a single Russian soldier broke open the barrack door. He managed to explain in Hungarian that the camp was liberated and they were free to stay or go. As for the SS guard who had conscripted Rezina to sew for him, the day after the liberation of Auschwitz, he poisoned Lilly and shot himself.[8]

The Russians arrived mid-afternoon on 27 January 1945. Even though the Red Army had already liberated Majdanek extermination camp, nothing could prepare these frontline veterans for what they encountered within the barbed wire of the Auschwitz camps. Amid more gruesome discoveries, they found what was left of the Kanada booty, well over a million items in total. One Russian soldier in bulky winter combat gear was photographed standing by a pile of shoes far higher than his head. Those who had worn the shoes were long reduced to ashes and bone shards, to living skeletons, or to shivering figures struggling west in what would become known as *Todesmärsche*. Death Marches.

On the march, leather shoes became sodden. Wooden shoes were worse – heavy and cold. Blisters bulged and burst; skin rubbed raw left blood in the footprints. Everyone was frosted with snow and splashed with slush as they were forced to the side of the road by convoys of frightened Reich-born Germans in heavily loaded cars and trucks, heading for the supposed safety of their Fatherland. All prisoners were tormented by foul winter weather.

Occasionally there were demands for identification from marching groups. Hunya heard voices calling out. First men shouting, 'Here the Tailor's Kommando; here the Shoemaker's Kommando . . .' Then women shouting, 'The Laundry Kommando', 'the Dressmaker Kommando . . .'

The dressmakers kept together as best they could, even as the column of marchers inevitably became less organised and less compact. Hunya was still weak from illness, but strangely calm. She had her friend Ruth Ringer to look after now, whose experiences in Birkenau had left her in far worse condition than those who had found shelter in the Stabsgebäude.

Some of the marching column split to head north-west. The dressmakers were part of a stream of unfortunates being led on a more westerly route. How long would they march? Even the strongest of them could barely move one foot in front of the other. Still they kept together, in a serpentine column along country lanes and village roads.

Those who stumbled were lifted by friends and half carried, half dragged. Those with no friends able to help were shot dead where they lay. After the long columns of prisoners had passed, local Polish people came out to stare at the corpses and to bury them. Thousands of them. They went to their graves without names, only their tattoo numbers and their meagre clothing to show identity or individuality.[9]

On the first night – in fact, it was dawn of the next day – the dressmakers collapsed exhausted in a pigsty when the order came to rest.

Hunya's feet were horribly swollen, but she knew better than to remove her shoes, or she would never get them back on again. Bracha had already been warned, 'Don't take your shoes off or your feet will be frozen!'[10] Unguarded footwear was snatched and stolen in the night. Walking barefoot meant frostbite and certain death.

Irene did not even make it to the pigsty. She was finished; no strength to go on. When she heard the order to *Stop*, she collapsed on the road and fell fast asleep.

Renée shook Irene awake.

'Can we escape . . . ?'

Bracha thought the plan was too risky, but Renée was reckless, and Irene could not bear the idea of marching further away from the liberating Russian army. In the end, Renée and Irene hid in straw bales near the pigsty, determined not to keep marching west. The coterie of dressmakers was to be separated.

Bracha, Katka and the others said their farewells as irritable

SS guards urged them on for the next leg of the march – 'Faster, faster! Whoever stays behind will be shot!'[11]

It was no idle threat. As the column snaked away, guards were stabbing the straw bales with bayonets. Had the young dressmakers been found? Not knowing was agonising for Bracha and the others moving off with the Death March, but soon all thoughts were numbed by cold, fatigue, and the need to keep trudging on. They held out their bowls for food when they passed houses and farms; soldiers beat them back. In this chaotic, menacing atmosphere Polish villagers rarely dared give, even if they felt pity for the prisoners. They were, however, witnesses to the suffering of those who marched. They saw Auschwitz on the move.

The prisoners marched through a monotonous landscape of woods, hills and snow, always more snow. Somewhere ahead Allied planes were bombing a column of retreating Wehrmacht soldiers. Prisoners and SS ducked for cover. Hunya tried to reassure her friend Ruth, who was whimpering with fear. A guard gestured to the nearby trees, tempting them: 'Go on, run. There's a wood. I promise I won't shoot you.'

For a moment the two women were tempted, but Hunya's common sense soon asserted itself. What if other soldiers spotted them? When the bombs stopped falling, she dragged Ruth upright and on they all went.

At the second rest stop, the dressmakers were herded into another farmyard to sleep. Hunya fought for space in a filthy shed. She had already been turned away from a crowded barn by prisoners snarling, 'No room for Jews here!'[12] After all their common suffering, antisemitism still corrupted some inmates.

Then – relief! – a destination of sorts. A vast confluence of prisoners gathered at a railway hub in the coal-mining town of Wodzisław Śląski, called Löslau by the Germans. It was here

that Marta made her long-anticipated escape bid, not from the
camp but from the crowds.

We were snowed-in standing sardines – Lidia Vargo[13]

For nearly three years Marta had used her skills to survive
Auschwitz, and her compassion to help others live too. Now,
having entrusted the care of little Rózsika – the youngest girl
of the fashion salon – to other dressmakers, she was finally
going to seize the opportunity to break free.

She would not be going alone. Joining her from the Upper
Tailoring Studio were cutter Boriska Zobel, mischievous Lulu
Grünberg and sturdy Baba Teichner. Marta would also be
escaping with another close friend from the Stabsgebäude, Ella
Neugebauer, a clerk at the *Standesamt*, the civil registry. Ella
was an optimist through and through, always ready to spread
encouragement and help others. The final member of the escape
team was a Polish woman, chosen to be their guide while on
the run.

During the mass confluence of evacuated prisoners at Löslau
train station, the conspirators deftly altered their outfits to blend
in with local Poles, hiding any evidence of camp garments. This
civilian clothing had been prepared well in advance.

The escapees made their way north to a station in the town
of Radlin, joining the crowd waiting to find a seat in one of
the compartments of a regular passenger train. They managed
to travel unchallenged as far as the town of Żywiec, not far
from the Polish/Slovak border, arriving in time for a massive
attack on the area by the Russian Red Army. The greatest
danger still came from German troops, who fired on the
exhausted group of women on the morning of 23 January. They
had come so far, so bravely. Now bullets spattered into them.
Boriska, Baba, Lulu and Ella were shot dead on the spot. Marta

and her Polish companion ran for their lives. Marta was shot next, in the back.

This was the version of the story Hunya heard later. Bracha and Katka were told a similar version: that Marta, Baba, Lulu, Borishka and Ella had been chased out of hiding places in a barn and all shot in the back as they scattered for shelter in nearby houses.

None of the remaining dressmakers saw exactly what happened. They were still in Löslau, and they had troubles of their own.

The next stage of their evacuation would be by railway, but not on passenger trains, and not even in the shelter of closed cattle wagons. To the accompaniment of shrieks, beatings and shootings, the dressmakers were loaded onto open coal wagons that were slippery with ice. In some wagons there were 180 women and girls pressed together. They had to use their food bowls to try to bail out snow. It was standing room only. *Packed in like upright herrings*, said one survivor. *Like sardines*, said another.

The train journey was the worst yet. When women jostled or fought, drunken SS men sent sprays of bullets into their midst. In open cars a bitter wind froze their faces; their legs burned with cold. Bracha and her sister Katka were still together, and Hunya huddled with Ruth. As night turned into day each prisoner sank into their own private hell, sent half-mad or full-mad from fever, exposure, hunger and thirst.

They left mountains behind and passed into lowlands. As they crossed the border into Germany, Hunya was vaguely aware of signs for familiar places: Frankfurt-am-Oder and Berlin. At one point Bracha looked through gaps in the wooden wall of the wagon to see a landscape of bombed out buildings with only chimneys standing. It was the exact scene from a dream she'd once had. A premonition?

When the train stopped, the dead were tossed out. German

civilians stared at the wild, ice-rimed creatures from another universe: impossible to believe that they had once been students, seamstresses, wives, mothers, teachers, doctors . . . human beings.

A new sign: *Ravensbrück*.

Female prisoners were being dumped into Ravensbrück concentration camp like refuse scraped into a rubbish bin. The camp was already overflowing when the survivors of the freezing train journey staggered in. It was 3 a.m. Arc lamps dazzled. Women fell onto freshly fallen snow and began licking it as food. Bracha looked up from the ground to see SS guard Maria Mandl standing above her. Mandl calmly observed, 'You should all know very well you have no right to be alive.'[14]

Some of the Auschwitz prisoners collapsed onto the floor of a huge Siemenswerke building, some squatted in a canvas tent already holding 8,000 women. It was a quagmire of urine, faeces and despair.

Veterans of Ravensbrück crowded round the new arrivals, desperate to barter anything for quilts or blankets. Those with nothing to barter stole what they could. There was a horrible reek in the air.

'They're going to gas us!' cried Hunya's cousin Marishka in the tent, recoiling at the stink. 'We won't wake up in the morning!'

Hunya, calm as ever, told Marishka to sleep and be at peace. Either they would wake or they would not.[15]

In the morning they recognised the smell. Not gas, but petrol fumes.

Camp police with rubber truncheons hit out at the wild surge of starving women when vats of soup appeared. Hunya failed to get anywhere near. Her friend Ruth could not even walk, let alone fight for food.

Somehow Hunya learned where the rest of the Auschwitz dressmaking kommando were quartered. Once again, the solidarity of the seamstresses was a life-saver. They were grouped with the former Stabsgebäude block leader, communist Maria Maul. Maul had arranged food and even some work, sewing sacks. Hunya and Ruth came to this refuge and Hunya was put in charge of the kommando's food distribution. Instead of noting inches with a tape measure for dressmaking clients, Hunya now measured bread portions with a yardstick and pencil.

Everyone wanted to know, 'Where's Marta?'

No one could answer.

They did not find their French friends from the salon in Auschwitz. Alida Delasalle and Marilou Colombain had already been transferred with other political prisoners to Mauthausen concentration camp in Austria, where they were working cleaning rails at the train station.[16]

Bracha did have a surprise reunion on the Ravensbrück main street. Among the mass muddle of neglected prisoners she met Irene's sister, Käthe Kohút. Käthe's husband Leo had worked an underground press, and for a long while they had both escaped deportation. When Leo was arrested, Käthe could not cope alone and gave herself up to the Gestapo. Her only 'crime' was being Jewish. Now she was starving and hollowed out by typhus.

'Come with me,' Bracha urged, never one to give up.

Käthe shrank away, saying, 'I will die here because I know Leo has died too. He couldn't survive this.'

Bracha was not able to persuade her otherwise. Not long after the encounter Käthe did die, another victim of the Nazis. She was only twenty-six.

Peace will come soon – Hunya Volkmann[17]

One bright day Hunya, Bracha, Katka and their friends from the dressmaking kommando were gathered in a group and told they were leaving Ravensbrück, for better or worse they did not know. Under the supervision of block leader Maria Maul, they walked to the nearest train station. Away from the camp, the air seemed unbelievably fresh. They were allocated seats on a real passenger train, along with rations of bread, jam and margarine. Such extraordinary gestures left the women almost hysterical with delight.

After a long ride they walked along a tree-lined road into their new camp, Malchow, one of Ravensbrück's satellites, a camp of well-organised scarcity and orderly starvation. Their barracks – only ten small blocks for roughly 5,000 women – were green-painted wood. The forest grew thick and dark all round. It was not long before inmates of Malchow were eating forest grass and tree bark because food supplies dwindled.

Some women went to work at the nearby ammunition factory, which was camouflaged as part of the forest. They managed to smuggle potatoes and carrots back to the others in camp, hidden under their dresses. Bracha was lucky to get the indoors job of *štubová*, room orderly, making sure the barracks were clean and the food was distributed.

Hunya appreciated being taken care of by her younger friends, who jokingly referred to her as 'old woman'. Even so, she suffered labouring with timber kommandos in the forest, and even struggled with the lighter work in the hospital kommando. Her luck improved when one of the factory managers, a German civilian from Stettin named Herr Mattner, called Hunya over and began to question her. He was interested when she said she was a seamstress, asking her to come and work for his wife. Once again, sewing skills saved the day for her.

First Frau Mattner made Hunya a meal of meat and fried potatoes. Hunya knew it was not wise to gorge on rich food when her stomach had shrunk so much, but her hunger was too intense. All night she was cramped from the meal, and all the next day too faint and ill to sew. Frau Mattner calmly brewed a cup of tea – *real* tea, as if Hunya were a real human being. They sat together until Hunya was well enough to sew and iron once more.

Hunya wryly commented, 'Roast pigeons aren't really good prisoner food.' She kept to plain fare afterwards, although she did accept Frau Mattner's offer of real coffee with sugar stirred in.

In the Mattner home it was such a thrill for her to pick up a needle again, and to touch fabric that was not sodden, frozen, bloodied, crusted or verminous. Hunya's dignity returned thanks to this unexpected German generosity. In return, she sewed perfect garments. Frau Mattner begged her to accept warmer clothes. Hunya refused, saying, 'I'll accept your food gladly because I'm so hungry, but I won't take clothes as long as this dress I'm wearing stays whole.'[18]

By April 1945, the noise of explosions seemed never-ending. Red Cross trucks appeared at the camp gates and parcels for the prisoners were unloaded: food!

The SS stole the lot.

One day Bracha spotted the Malchow camp commandant bicycling out of the main gate wearing civilian clothes.

'What's going on?' she asked him.

'The Russians are coming! I'm heading west to the next village, to be liberated by the Americans . . .'[19]

Russians, British and Americans were all converging on the area.

On 2 May, the same day as Berlin surrendered, the prisoners of Malchow were free to roam. The SS guards who marched Hunya and others out of the camp simply abandoned them saying, 'The Russians are coming, we're saving ourselves, we don't care what you do.'

Dazed, the dressmakers tentatively explored new possibilities, some heading west towards the Americans, some east to the Russian lines.

Marta's cousin Herta Fuchs ended up in a British zone of occupation, eventually recuperating at a Displaced Persons camp at Lüneberg. Here, in Lüneberg, notorious SS guard Irma Grese was incarcerated, having transferred from Auschwitz, and here she faced trial. Like many SS, Grese had a wardrobe of non-uniform clothes all ready for when the Allies arrived, so that she could try to pass as a civilian or a prisoner. She had been stationed in Bergen-Belsen, presiding with Commandant Kramer over a cesspit of appalling conditions. Right until the end, Grese demanded bespoke fashions from inmate-seamstresses. She called on Ilona Hochfelder, former couture sewer from the house of Chanel in Paris, who had endured Auschwitz in the Birkenau sewing factory. The last thing Ilona made for Grese was a civilian skirt, and she detested every stitch of work for such a hideous woman.[20]

Away from the camp, Hunya watched white flags waving over the nearby town and the sky was filled with fluttering leaflets dropped by Allied planes. With her companions she joined crowds of displaced people looking for food and shelter. Very quickly they were lost in the forest, footsore and ravenous. Exhausted and dispirited, they trudged on until they could walk no further. When they sat down to rest, they noticed a sack on a pile of branches by the path.

'It's explosives!' someone warned, well aware that liberated prisoners had already been killed by landmines seeded around the German countryside.

Hunya disagreed. She opened the sack to discover a miraculous feast of bread loaves, butter, sausage and smoked meat. She advised everyone not to gorge themselves, remembering her own difficulties after over-eating with the Mattners in Malchow. Later, jammed into a shed for the night alongside other prisoners, the bounty was shared further, with good manners and jokes: no need to fight savagely for every scrap now they were free.

A torch lit up the darkness. Russian soldiers called in German, 'Who's there?'

'Prisoners!' they all replied.

Dozens of arms were raised to show their Auschwitz numbers. The Russians announced their liberation.

The liberation, though undramatic, was especially poignant for Jewish survivors, who had been systematically searched out for robbery, slavery and death from every city to every hamlet in Nazi-dominated territories.

The following day Hunya sat in a meadow and wondered what to do next. Suddenly three jeeps drove up from different directions. Men jumped out, shaking hands and sharing cigarettes. They were Russians, British and Americans, making a historic rendezvous on German soil after many years of battle. Witnessing the meet-up, Hunya thrilled with the realisation – *they were free*.

Bracha and Katka went east to a nearby village, and asked for shelter at a farmhouse. The old woman inside cried that her sons were at the front and she did not know if they were dead or alive. She did at least allow the exhausted prisoners to sleep on straw in an attic room. The next morning they woke to find a Russian soldier in the yard, flourishing a revolver. There were stories, of course, that Russian soldiers raped whatever women or girls they found, partly out of revenge for German atrocities against Russian women and partly because sexual violence was hideously endemic.

Bracha was an optimist, as usual. She reasoned, 'What can happen to us . . . we have tattoos?'

Their status as former Auschwitz inmates would hopefully act as some kind of protection, since it clearly showed that fascists were a common enemy. Sometimes it was a successful deterrent, as was the women's haggard, emaciated appearance. Often there was nothing that would stop the rapes. Yet another horror on the back of so many. As in the camps and in wider society, victims of rape had to absorb the shame themselves. In post-war accounts there are many stories of *other* women who were attacked; it is rare that survivors feel at ease enough to admit that they themselves were the ones who were raped.

Bracha and Katka showed their tattooed camp numbers to the armed Russian soldier in the farmhouse yard. He understood the significance and then asked where the young women were sleeping. He was outraged at the answer.

'On straw? *Germans* should sleep on straw . . . *you* should have the bed!'

He looted the house and eventually went on his way.[21]

One of the Russians Bracha and Katka met later was Jewish. He warned them not to mention that they were Jews, because antisemitism had by no means abated. 'Head home,' he advised. 'You don't know what's going to happen.'

Head home.

It was not so simple. Everything they owned had been stripped from them by the Nazis. They had the clothes they stood up in, nothing more.

Hunya's group were led by a Russian officer to a German house. The house owner had locked as many of her belongings away as she could, keeping hold of the keys, and asking that they did not damage anything.

'We've suffered enough from these bastards,' said some of the camp survivors. 'It won't hurt to enjoy the spoils now.'[22]

The women took over, rummaging in every cupboard then savouring a brew of good coffee. It was extraordinary to be in a house once more, to be able to bathe and scrub oneself clean. Hunya's cousin Marishka luxuriated in the feel of a looted, white, cotton nightgown.

'Don't look too tempting,' the others warned her.

There was a loud knocking at the door. Feeling responsible for the group, Hunya went to open it. She was faced with four smart Russian officers who went off to explore the house. Hunya followed the sounds of protest as Marishka, in a now crumpled white nightgown, struggled to free herself.

'Who do you think you're revenging yourself on?' Hunya shouted at the Russians. 'Look at us! We're hungry, we're tired!'

Her words somehow resonated with the senior officer. He shrugged and conceded, 'If she doesn't want to, let her go!'

Remarkably, Hunya prevailed and the officers left. When the window was opened to let in a breeze, the night air was shrill with screams from others further away who were not so fortunate.

Defiant as ever, the next day Hunya put on a headscarf and shawl, walked to town, pushed her way into the new Russian HQ and demanded to see someone in authority. The officer she spoke with was sympathetic about her concerns: that they were eight defenceless females. He explained there was nothing he could do, and that they should protect themselves as best they could.

Back at the requisitioned house, other liberated inmates broke in to loot. Hunya did her best to stop them, saying they should not stoop to behaving as the Germans had. Realistically, she knew she would have to take some clothes for herself at the very least. The other women persuaded her to replace her worn woollen dress with a decent blouse and skirt. When the German homeowner complained it was theft, Hunya finally lost her temper, asking, 'Aren't you ashamed to demand honesty and decency, after all you've done to us?'[23]

Re-dressing oneself was a significant part of liberation. To set aside camp stripes, camp rags and all tokens of prison life, to put on proper garments once again, this was a powerful transition. From number to woman; inmate to person. Shedding rags helped shed humiliation. Erika Kounio, one of Bracha's friends from the Stabsgebäude, later said, 'We had to change our clothes, to become human again.'[24]

There was also the matter of getting decent footwear. Hunya's group somehow became adopted by a lovely young Russian soldier named Stephan. He turned his nose up at her battered shoes.

'They've seen a lot of miles!' she chided him.

'What size are you?' he asked. Later he appeared with a pair of plimsolls and a pair of slippers. She wanted to know where he had got them.

'I saw a shoe shop . . . ,' he began.

'The shops are closed!' she countered.

Stephan gave a conspiratorial smile. 'True, it was closed at the front, but I found a door at the back.'[25]

Hunya could hardly complain, not with a long journey home still ahead of her. She would not be making the journey alone. She was still with several of her companions from the camp. When they finally set off it seemed as if the whole of Germany was on the move. From 8 May 1945, perpetrators, bystanders and victims, all were adjusting to the country's unconditional surrender, and to Allied reckoning.

We do not speak of things – Hedwig Höss[26]

While former prisoners resumed a life of freedom, symbolised by fresh clothing, the SS underwent a different kind of transformation: a reversal of fortune from power and riches to metaphorical rags.

All around the defeated Third Reich, roadsides were littered with torn insignia and discarded uniforms. In German homes seamstresses began *Entnazifizierung* – denazification – of clothes. Panzer uniforms became pyjamas. Fabric from Hitler Youth outfits was used to patch dresses. Swastika patches were unpicked from red flags.[27]

No more jack boots and whips: SS women buttoned up floral frocks and zipped on civilian skirts. With uniforms they had been *somebody*, and part of an organisation; without them they were suddenly left to their own devices, and perhaps their own consciences.

The Allies rounded up those who were pointed out as perpetrators. Rapportführerin Elisabeth Ruppert, once guard at the Auschwitz dressmaking salon, was arrested because of her SS membership. She was charged with bodily harm to prisoners and participating in murderous selections at Birkenau.

Ruppert ended up incarcerated in the newly inaugurated SS prison at Dachau concentration camp. US film footage of the prison in May 1946 shows a fleeting glimpse into the cell Ruppert shared with none other than Oberführerin Maria Mandl, the woman who had so callously informed Bracha and her companions in Ravensbrück that they should not still be alive.[28] In the footage Mandl looks innocuous enough in a short-sleeved blouse and coloured collar. She was hanged on 24 January 1948 after a trial in Kraków. Next to her in the footage, Ruppert is relaxed and smiling in loose layered clothes. At her trial the court found the charge of participating in selections not proven, and that she had already served enough time for charges of bodily harm against prisoners. Ruppert left prison a free woman. No details of her post-war life have yet been recovered, or of her thoughts on the ludicrous juxtaposition of a fashion salon in Auschwitz.[29]

Where possible, the Allies also sought to capture and interrogate wives of high-ranking Nazi officials.

By the time of Germany's surrender, stylish Magda Goebbels

had already murdered her children then committed suicide with her husband Josef. This was shortly after Hitler and his new wife Eva killed themselves in Hitler's Berlin bunker on 30 April 1945. Whatever Magda wore at her death was doused in petrol along with her corpse then set on fire. Hermann Goering's wife Emmy quickly bundled together valuables in a hat box when the Allies came to arrest her. She went to prison wearing a coat by Balmain, purchased in Paris.

Marga Himmler and her daughter Gudrun were first incarcerated then eventually found work in a textile mill, now bereft of the many clothing gifts Heinrich Himmler had sent them over the years. Himmler himself was captured disguised with an eye patch and a fake uniform. He committed suicide rather than face the reality of defeat, with all his ambitions in shreds.

Hedwig Höss, instigator of the Auschwitz fashion salon, eluded the authorities for some months after the war's end. Like the Goebbels, she had planned a suicide pact with her husband, but they decided against it for the sake of their children. Rudolf lamented in his memoirs that it would have saved Hedwig a lot of trouble if they had died after all.

'Trouble' is all relative. True, Hedwig was separated from her husband, and true, she had to shed a great many of her treasures as they fled north-west from Ravensbrück, but she was not on foot like so many refugees. A network of Nazi support ensured that she was treated as a VIP, unlike civilian victims in the bomb-pitted, fire-gutted cities she passed in her classy chauffeur-driven car, on her way to a refuge.

This car drove into the small town of Sankt Michaelisdonn, up an avenue of chestnut trees, to Süderdithmarschen AG sugar refinery, and a sanctuary arranged by Käthe Thomsen, one-time teacher to the Höss children in Auschwitz. The car was followed by a lorry crammed full of belongings: baskets of food, fine French cognac and magnificent leather suitcases bulging with clothes.[30] Hedwig, gathering her five children from the car, was welcomed by the factory manager and his family. Her goods were then unloaded.

She was clearly bitter about the loss of her privilege, and of her husband, who had been told by Himmler to 'disappear into the Wehrmacht'.[31] After showing her host family photographs of her Auschwitz home and garden, Hedwig put the photo albums in the stove to burn.

'I'm proud of my husband,' she told her hostess.[32]

Eager to find and arrest the Auschwitz commandant, British Nazi hunters searched Hedwig's new home, commenting that she was surrounded by 'clothes, furs, fabrics and other valuable stuff'.[33] She told them Rudolf was dead, despite the fact that he had actually managed several trysts with her at Sanckt Michaelisdonn. The British eventually brought Hedwig in for more sustained, physical interrogation. She was described in the subsequent report as wearing a dirty blouse and peasant skirt, but retaining an air of arrogance. Either Hedwig or her brother Fritz revealed under pressure the truth about Rudolf's disguise as a farm labourer near Flensburg. Neither would accept responsibility for the betrayal.

One Sunday in April 1947, a British Army courier delivered an envelope to Hedwig containing farewell letters from Rudolf and his wedding ring. Rudolf Höss went on trial in Poland. Found guilty, he was put in a locked room in the basement of the Stabsgebäude building in Auschwitz for the last night of his life, not far from the rooms of the Upper Tailoring Studio. He was hanged by the old crematorium in the Auschwitz main camp, adjacent to the now neglected garden of the former Höss villa.

Hedwig and Rudolf's dream of a rural paradise in the East was over. Their children, now fatherless, played in shoes tied on with rags, or in wooden clogs that left their toes frostbitten, not unlike the inmates of the camps they had left behind.[34]

Lots of people said, why do I have to survive when my family is gone?
                                        – Bracha Berkovič

It was trains that took the dressmakers away from their homes, and trains that took them back, more or less.

After parting from her friend Ruth Ringer – who cried so much everyone said she looked like a wet cat – Hunya's group left Germany with a merry bunch of Czech men. They were repatriated in twenty-five lorries, which they decorated with fruit blossoms and wildflowers picked along the way. The returning prisoners were welcomed with smiles, gifts and sympathy in Prague. In fact, Prague railway station was overwhelmed with returnees, too many to be processed. Everyone was eager to find out who else had lived, and to tally up the dismal numbers of those who had died.

Hunya next took the local train line on to Poprad in Slovakia. Now she was met with sullen faces and indifference. The train she was on broke down as it reached Poprad station. Buffeted by strangers, bereft of her friends, Hunya suddenly saw something that made her scramble out of the carriage. There, on the platform from which so many Slovakians had been deported, was her brother-in-law Ladislaw, come to meet her and drive her home to Kežmarok. He'd had no actual news of her arrival, only a premonition that he should take the horse and cart to the station that day and wait. His optimism was rewarded with a joyful reunion.

Kežmarok was full of people, but almost empty of Jews. Hunya tiptoed into her sister Tauba's house so as not to wake the sleeping children, who were snug in their own beds now after fearful months in hiding.

Many years after leaving to run a dressmaking salon in Leipzig, she was back.

Bracha, her sister Katka and little Rózsika began their

homeward journey walking and hitching rides on carts until they reached a railway station. Auschwitz tattoos were their tickets to ride. The trains were jammed with displaced people, including many camp survivors. They wore a jumbled assortment of outfits including camp stripes, stolen civvies and oddments of military uniform. At every stop peasant women in shawls and head-scarves came to sell eggs or potatoes. No one had money, but a lucky few bartered bits of fabric, stockings or socks.

All items of clothing were precious, making Europe a frantic marketplace of buying, selling, bartering and looting. Near Frankfurt, one abandoned German goods train full of plunder from France and Belgium was quickly hollowed out by exuberant foreign forced labourers and German civilians, who wept at the sight of endless hats, skirts and fabric bolts. American military police looked on, saying, 'Let them have a good time.'[35]

Post-war portrait of Bracha Berkovič

Bratislava became a hub for returning Slovakian Jews, as well as a transit point for Jewish refugees from Hungary, Romania and Poland, heading to the American zone in Vienna. New arrivals sought out familiar faces. Although Bracha and Katka would soon discover that almost all their relatives had perished, they had the most extraordinary welcome at Bratislava train station from none other than their dear friend Irene Reichenberg, who had quite a story to tell.

Bracha had last seen Irene and Renée as they burrowed into straw bales to try to escape the Death March from Auschwitz. Now she learned they had been lucky not to get speared by bayonets. Once the noise of dogs and soldiers had died down, the two young women had dashed to a nearby forest and eventually found refuge behind the snowy gravestones of a cemetery. Hunger and cold drove them out into the streets of a Polish village, deserted during yet another air raid, and they happened to pass a woman leaning on her fence watching the sky light up with flares from the frontline fighting.

'Who are you?' she challenged them. They had buried their striped camp jackets in the snow, but Irene's dark blue woollen dress was still marked with a red stripe down the back to brand her as a prisoner, because she had not been able to pick off the crusted paint.

'We are refugees from Kraków,' Irene lied.

'I know what you are, I watched your sort of people march past. Did anyone see you come here?'

'No one.'

The villager nodded towards her shed. She told them they could hide there. Surreptitiously she brought them food and coffee hidden in a bucket, saying, 'When the Russians come, tell them that I helped you. If the Nazis come back, say nothing about it.'[36]

As soon as it seemed safe, Irene and Renée were invited into the Polish woman's house. They were to be a kind of insurance policy for when the Germans had been routed and the Russians wanted to know whose side the Polish peasants had been on. Irene and Renée sewed for the woman, and in fact for the whole village, to pay for the hospitality. Once again dressmaking saved them.

Later, Slovak soldiers fighting with the Russians let Irene and Renée join them for a long journey back to Slovakia. They arrived in February 1945 – the first of the deported Jews to return. They saw no one and knew no one, until one day, while lodging in a small village near Poprad, they opened the door to Irene's big brother Laci Reichenberg.

'How did you find us?' Irene asked in wonder.

Since a failed Slovak uprising in August 1944, Laci and his wife Turulka – sister to Marta Fuchs – had been with partisans in the mountains. Laci had been travelling through Poprad when someone told him his sister Irene was just up the road. It was unbelievable luck.

Irene had no news of Marta; no idea about the escape attempt back in Löslau, or the shots fired at Marta, Borishka, Baba, Lulu and Ella.

Once Bratislava was liberated from the fascists, Irene went back to Židovská Street. Her home at number 18 had been occupied by another family. Of the circa 15,000 Jews living in Bratislava in 1940, only about 3,500 survived the war.

Irene next set her heart on seeing Bracha again. She went every day to meet every train arriving from the west. Her persistence paid off. In June the friends were reunited.

Now they had to adjust to post-war life. There was no time for deep mourning or despair. Once again they had to work to survive. Various agencies did what they could to help survivors, but the handouts were barely enough to buy food for a day.

Then Katka got hold of a sewing machine.

Recovering pre-war possessions was far from easy. Bracha

and Katka were extraordinarily fortunate in that Catholic neighbours had safeguarded a few family photographs. These were precious beyond belief, particularly when they came to understand that most of the beloved faces in the photos were dead.

In Auschwitz-Birkenau, inmates had learned very quickly that there were few personal possessions actually essential to life: clothes, shoes, food bowl. Beyond that it was friendships and loyalty that counted. Recovering belongings was less about owning items than about re-establishing some kind of home life after the distorted reality of the camps.

However, the domestic items stolen or dispersed when Jews were transported were far more important than ordinary paraphernalia. Everyday objects such as curtains, bedspreads and knitting needles were memorabilia too – reminders of lost loved ones, of the people who had once drawn the curtains, snuggled under the bedspreads or knitted gloves, socks and sweaters by the fire.

Across Europe there was definite hostility to Jewish people returning and wanting to recover lost property and belongings. When Hunya went to reclaim crockery deposited with a neighbour, the woman said she had long since lost it, yet promptly served Hunya a snack on one of her own plates.

Another former Stabsgebäude admin worker got home, knocked on her own front door, and was told, 'It seems the gas chambers had holes . . .'[37]

Bracha herself was horrified to hear from a Jewish doctor, who had to listen to her colleague complaining, 'One thing I hate about Hitler . . . he didn't kill all the Jews.'[38]

Transylvanian dressmaker Rezina Apfelbaum acquired a friendly policeman as escort when reclaiming belongings given to truculent neighbours for safekeeping. Rezina went through the house saying, 'This is mine, and this is mine . . .' and then straight away used her recovered sewing machine to start making clothes for herself and for the family members she had saved in Birkenau.[39]

Not all survivors from the Auschwitz dressmaking salon were well enough to work. In France, Alida Delasalle and Marilou Colombain were initially fêted on their return to Paris from Mauthausen concentration camp. They arrived in the capital by train on 30 April 1945, and were taken to Hotel Lutetia to sleep in real beds with clean white sheets. They were two of only forty-nine female French political prisoners to survive, out of 230 who had originally been deported.

Although there was a parade in the city on 1 May – the day before their dressmaking friends were liberated at Malchow camp – there was no happy-ever-after. A liberation indemnity gave them two hundred textile points to be exchanged for a dress, slip, underwear, stockings and handkerchief, but French society quickly evolved a mythical image of a heroic male resistance fighter that effectively pushed women into obscurity.

Mentally and physically survivors were wrecked. Marilou, relatively young, took up dressmaking professionally once more. Alida, older and less robust, endured long-term hospitalisations due to concentration camp illnesses and was never able to sew full-time again.[40]

Olga Kovácz, one of the older Slovakian seamstresses from the Upper Tailoring Studio, was on permanent disability after the war. She did marry in 1947 and have a son, but she commented bitterly, 'The material help I received can't replace the years in concentration camp Auschwitz.'[41]

Things aren't important, but beauty is – Edith Eger

The Czechoslovakian fashion industry had taken a thorough beating during the war, with the imprisonment and murder of Jewish specialists, Nazi bullying and the general strangulation of business during the German occupation. In the months after peace, old fashion houses were revived and new salons opened. Within weeks of her return to Bratislava, Bracha received an invitation to work at one of these new salons in Prague. How could she refuse? The invitation was from none other than her remarkable former kapo: Marta Fuchs was alive.

Meeting Marta at a centre for Jewish returnees was another end-of-war miracle.

Marta had indeed been shot during the brave bid for freedom back in January. German bullets felled Baba Teichner, Lulu Grünberg, Borishka Zobel and Ella Neugebauer on the morning of the 23rd. Marta was hit in the back, but the bullet was blocked by a book in her rucksack. She kept on running until she reached the safety of a Polish house. The Germans did not dare hunt her further, because Polish partisans were so active in the area.

Marta's Polish friend also survived the escape. The two of them promptly took up their needles to sew clothes in return for food and sanctuary with various Polish families. At times they had to go into hiding for fear of discovery; at times they endured Russian bombardments. Between 29 January and 12 February, Marta spent fifteen days in an underground bunker, sharing sanctuary with a cow. The area was late being liberated and Marta next had an arduous journey home via Kraków and Budapest.

Once safe, she wrote a diary of these fraught months – January to May – on office paper possibly taken from the Stabsgebäude. In an entry for 28 April, en route for Budapest, she noted, 'We are hungry as wolves, but not able to swallow the bacon stolen yesterday.'[42] She was desperately anxious to discover if her parents and sister Klári were alive and well, having last heard from them via postcards to/from Auschwitz.

It was lucky there were former comrades from Auschwitz

along the route who could vouch for the fact that Marta was genuinely from the camp, and that she had been part of the communist underground, because Russians were hunting for Nazis posing as liberated prisoners. Marta's brave resistance work was acknowledged by other communists and she was given papers by the Kraków Polish Labour Party permitting her to return home. One of the former prisoners who vouched for her was none other than Franz Danimann, one-time gardener at the Höss villa.[43] Miraculously, Marta was eventually reunited with many dear friends and family members. A diary entry for 8 May 1945 notes, 'Sirens sound an announcement of peace.' From Budapest she made her way back to Prague.

Survivors found being in Prague an experience in itself. Seeing fashions on display in shop windows and an array of goods for sale reaffirmed a sense of civilisation, even if they had no money to spare for purchases. It was hard to believe that normal shops even existed after the grotesque experience of the Kanada warehouses in Auschwitz.

Establishing a new textile-related business in post-war Prague was immensely challenging, not least because it meant dealing professionally with customers and suppliers who had potentially welcomed Jewish persecution, and even profited from appropriation and deportations. Unlike the German plunder stores in Auschwitz, there was no abundance of supplies. Needles were so rare they were considered a luxury item. The best fabrics were being produced for export only, to create revenue for the recovering Czech economy.

Marta was as resourceful and capable as ever. She adapted to the post-war drive for producing good-quality practical clothes at reasonable prices. Women wanted attractive garments that were also easy to put on, easy to wash and good for busy, working lives. Pockets were popular. As ever, there was also an elite who could afford high fashion, even adopting the exuberant new styles launched by Christian Dior in post-war Paris. New fashion magazines printed inspirational new designs.

Of course, a good salon needed good seamstresses. To staff Salon Marta, Marta could call on the skills of her friends from the camp. Hunya travelled to Prague from Kežmarok. Manci Birnbaum, another veteran of the Upper Tailoring Studio, also came. And so, in turn, Bracha Berkovič took the train from Bratislava.

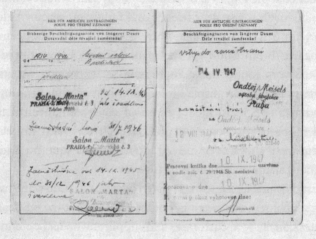

Marta's post-war work card with details of Salon Marta

Journeys often meant poignant reminders of happier times pre-war and also of lost lives. Sometimes there were chance meetings. On one occasion Bracha was travelling by bus in Bratislava when she saw someone she recognised.

'Are you Borishka?' Bracha asked, hoping against hope that Borishka Zobel from the Auschwitz salon had somehow survived being shot with Baba, Ella and Lulu.

'No, I'm her sister,' came the reply. 'Do you know what happened to her?'[44]

On her journey to work for Marta in Prague, in June 1945,

Bracha had an even more fateful encounter. She spotted a man named Leo Kohút while changing trains at Brno. She knew Leo from Bratislava before the war, when he had come courting Irene's sister Käthe, under his pre-war name Kohn. Now she had to tell him that she had last seen his wife Käthe in Ravensbrück.

Twenty-eight-year-old Leo had graduated from pre-war Zionist youth organisations to fighting with the Slovak army, as well as setting up a cell of Jewish communists that included Alfred Wetzler, the man who had escaped from Auschwitz with Rudolf Vrba to tell the world about plans to murder all Hungarian Jews. Leo had been classed as an essential worker in the Slovak State Printing Plant in Bratislava, where he secretly created falsified ID papers for the resistance. In January 1945, he was imprisoned in Sered', then Sachsenhausen, then Bergen-Belsen and a sub-camp of Dachau, barely surviving until liberation in Bavaria by the Americans. Of his entire family, only one brother and one sister survived.[45]

Leo and Bracha parted that day, but the meeting stayed in her mind. After two weeks in Prague, she returned to Bratislava. She rejoined Katka, Irene, little Rózsika and others in a large apartment belonging to Irene's brother Laci. People came and went, using the apartment for stopovers and reunions. Marta's sister Turulka, Laci's wife, did her best to keep everyone fed, clothed and laundered. The young people clung to these connections in the absence of other close family. They had to parent themselves now.[46] Family life for Bracha was focused on her loved ones. After the war she said she only wanted one room with one bed and somewhere to sit, with a corner as a kitchen.[47]

For Bracha and Leo, friendship slowly evolved into something more intimate. Like many survivors they gravitated towards marriage as a sensible choice, for mutual support, to stave off loneliness and to begin new generations. They married in 1947.

Bracha wore a blue dress and white blouse, and a wedding ring borrowed from Leo's sister. Her only wedding present was a tablecloth. She was now Mrs Kohút.

Leo persuaded Bracha to have her inked-on Auschwitz number removed, saying, 'Why should everyone know your life story because of the tattoo?'

Bracha and Leo Kohút in the early 1950s, with sons Tom and Emil.
She stitched her blouse and the children's clothes herself.

The scar tattoo-removal left on her left arm was nothing compared to the scars on her psyche. There were no parents, no grandparents at her wedding; no mother to help her through the birth of her sons in 1947 and 1951. The oldest son was Tomáš. Bracha named her second son Emil, after her brother murdered in Majdanek. She continued to sew to make ends meet, and to clothe her family, until Leo said she should quit this manual labour for work in publishing, and here she thrived, finding an outlet for her intelligence and organisation.

After food, clothing is the most important of life's necessities
– Žena a Móda magazine (*Woman and Fashion*), August 1949

Wedding of Marta Fuchs and Ladislav Minárik

Between September 1945 and December 1946, Marta was manager of Salón Marta in Prague.[48] After the war she had changed her surname from Fuchs – Fuchsová in its female form – to Fullová, after L'udovít Fulla from Bratislava, one of Slovakia's most talented artists. This action reaffirmed her love of the arts, and also made a break with the past. Her name would change again with marriage.

Marta already had connections with her husband-to-be, thanks to Kanada contact with Rudolf Vrba. As soon as possible after his escape from Auschwitz, Vrba had joined mountain guerrilla fighters in the Slovakian hills. He ended up sharing tent space with a partisan doctor named Ladislav Minárik. (Ladislav was also friends with another Auschwitz escapee, Arnošt Rosin.) Ladislav took care of injured comrades.

Once the Nazis were ousted, Ladislav returned to hospital work in Prague, first finishing medical studies that had been interrupted by university closures in 1939. He and Marta were a very striking couple when they married on 6 September 1947, both in well-cut suits. They'd had their fair share of wartime trauma and continued to devote their lives to supporting others. Marta's sewing skills would eventually turn to crafting baby clothes for her own growing family.

For some salon owners, the communist takeover of Czechoslovakia in 1948 meant the eventual closure or nationalisation of privately owned businesses. Marta, however, only made the decision to move to the High Tatras of Slovakia in 1953, with her husband and three children – Juraj, Katarína and Peter.[49] While Ladislav worked as a tuberculosis specialist, Marta used her exceptional talents to help patients learn sewing and crafting skills during rehabilitation, for physiotherapy and general wellbeing.

Both family ties and friendships forged in Auschwitz would come to stretch across borders and oceans. Some of the dressmakers found they could not settle in Europe post-war. There were too many painful reminders of the past, and too much anti-Jewish hostility in the present. Marta's cousin Herta manoeuvred her way through German bureaucracy to secure an emigration visa to the US, where she married and settled in New Jersey. Her camp traumas inevitably travelled with her as emotional luggage, along with distressing physical repercussions.

Irene's friend Renée, the rabbi's daughter, chose to go to Palestine, securing a rare immigration visa thanks to her brother Shmuel, who had emigrated there in the 1930s. In Haifa, Renée met German Jewish refugee and former POW Hans Adler, an agricultural labourer. They married and raised three boys – Rafi, Rami and Yair.

Renée Adler, née *Ungar, with her husband and oldest son, in Israel*

Irene herself came to Israel, though far later than Renée, and via a very lengthy sojourn in Germany. She married quite late, in 1956, to another survivor. By coincidence her husband, Ludwig Katz, had also worked in the Kanada warehouses of Auschwitz-Birkenau. While hauling suitcases at the plunder huts, Ludwig witnessed endless tragic scenes as columns of Jews lined up for the gas chamber. Aged only seventeen when deported, he had endured a great deal of suffering, and had also meted it out in his role as kapo, appreciating and abusing the power it gave him. After the war Ludwig was paranoid he would be denounced. Irene, carrying trauma of her own, called her marriage 'a second Auschwitz'. Ludwig simply could not contain the after-effects of the trauma he had witnessed, or the guilt from violence he had meted out as a kapo in the camp. Depression and ill health became unbearable and he tragically committed suicide in 1978.

Post-war portrait of Irene Reichenberg

Irene moved to Israel. Her son Pavel grew up remembering visits from Auschwitz escapee Alfred Wetzler and, of course, from Irene's dressmaker friends.[50]

Bracha's sister Katka married at a detention camp on the island of Cyprus, hundreds of miles from her home town and separated from what was left of her family. Katka had decided to settle in Palestine. When she embarked for emigration, the British Mandate still controlled the country, allowing only minimal numbers of immigrants and patrolling the Mediterranean to stop illegal entries. Katka's non-lawful ship was capsized by one of these British patrols.

Behind barbed wire on Cyprus, Katka once again turned to sewing to earn a subsistence, this time cunningly making clothes out of British tent fabric and selling them to other internees. Her marriage was a sort of *carpe diem* affair. Her husband, Josef Lahrian, was called for military service as soon as they legally arrived in the new state of Israel in 1948, and the marriage did not survive. Her next marriage to Josef Landsman gave her the great joy of a daughter – Irit. Her third and final marriage was where she finally found happiness.

Katka's fingers were never still. In freedom she did not sew high fashion for a Nazi elite, but ordinary, everyday clothes for her daughter, whom she adored, and the grandchildren that would follow.

And then there was strong, confident Hunya.

Hunya's ship the SS *Kedma* headed east, avoided British blockades and arrived at the port of Haifa in September 1947. *Kedma* meant 'going forward'. On this occasion, it was a very different connotation from the trains going east with Jews to Auschwitz. Now *going east* meant meeting her family who had escaped from Europe before the Final Solution reached its most murderous phase.

'Just wait until you see her,' one of Hunya's Israeli nieces was told. 'She wears *nail varnish*.'[51]

For a while Hunya went to live with her sister Dora in Tel Aviv. It was a dramatic contrast to Kežmarok, Prague and Leipzig. Tel Aviv – called the White City because of its amazing 1930s Bauhaus architecture – was a new town, literally raised on the sand banks of the Mediterranean. Having survived a Death March, Hunya could now walk at her leisure along Tel Aviv's beautiful boardwalk, watching palm trees in the breeze and listening to blue sea waves roll onto golden beaches.

Life in the new nation of Israel was no holiday, however. Dora and her family did their best to adapt to Hunya's arrival. They knew something of the tragedy of Jews in Europe, but it was clear that only those who had been through the camps could truly comprehend the extreme experience. Having such a strong-willed woman in an already crowded apartment was not easy, particularly when Hunya took over the living room as a sewing workshop, and the main bedroom as a fitting area for clients.

Hunya was happy to make clothes for the family as well. New outfits were especially popular for Passover, and she also created bridal clothes. The only price for her generosity was to accept her advice, opinions and criticisms, which were always given with great confidence.

For all that she was quick to anger in the difficult years adjusting to life in a new country, Hunya also inspired deep affection and loyalty. She married baker Otto Hecht. After his death she got an apartment of her own, where her father was a regular visitor, as were her nieces, who sat and listened to endless stories of life in Europe before the war, and in Auschwitz.

Hunya gained positions at some of the most prestigious fashion shops in Tel Aviv, including the upmarket store Gizi Ilush on Allenby Street; also Elanit, and the Englander Sisters. Israel, as a fledgling country with contested borders and powerful enemies, struggled with wars and austerity in the 1940s and 1950s. Clothes in Israel reflected the hardship and the hard work of all those who were striving for a strong nation and robust economy. Status dressing was of no interest to people doing kibbutz work, or serving in the military. Dark skirts, plain blouses and headkerchiefs were usual workaday women's wear, with perhaps a modest floral frock for Sabbath and special occasions. Austerity programmes and rationing curtailed fashion extravagance for all but a cosmopolitan elite.

As mass production slowly replaced the work of home dressmakers and self-employed seamstresses, Hunya wisely decided to retrain in factory techniques, returning to Germany to learn industrial sewing for the Israeli-based company Gottex, which was founded by Lea Gottlieb in 1956. Back in Tel Aviv, Hunya became proficient at making luxury leisure wear and swimsuits. These aspirational leisure garments were a far cry from her modest life in a small apartment, where local prostitutes came to shelter under her balcony in wet weather, and where she fed a stray cat – she named it Puza – on the fire-escape stairs.

You are alive. Nothing is impossible – Rezina Apfelbaum[52]

New lives, new families, new countries. Through the later decades of the twentieth century and into the twenty-first, fashion glorified in transformation – *nylon, plastic, fast, disposable!* As women, seamstresses, mothers, the dressmakers might be forgiven for supposing that their wartime and lifetime experiences would be treated as disposable too, forgotten by history, as ephemeral and anonymous as the clothes they once stitched in Auschwitz.

Fortunately there were threads of history to follow for those who went looking . . .

They Want Us to Be Normal?

And they want us to be normal? – Hunya Volkmann-Hecht[1]

Mrs Bracha Kohút, *née* Berkovič, stops speaking for a moment. I wait. The house in California is still.

Of all the objects around us – flower bouquets, Slovakian embroideries, books and ceramics – it is the photograph on the coffee table that constantly draws her attention: an enlarged, colourised portrait of her family in 1942, taken shortly before her deportation to Auschwitz. Now this image is a focus for her memories. I too am held by their gazes; people I have never known and can never meet. I look at Katka and Bracha in the photograph, then at the Bracha who sits beside me, running her fine fingers along the seams of her slacks.[2]

Only two years short of reaching 100 when I first meet her, Bracha is still independent and very bright, despite the inevitable fragility of old age. Now widowed after a long happy marriage with Leo Kohút, she cooks for herself and for her visitors. I am invited to a small kitchen, where she serves delicious rissoles, creamed spinach and cauliflower soup. She prepares kosher chicken and matzo balls, just as she was taught at home in Slovakia so many decades before. Her movements in the kitchen are long practised. They remind me of my grandmother, who cooked and baked every day of her adult life.

Bracha eats in silence, with concentration. I cannot help

thinking of meal times in camp, where desperate women fought for what little was on offer. I try to bridge the gap between this composed woman, and the twenty-year-old who endured experiences almost beyond imagination. What I have studied, she has lived.

'I was in Auschwitz for one thousand days,' she tells me. 'Every day I could have died a thousand times.'

One day I arrive at her house early, before any of the family join us, and Bracha simply sits to tell me about friends she knew before the war: all dead in the Shoah. Her experiences are compartmentalised, but these compartments are not watertight. At times emotions spill over – brief glimpses of anger and sorrow. The rituals of everyday life are one way of structuring turbulent memories, of creating neatness and order: when Bracha's daughter-in-law Vivian visited wearing fashionably torn jeans, Bracha innocently offered to sew up the rips.

The long-term process of remembering and forgetting is fraught. These days Bracha speaks freely of her time in the camps, slipping from one language to another as she searches for the best way to convey her memories. However, when her two sons Tom and Emil were young, the Holocaust was a taboo subject. Keeping silent left more room to nurture an apparently normal life. It was also a wise survival tactic: if the boys did not even know they were Jewish, their parents hoped they would not suffer antisemitism, which was still a pervasive threat in socialist Czechoslovakia.

The boys only learned that their parents were Holocaust survivors when their Aunt Katka began to talk on the subject. Since then it seems one son has embraced knowledge about his family legacy; the other cannot bear to dwell on his family's suffering.

Keeping silent about the past was not unusual among survivors, who wanted to look ahead to personal and professional fulfilment in the post-war years. Dressmaker Renée Ungar, who escaped from the Death March with Irene Reichenberg, wrote a long, savagely honest letter in 1945 detailing her wartime fate, but she would not discuss the camps with her two sons.[3] 'The disaster that happened there is impossible to grasp and the human mind cannot believe it,' her letter stated. That was part of the problem: if and when survivors did try to speak of their experiences, the reaction was often disgust, indifference, or sheer disbelief.

One of Bracha's friends from the Stabsgebäude, Erika Kounio, wrote in her memoirs about the initial difficulties of trying to communicate: 'People wanted neither to listen to me nor to believe my story. They would look at me as if I were from a different planet.'[4]

Irene had her tattoo removed, saying she could not bear to look at it, it was so ugly. The number was gone but the scar remained. The wounds stayed fresh whether she repressed memories or spoke about them. Irene's son Pavel grew up hearing talk about Auschwitz at home, and inevitably absorbed some of his parents' distress.

Irene's intellectual curiosity, stimulated by clandestine classes in the Stabsgebäude, continued all her life. She educated herself about the Holocaust, the Nazi regime and fascist psychology. It was a compulsion for her to know and to understand. Rows of books on these subjects were not so much reminding her of the past, as symbolic of her inability to forget. When she spoke of Auschwitz, she tried to shut down emotions that would otherwise overwhelm the narrative.

There were two incidents in particular Irene never stopped talking about. One was returning to the hospital barrack to find her sister Edith gone – gassed – and the other was finding her murdered sister Frieda's coat while sorting through clothes in Kanada.[5]

Understandably, some survivors were not able to open up about the camps until the third generation, the grandchildren, began asking questions. Their long silences did not mean a reprieve from the memories. The past could be triggered by the sight of uniforms, the barking of dogs, smoke rising from chimneys, banging at the front door, or even stripes on fabric.

Anxiety was a semi-constant companion for many survivors. They knew from bitter experience how easily trusted neighbours, colleagues and school friends became passive bystanders instead of allies, or even active perpetrators. They knew that a nice house, clean clothes and good conscience were absolutely no protection against abuse. They scanned the faces of people they met, wondering how they would behave in a camp situation.

Memories were embedded in the body and mind, causing lifelong symptoms of distress and physical illness.[6] Nightmares broke through emotional defences that maybe worked well enough when awake. In the 1980s, Bracha and Irene travelled together to Japan, as ambassadors for Cultural Homestay International, an impressive educational enterprise run by Bracha's son Tom and daughter-in-law Lilka.[7] During the day, the two friends explored Japan. At first they marvelled at people carrying umbrellas and parasols when it was not raining, then they realised it was as protection from the soft fall of ash from a relatively modest volcanic eruption. At night Irene had terrifying dreams, screaming in her sleep. Bracha sat with her and soothed her friend by stroking her arm gently. When she woke up, Irene had no memory of the horrors she had relived in her subconscious.

Former prisoners who survived Auschwitz because of relatively 'safe' positions had the added complexity of living with the guilt at being alive because of this privilege – even if they had not taken advantage of anyone – when so many others died. The dressmakers of the Upper Tailoring Studio had to carry the knowledge that under extreme duress they had worked for the SS, that they been coerced into clothing the commandant's family, and that this had kept them from the gas chambers.

Rudolf and Hedwig Höss personally intervened to save the life of Marta Fuchs on more than one occasion. Was this one reason for Marta's relative silence on the subject of Auschwitz post-war? Bracha's sister Katka seemed to think so.[8]

Marta made a joke about her camp tattoo number 2043. When her grandchildren asked, 'What is that?' she answered, 'God's telephone number.'

Marta did not hide the tattoo, nor did she hide from world affairs, keeping well informed about the news throughout her life. Her husband kept in contact with partisan comrades from the 1944 Slovak National Uprising against occupying German forces, and with Auschwitz escapee Rudolf Vrba. It was Vrba who asked Marta to testify against Rudolf Höss at his 1947 trial in Kraków. Marta would not go; she kept her secrets.

Marta expressed some of her humanity through feeding people. She is remembered by her family for chicken soup, cake with jam and whipped cream, and chocolate puddings galore. With her husband Ladislav, she roamed the forests around Vyšné Hágy in the High Tatras Mountains, gleaning mushrooms, rosehips, strawberries, raspberries and blueberries to make into jam, to gift to others.

Perhaps she did not talk directly about the dire experience of starvation in Auschwitz, but her pantry spoke for her: it was always well stocked with supplies such as flour, sugar, rice and honey. Having known squalor and filth in Auschwitz, it is also telling that she loved bathing when she had free time, travelling to visit nearby spas and swimming pools.

Marta also communicated with needle and thread. Her days

of acquiring goods in Kanada warehouses for greedy SS clients were long gone. After her Prague salon was closed, she sewed for loved ones from a stock of fabrics and notions stored on the house balcony and in the garage. 'Sewing saved my life,' she told them, 'so I won't do anything else.'[9]

Hunya never stopped sewing post-war, and it seemed she never wanted to stop talking about it either. No silence for her. Young nieces Gila and Yael would visit her apartment each week. Even after a stay of several hours, when the girls made a move to leave Hunya would object, '*Gehst du schon?*' – 'Are you going already?'[10]

Gila asked her aunt Hunya if she would tell her story so that she could submit it to a high-school writing competition. While Hunya cut and pressed and stitched in her sewing room at home, Gila listened to her endless memories and wrote them down, pausing only to help Hunya thread needles. Gila's school project won first prize in the competition, but this was more due to her outstanding writing flair than to the content: stories of camp life were not considered particularly significant, and there was very little Holocaust education in Israeli schools in the 1950s.[11]

Rezina Apfelbaum, the Transylvanian dressmaker who saved the lives of her close family by sewing for the SS in secret at night, found that life in the new state of Israel was hard enough in the present tense, without looking backwards. She was never eager to talk about her Auschwitz experiences, and did not tolerate self-pity. Her resilience lay in emphasising the triumph of survival and pushing the next generation to excel.

However, in the 1960s Israel's focus was pushed back to the war years, and the world also watched with horrified fascination, as Adolf Eichmann – one of the most prominent architects of Holocaust logistics, ultimately responsible for the deportation of all the dressmakers – was forcibly brought to trial.

Photograph of Raya Kagan with a fabulous up-do, found among Marta's personal papers. An inscription on the back reads: 'A ma chère Marta, en souvenir de notre rencontre, Raïa, Prague, 3.VII.47' – *To my dear Marta, in memory of our meeting*

In 1961, witness after witness took the stand to testify for the prosecution. Their words were translated, transcribed and televised. They were heard and seen and believed. Raya Kagan, one of Marta's friends from the Stabsgebäude, who also gave language and literature lessons to other young women there, spoke eloquently about her experiences at Auschwitz. Marta remained silent. Political and cultural shifts led to more judicial appetite for Nazi war crimes prosecutions. Further trials against Auschwitz perpetrators were held in Germany between 1963 and 1965. In the dock, defendants without the impact of their SS uniforms no longer looked powerful or superhuman.

Among those required to testify in the 1960s was none other than Hedwig Höss. She had spent the intervening years lamenting her losses to friends from the Nazi glory days: no more luxury, power, status or servants. Hedwig was photographed arriving for a trial at the courthouse in Frankfurt-am-Main, wearing a flowerpot hat and neutral-coloured coat. Ever ladylike, her dark bag, gloves and shoes all matched. A silky scarf and telescopic umbrella completed the ensemble.[12]

One grandson, Kai Höss, called Hedwig 'quiet and very correct', a 'real lady'.[13] Another grandson, Rainer Höss, claims she was nicknamed *Generalissima* in the family, because of her chilling tyranny at home. According to Rainer, Hedwig's friends were informed that 'the story of the gas chambers was completely made up – lies spread by Jews to extort money,' and that there was no starvation in Auschwitz. Hedwig told Rainer the 'hard times' of the war years were 'best left forgotten'.[14]

Hedwig changed neither her infamous surname nor her attitude towards the Nazi era. She was one of those who chose not to listen when survivors spoke. In later years, she told a historian who requested an interview that she did not have the strength to face the horrors of the past again and again.[15] Survivors who had actually lived through the horrors had no choice but to cope with the aftermath.

We all should have testified long ago, but I believe it is never too late
                                                        – Dr Lore Shelley[16]

A family photograph from 1981 shows Hedwig Höss relaxing on a vibrant orange and brown sun chair in a garden. Her hair is permed and she wears a pearl necklace. There is an open book on a green floral tablecloth, wind chimes dangling above her head, and sunlight shining on red geraniums. A rake and parasol are propped up behind her. She looks away from the camera.

In the same year, the first ever World Gathering of Holocaust Survivors was held in Jerusalem. It would have far-reaching implications for the recording and sharing of the dressmakers' stories thanks to the scholarship and dedication of one particular attendee, a survivor named Dr Lore Shelley, *née* Weinberg.

By the 1980s, there was an increasing respect for the importance of survivor testimonies, rather than endless scrutiny of the perpetrators. Lore Weinberg, a young Jewish German deported from Lübeck to Auschwitz on 20 April 1943, had the good fortune to be saved from Birkenau and escorted to work at the Stabsgebäude by none other than brave Mala Zimetbaum, the camp courier who was captured and hanged after her escape from Auschwitz with her lover Edek. Lore's other companion on this short journey was French dressmaker Marilou Colombain.

While Marilou joined Marta in the Upper Tailoring Studio, Lore took up secretarial work in the SS Civil Registry. Along with the dressmakers, Lore was evacuated from Auschwitz to Ravensbrück in January 1945, and liberated from Malchow camp, at which point she was barely clinging to life. During her long recovery to better health, she met and married another survivor, Sucher Shelley. They eventually settled in San Francisco to run a watch shop. Their home was overflowing with books, and Lore was rarely seen without a pen in hand.

In-between work, travels and raising a daughter, Lore attained two Masters degrees and a PhD. Combining keen academic integrity with compassion borne out of suffering, Dr Shelley gathered and analysed information from survivors. Her scholarship was motivated by a fervent desire to counter the insidious pervasiveness of Holocaust denial. She was also combating three decades of 'apathy, lethargy and indifference' towards Holocaust survivors, as she described it to fellow survivor and writer, Hermann Langbein.[17]

At the 1981 World Gathering of Holocaust Survivors, Dr Shelley handed out questionnaires. If people did not feel

able to *talk*, perhaps they would be willing to *write*. She ultimately handed out 1,900 questionnaires in Israel, Europe and
the USA.

Among the hundreds of testimonies collected and analysed
was a questionnaire response from dressmaker Hermine Hecht,
née Storch: Hunya.[18]

I came across Hunya's questionnaire after many hours of
browsing brown archival folders in the Tauber Holocaust
Library, in San Francisco. At this stage in my trip to the USA
to meet Bracha Kohút, I had seen very little of the city beyond
views from a car window. My world had shrunk to the utterly
peaceful library reading room and the tantalising boxes of
documents from Dr Lore Shelley's papers, deposited in the
archive after her death in 2012. Every single manila folder held
a life of memories and a story. It was quite a jolt when I got
to folder number 624 and finally saw a name I recognised.

Dr Shelley had crafted a tri-lingual questionnaire with questions in English, German and Hebrew.[19] Hunya had written
her responses in German, in blue biro, with firm, elegant handwriting.

I saw the basic biography of Hunya's camp experiences set
out in answers to ninety-four core questions. For trade, she
wrote *Schneiderin*: Tailoress. She gave sparse details of her
husband Nathan's death in 1943, of her deportation and eventual evacuation. There were ticks in boxes about chronic ill
health, an inability to forget the past, a loss of purpose in life.

On the subject of reparations, Hunya had to reflect on the
greed enabled by the Nazi regime. She responded *Strongly
Agree* to the printed statement, 'Many Germans nowadays know
how many billions of Deutschmarks have been paid to Israel,
or to survivors, for reparations, but nobody seems to remember
the billions that were stolen from the Jews by the Germans.'

Hunya completed the questionnaire at her apartment not far

from the boardwalk in Tel Aviv, an address I later went to visit, standing under Hunya's balcony on a blustery winter's day. It was only the beginning of the discoveries in Dr Shelley's archives.

Lore Shelley had experienced the surreal alternative 'civilisation' of Auschwitz bureaucracy and SS daily life. She knew the secretaries, dressmakers and hairdressers of the Stabsgebäude, as well as the biologists and chemists drafted in to work at Himmler's agricultural passion projects nearby. Her next projects centred on retrieving the full testimonies of women and men of the admin block, to give a unique insight into the way Auschwitz functioned as a commercial and exterminatory enterprise. The research would eventually fill four books. In the pre-internet era, when transatlantic telephone calls were prohibitively expensive, research such as this meant correspondence. *Lots* of correspondence.

The tactile experience of archive work is akin to the sensations of handling antique or vintage textiles. My fingers felt the weight of classy water-marked note paper, the crinkle of semi-transparent typewriter sheets, purple-edged photostats and the light blue folds of aerogrammes. Each piece of paper told a story. Among them were glimpses of the dressmakers: a pencilled list of names under the heading *Obere Nähstube*, an address on a mailing list, a passing mention in a letter. Some I recognised, some were new to me. They switched between maiden names, married names, Hebrew names and nicknames.

Marta, Mimi, Manci, Bracha, Katka, Irene, Hunya, Olga, Herta, Alida, Marilou, Rahel . . . Over time I would expand the initial list of dressmakers' names from these few to twenty-five.

In Lore Shelley's archives, among the jottings, book plans and memos, I found documents of even deeper significance, such as typewritten testimonies from Hunya and her companion in the dressmaking workshop, Olga Kovácz, who travelled on the same transport to Auschwitz as Marta Fuchs. There was also an airmail envelope decorated with beautiful yellow and red fuchsias containing a charming letter in French from Alida Delasalle, now Alida Vasselin, and with it a photograph of Alida from her camp registration, and the message: 'Dear Lore, in memory of our meeting at my place, in friendship, Alida.'

Encountering the dressmakers through their correspondence was a profoundly moving experience, particularly as so little was known generally about their lives and fates. Dr Shelley was very much aware of the importance of her work in memorialising survivor experiences. On 5 October 1988 – anniversary of a major selection at Auschwitz-Birkenau – she wrote to Hunya in Israel: '. . . you said it to Lulu and the others who died (. . .) that their names and deeds would be snatched from the past and oblivion.'[20]

Thanks to Dr Shelley's archive, I now had a multitude of leads to follow. Like Dr Shelley, I would be reaching out to contacts around the world. One name would lead to another, and another. Also like Dr Shelley, I would appreciate the frustration of any researcher asking questions that are not answered. In 1987, she wrote a lengthy letter to a contact in Israel, begging for answers about the dressmakers.

Her list of questions echoed my own:

What type of clothing did they sew: dresses, skirts, coats, suits, blouses, other items? Did they have patterns? Who did the cutting?
   Who took the measurements or did the fittings?
   Which SS woman was in charge of the Kommando?
   What happened if the dress or suit was not ready in time or did not fit? Were there punishments? Please give examples.[21]

Dr Shelley ended this particular letter thus: 'Thanks very much in advance for everything. I hope to hear from you soon.' If her contact ever replied, his letter is not in the archive, and the answers were not collected or published. The task of answering the questions would fall to me, and it has been a great honour to continue Dr Shelley's work in this respect.

Perhaps the most remarkable element of Dr Shelley's archives is the overwhelming evidence of *friendship* among the correspondence. Alliances formed in childhood, on the transports, in Birkenau and the Stabsgebäude are as strong and loyal as ever decades later, and they come to encompass spouses, children and grandchildren.

In Dr Shelley's 1981 survey, question 61 required a response to the following statement:

'The mutual friendship and trust of two persons was the basic unit for survival in camp.'

Hunya marked *Strongly Agree* on her survey.

*Sisters Bracha and Katka before the war, and again
in their eighties, recreating the pre-war pose*

A more open question in Dr Shelley's survey asked, 'To what do you attribute your survival?' Example answers were suggested – *Faith, Friends, Coping Skills, Luck*. Of the answers I reviewed, the majority of respondents ticked boxes for *Luck*, followed by *Faith* and *Friends*. There was space to expand on the reply. Here I noted comments such as 'being so young', 'inner strength', 'will to live and take care of two sisters' and 'I thought my sister would stay alive and I didn't want to leave her alone.'

I inevitably thought of Irene's anguish at losing her sisters, and Bracha's commitment to her little sister Katka.

Hunya's pen had gone deep into the paper when she wrote her reply concerning survival: 'Good skills and a good kapo.' She gave credit to sewing talents and to Marta Fuchs.

An unsuspecting listener might have believed that these women were exchanging beautiful memories of their youth

– Hermann Langbein[22]

Among the papers of Dr Lore Shelley is a photograph without names or date. It shows a group of middle-aged women with well-styled hair but comfortable clothes, almost certainly a group of Stabsgebäude survivors. Handbags and glasses of wine are to hand. They are all physically close, and all smiling.

Hunya's niece Gila remembers friends from the Auschwitz days meeting in her house and giggling like girls on summer camp. Irene's niece Thalia remembers 'the girls' gathering at her parents' place when Irene visited from Europe. Renée would come by and the gang used to sit out on the porch having great fun together. Gila and Thalia were teenagers at the time. They could not understand how reminiscing would lead to such laughter.

In France, dressmaker Alida Delasalle – remarried as Alida Vasselin – attended an annual reunion of former Auschwitz prisoners each January, when her health permitted. She appreciated the friendly atmosphere, writing, 'We feel tremendous joy and great moral comfort.'[23]

Friendship bonds woven in childhood and in camp went deeper than euphoric fun at reunions. During all their post-war difficulties, the dressmakers had a strong support network operating around the world. In later years Bracha spoke with her sister Katka almost every day. When Marta's niece Eva needed a refuge in Germany while escaping repression in Czechoslovakia, Irene welcomed Eva to her home there.[24] When Bracha and her family took a similar route across Europe to the USA, it was Manci Birnbaum from the Upper Tailoring Studio who offered support, helping Bracha find housing and employment. When Bracha was finally able to travel to Israel, she was very happy to have the chance to visit Hunya, now in a retirement home.

'I liked Hunya,' Bracha told me with a smile.

Thanks to the endeavours of Lore Shelley, and all the relatives and interviewers who have collected the dressmakers' stories, we have their words. This is not all.

Remember that back then there was no leaf and no tree or flower growing   – Irene Kanka, *née* Reichenberg[25]

Much of the Auschwitz-Birkenau complex still stands, although in far different conditions now than when the dressmakers endured its nightmare landscape. Bracha made two return journeys to Auschwitz, once in the 1950s and once in the 1960s, both as part of tours organised by the Czechoslovak *Zväz Protifašistickych Bojovníkov* – Union of Antifascist Fighters – of which she was a member along with her husband Leo.[26]

The geography of the site was overlaid with her own memories.

Modern visitors enter the main camp of Auschwitz through the brick building complex where newly arrived deportees were processed from 1944. It now has ticket wickets, souvenir shops and snack machines. You can pass under the *Arbeit Macht Frei* gate arch hearing only the muted words and footsteps of other tourists, not orders at scream-pitch, barking dogs, or surreal orchestral music. You can enter the brick barrack blocks where the first female prisoners in Auschwitz slept on straw and supped on weak soup. You can see for yourself how close they are to the punishment block and the original crematorium.

Beyond a barrier you might spot the dull grey walls of the former Höss villa. Hedwig's beautiful house – furnished from the camp, decorated and cleaned by prisoners – was taken over by Russians after the German retreat. When the original Polish owners returned, the nine-year-old daughter of the family got a child's-eye view of scratches on the parquet floor and piles of animal excrement. This little girl then marvelled as Hedwig's 'paradise' garden bloomed in spring. Subsequent owners of the house avoid looking from the attic windows of Marta's former sewing room, which give a view of the camp.[27]

A few minutes' walk from the Auschwitz main camp and Höss house is the beautiful white building that became the SS administration block – the Stabsgebäude. Here, in January and February 1945, Soviet NKVD personnel acquired several hundred boxes of papers that were not destroyed in time by the Nazis. The forms that inmate-secretaries had so diligently filled, and the documents they so carefully typed, were to be used in war crimes trials against the SS. In time the building became a vocational college. Visitors can count the floors and speculate which windows gave light to Marta's dressmakers, in the Upper Tailoring Studio.

A few kilometres away from the Stabsgebäude, past the railway sidings where the dressmakers first jumped down from cattle cars with their remnants of luggage, is the emotionally charged landscape of Birkenau. Remaining barrack buildings still hold their concrete and wooden bunks, where Bracha, Irene, Hunya and the others were tormented by hunger, sickness, thirst and lice. A short walk along the rail spur brings the site of Birkenau's Kanada warehouses into view. Blasted concrete among the grass and wildflowers is all that remains of gas chambers and underground undressing rooms. Beyond the barbed wire are miles of fields that once formed part of the Auschwitz agricultural enterprises, fertilised with human ash and bone.

Off the visitor route in the Auschwitz main camp are brick and wooden buildings that served as Nazi workshops and storerooms. Nearby, the former camp extension – *Lagerweiterung* – where the dressmakers were quartered from May 1944 until their evacuation on the Death March. Now the twenty blocks are a housing estate named after one of the most significant inmate members of the Auschwitz Underground, Captain Witold Pilecki, a man who had pitied the plight of early transports of Slovakian women and ultimately admired all those brave enough to be part of the camp resistance.

When Soviet soldiers arrived at Auschwitz on 27 January 1945, they were staggered to find booty from Jewish despoliation in Eastern Europe and mountains of plunder in remaining Kanada warehouses, including well over a million garments. The goods – including 239 bales of hair estimated to have been shorn from 140,000 women – were sorted and stored in the camp extension buildings. The remaining clothes of murdered Jews were no longer merely suits, frocks, shoes and shirts. Under the aegis of the Extraordinary State Commission of the Soviet Union for the Investigation of the Crimes of the German-Fascist Aggressors, they became evidence of war crimes and the evils of capitalism.

Detail of the shoe exhibit in the Auschwitz State Museum.

With the opening of the Auschwitz-Birkenau State Museum, a select few clothes and a mountain of footwear were carefully set on display, poignant reminders of the human bodies who had once worn them. The empty slippers, dance shoes, galoshes, sandals and boots need no words. The leather slowly rots; the silk, cotton, cork and linen collapse and decay.[28]

Clothes and shoes displayed at Auschwitz were stitched by unnamed hands, almost all dead now by murder or a natural ending. What of the fashions made in the Upper Tailoring Studio?

Over the years Hedwig Höss would have shed shabby, out-of-date clothes. Who knows if they were passed on to needy friends, or sold to a rag-and-bone merchant, or cut up for cleaning cloths? Or did they find their way into the growing market for vintage clothing, even ending up as items sold via online auction sites? It is impossible to verify; no labels were sewn into the creations from Marta's workshop.

One garment that does survive from the Auschwitz plunder is the grey wool Bavarian waistcoat brought from Kanada I to the Höss villa and signed for by Hedwig herself. It was worn first by Hedwig's little son Hans-Jürgen and then by his son Rainer in turn.

Hedwig died in September 1989 while making her annual visit to her daughter Brigitte in Washington DC. At Christmas, Brigitte still hangs up an ornament knitted by her mother Hedwig – a little textile link to a past life.

During our time together in California, I asked Bracha Kohút if she had saved any mementoes from her time in the camps. She shook her head vehemently. Nothing. All she has is memories and her photographs.

One day I received a parcel from Hunya's niece Gila, containing perhaps the most significant item ever to be added to my collection of antique and vintage clothes. It is a two-piece 'costume' that Hunya sewed for Gila out of one of her own silk dresses. Each time I see the design details, the stitches, I think of Hunya's deft hands working at sewing machines in Kežmarok, Leipzig, Auschwitz and afterwards.

When I visited Katka's daughter Irit in Israel, she brought out clothes Katka had made and worn, still kept in the wardrobe after Katka's death. They are simultaneously nothing special and extraordinary. In fact, the house where Katka lived – home to three generations now – is still softened by her handiwork. Her tapestry pictures colour the walls, and she knitted chair-back covers and door-handle protectors so that nothing would bash on the plaster or paintwork. One of the tapestry pictures is visible in the background of Katka's video testimony for the Shoah Foundation. In the testimony Katka's voice has a lilt as soft as the neat blouse she wears. She frequently pauses to say, 'How shall I explain . . . ?'

Words are not sufficient.

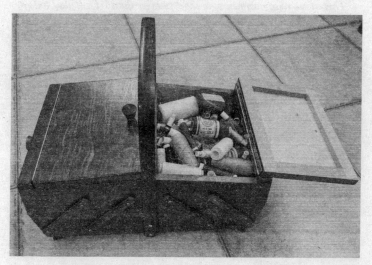

Irene's sewing box

While I was in Israel, Irene's son Pavel invited me to his home, filled with the amazing textile art and photography of his wife Amy. Irene's bright pink umbrella was still propped in the front porch. Pavel fetched Irene's sewing box, crammed with threads, tape measures and notions, just as she had last left it. Amy showed me what she considered to be the best portrait she ever took of Irene. It was from 23 April, Irene's birthday. Decades before, in Bratislava, Irene's mother had somehow found an egg to gift her daughter. Later, in camp, Marta arranged for the miracle of a boiled egg in tribute to this kindness. On this day, Irene's last ever birthday as it happened, Amy jokingly gave her an egg from the Passover seder meal of the day before. Irene held it up – the camera clicked.

Three generations of love and generosity – beyond words. Irene died in February 2017.

It is hard to fathom why the Fates picked me to be the last one. There were many women who were younger than I. I am glad today that I can share with others all that I know about this accursed time and place   – Bracha Kohút *née* Berkovič [29]

As we sit in her sunny home, I ask Bracha how it feels to be the last surviving seamstress of the Upper Tailoring Salon.

'You should have come ten years ago,' she replies, 'when more of us were still alive.'

If only.

As each year passes, so do the survivors. In their last months some of the dressmakers felt their careful emotional compartments collapse. They returned in their minds to happy memories of childhood and terrifying memories of the camps. Love and bitterness are woven together.

Their words, their stitches, their stories must not be forgotten.

Each of the dressmakers reflected on their experiences. Alida held on to her anger against the Nazis, writing, 'My heart cannot forgive.' She also pledged commitment to the goal of 'international peace and indestructible friendship among all the people of the world.'[30] Her compatriot Marilou Colombain – remarried as Marilou Rosé – saw her wartime resistance fighting continuing through life as dedicated combat against antisemitism.

Irene spoke passionately against xenophobia, tribalistic divisions and all racism. Despite the horrors she endured in Auschwitz, she knew through her friendships with the dressmakers there that love and loyalty were never extinguished entirely. In later life she paid tribute to all her friends in camp, saying, 'This was hell on earth, but there were people who still kept the face of humans.'[31]

Bracha freely acknowledges her lack of trust in humanity, but still urges young generations to build united communities by accepting individuals and celebrating diversity.

I wave goodbye to Bracha, standing bright-eyed, waving and smiling in the porch of her little house in California. This small, resilient woman has faced deprivation, deportation, starvation, humiliation, brutality and bereavement. Now she calmly endures Californian wildfires, political upheaval and Coronavirus lockdown. When I made a video call in spring 2020 to ask how she was faring, she simply answered, 'I'm alive.'

February 2021
With deep sadness I now write that Bracha Kohút, née Berkovič – known as Betka to her family – died in the early hours of Valentine's Day 2021. She will long be remembered for her energy, loyalty and resilience. She is now at peace. It was a privilege and a pleasure to have known her.

ACKNOWLEDGEMENTS

Crafting this book has not been a solo enterprise. I am grateful for the time, expertise and experience generously gifted by many individuals, not least the families of survivors who shared precious mementoes as well as heartful memories. In addition, I have appreciated the immense resources of archives such as Yad Vashem World Holocaust Remembrance Center, the United States Holocaust Memorial Museum, the Tauber Holocaust Library, the Wiener Holocaust Library, the Visual History Archive USC Shoah Foundation, the British Library, the Ghetto Fighters' House Museum, and the Museum of Jewish Heritage.

Researching such a deeply important and deeply harrowing aspect of history is no easy task. Throughout my studies and writing I have been supported by patient friends, insightful literary agents and, in the final stages, by the talented editors of brilliant publishers. Despite the hard work, it has frequently been an uplifting experience to be able to commemorate the experiences of women so unjustly persecuted, and to become part of a new worldwide weave of connected lives.

Of course, any faults in the book are my own. I hope I have done justice to the memories of the dressmakers – particularly those unable to speak for themselves – and that I have honoured the trust placed in me by their relatives. I now look forward to learning more as archives re-open after the Covid19 pandemic, and the book goes out into the world.

In the meanwhile, my particular thanks go to:

Yael Aharoni, Lilka Areton, Tom Areton, Emil Areton, Avri Ben Ze'ev, Katarína Blatná , Rosalind Bryan-Schrimpff, Hilary

Canham, Angela Clare, Vivian Cohen, Clementine Gaisman, Oshrat Green, Irit Greenstein, Avri Greenstein, Allison Hellegers, Richard Henley, Rainer Höss, Yedida Kanfer, Pavel Kanka, Amy Kanka-Valadarsky, Ellen Klages, Bracha Kohút, Gila Kornfeld-Jacobs, Rupert Lancaster, Elisa Milkes, Juraj Minárik senior, Juraj Minárik junior, Alice Natali, Sara Nelson, Fred Parker, Jan Parker, Rosalind Parker, Thalia Reichenberg Soffair, Rafi Shamir, Kate Shaw, Gabriela Shelley, Eva Vogel, Helen Westmancoat, John Westmancoat, Maxine Willett.

ILLUSTRATION CREDITS

1. Irene Reichenberg photograph detail, Amy Kanka-Valadarsky
2. Renée Ungar, 1939 photograph, private collection
3. Bracha Berkovič, elementary school photograph, family archives © Tom Areton
4. Marta Fuchs, Schneider 1934 family wedding photograph, private collection
5. Bracha Berkovič, pre-war Mizrachi group photograph, family archives © Tom Areton
6. Prague fashions, *Eva* magazine, 1940, author's archive
7. *Fürs Haus*, 8 November 1934, author's archive
8. *Eva* magazine, 1940, author's archive
9. *Eva* magazine, 1940, author's archive
10. Spring fashions, *La Coquette*, undated, author's archive
11. Hunya Storch, 1935 photograph, Gila Kornfeld-Jacobs
12. *Mode Und Heim* cover, 12th edition 1940, author's archive
13. Detail of ADEFA label on a late 1930s rayon crepe dress, author's collection
14. Renée Ungar, pre-war photograph, private collection
15. Katka and Bracha Berkovič, pre-war photograph, family archives © Tom Areton
16. Aprons, *Deutches Moden Zeitung*, 1941, author's archive
17. Paper pattern detail, *Deutches Moden Zeitung*, 1941, author's archive
18. Nathan Volkmann, pre-war photograph, Gila Kornfeld-Jacobs

19. Fur fashions, *Eva* magazine, December 1940, author's archive
20. Furs, *Bon Marché* shopping catalogue, France, winter 1939/40, author's archive
21. Käthe Kohút, *née* Reichenberg, pre-war photograph, family archives © Tom Areton
22. *Mode und Wäsche*, 1942, new fashions for spring coats, author's archive
23. Berkovič group portrait, 1942, family archives © Tom Areton
24. *Bon Marché* catalogue goods, winter 1939/40, author's archive
25. 1941 German atlas page of occupied territories bordering Slovakia, author's archive
26. Bracha Berkovič before deportation.
27. Moritz Mädler luggage Leipzig, Berlin, Hamburg, advert, *Die Dame*, 1939, author's archive
28. Watches for sale, *Bon Marché*, winter 1939/40, author's archive
29. Kanada II barracks, The Archive of the State Museum Auschwitz-Birkenau in Oświęcim. Nr neg. 20995-482
30. Bracha Berkovič, 1937 photograph, family archives © Tom Areton
31. Gardening outfits, Beyer's *Mode und Wäsche*, author's archive
32. Knitting patterns from *Die Hausfrau*, October 1939, author's archive
33. Girls' outfits, Beyer's *Mode Für Alle*, 1944, author's archive
34. Höss family portrait, 1943, Institut für Zeitgeschichte München–Berlin, IfZ BA-00019962
35. Autumn fashions for suits, *Beyer's Mode Für Alle*, 1944, author's archive
36. Detail of postcard from Marta Fuchs, 3.3.44, private collection

37. Alida Delasalle identification photographs, Tauber Holocaust Archives, Jewish Family and Children's Services Holocaust Center, Lore Shelley Collection, 2011-003. Orig. Stabsgebaude, M-Z. Alida Vasselin

38. Elegant afternoon dress designs, *Les Patrons Universels*, 1943, author's archive

39. Rezina Apfelbaum photograph, private collection

40. Nightgown and lingerie designs, *Les Patrons Universels*, 1943, author's archive

41. Marta Fuchs postcard, 3 March 1943, private collection

42. 23.9.44 photograph, Pictorial Press Ltd/Alamy Stock Photo, 2BFCN18

43. Bracha Berkovič, post-war photograph, family archives © Tom Areton

44. Marta Fuchs post-war work card, private collection

45. Kohút family photograph, family archives © Tom Areton

46. Marta and Ladislav Minárik wedding photograph, private collection

47. Renée Adler, *née* Ungar, and family, private collection

48. Irene Reichenberg, post-war portrait, private collection

49. Raya Kagan photograph, private collection

50. Bracha and Katka Berković photograph, family archives © Tom Areton

51. Photograph of shoes on display at the Auschwitz-Birkenau State Museum, author's collection

52. Irene Reichenberg's sewing box photograph, author's collection

BIBLIOGRAPHY

Aalders, Gerard, *Nazi Looting: The Plunder of Dutch Jewry During the Second World War*, trans., Arnold Pomerans and Erica Pomerans, Berg (2004)

Aly, Götz, *Hitler's Beneficiaries: Plunder, Racial War and the Nazi Welfare State*, trans., Jefferson Chase, Versa (2016)

Aly, Götz and Susanne Heim, *Architects of Annihilation: Auschwitz and the Logic of Destruction*, Phoenix (2003)

Arad, Yitzhak, Israel Gutman & Abraham Margaliot (eds.), *Documents on the Holocaust*, trans., Lea Ben Dor, University of Nebraska Press and Yad Vashem (1999)

Berr, Hélène, *Le Journal de Hélène Berr*, trans., David Bellos, McClelland & Stewart (2008)

Birenbaum, Halina, *Hope Is the Last to Die*, Auschwitz State Museum (2016)

Bogner, Nahum, 'Cyprus Detention Camps', *Encyclopedia of the Holocaust*, ed., Israel Gutman, Macmillan (1990)

Borden, Harry, *Survivor*, Cassell (2017)

Bourke-White, Margaret, *Dear Fatherland, Rest Quietly. A Report on the Collapse of Hitler's Thousand Years*, Arcole Publishing (1946/2018)

Boyd, Julia, *Travellers in the Third Reich*, Elliott & Thompson Ltd (2017)

Brosh, Hilary, *Threads of Life*, unpublished MA dissertation, Leeds Metropolitan University (2012)

Buber-Neumann, Margarete, *Milena*, trans., Ralph Manheim, Collins Harvill (1989).

Burianová, Miroslava, *Móda v ulicích protektorátu*, Narodni Muzeum, Grada Publishing (2013)

Caldwell, Erskine, and Margaret Bourke-White, *North of the Danube*, The Viking Press (1939)

Chesnoff, Richard Z., *Pack of Thieves*, Phoenix (2001)

Chiger, Krystyna, with Daniel Paisner, *The Girl in the Green Sweater*, St Martin's Griffin (2008)

Clendinnen, Inga, *Reading the Holocaust*, Canto (2002)

Collins, Robert and Han Hogerzeil, *Straight On: Journey to Belsen and the Road Home*, Methuen & Co (1947)

Czech, Danuta, *Auschwitz Chronicle, 1939–1945*, Henry Holt & Co. (1997)

Czocher, Anna, Dobrochna Kałwa, Barbara Klich-Kluczewska, Beata Łabno, *Is War Men's Business? Fates of Women in Occupied Kraków in Twelve Scenes*, Muzeum Historyczne Miasta Krakówa (2011)

Delbo, Charlotte, *Auschwitz and After*, Yale University Press (1995)

Dojc, Yuri and Katya Krausova, *Last Folio: Textures of Jewish Life in Slovakia*, Indiana University Press (2011)

Dune Macadam, Heather, *999: The Extraordinary Young Women of the First Official Jewish Transport to Auschwitz*, Citadel Press (2020)

Eger, Edith, *The Choice*, Rider (2017)

Epstein, Helen, *Where She Came From: A Daughter's Search for Her Mother's History*, Holmes & Meier (2005)

Fantlová, Zdenka, *The Tin Ring: How I Cheated Death*, Northumbria Press (2010)

Feldman, Jeffrey, 'The Holocaust Shoe. Untying Memory: Shoes as Holocaust Memorial Experience', in *Jews and Shoes*, ed., Edna Nahshon, Berg (2008)

Fénelon, Fania, *The Musicians of Auschwitz*, Sphere Books (1977)

Fogg, Shannon L., *Stealing Home: Looting, Restitution and Reconstructing Jewish Lives in France, 1942–1947*, Oxford University Press (2017)

Flanner, Jean, *Paris Journal 1944–1965*, Atheneum Press (1965)

Frankl, Viktor, *Man's Search for Meaning*, Rider (2004)

Fromm, Bella, *Blood & Banquets: A Berlin Social Diary*, Birch Lane Press (1990)

Garliński, Jósef, *Fighting Auschwitz*, Fontana (1976)

Gensburger, Sarah, *Witnessing the Robbing of the Jews: A Photographic Album, Paris, 1940–1944*, trans., Jonathan Hensher, Indiana University Press (2015)

Gibas, Dr Monika, Dr Cornelia Briel, Petra Knöller, Steffen Held, *'Aryanisation' in Leipzig: Driven out. Robbed. Murdered*, touring exhibition. http://www.juedischesleipzig.de/arisierung_engl09.pdf

Gilbert, Martin, *The Dent Atlas of the Holocaust*, JM Dent (1993)

Goering, Emmy, *My Life with Goering*, David Bruce & Watson Ltd (1972)

Gold, Dina, *Stolen Legacy: Nazi Theft and the Quest for Justice at Krausenstrasse 17/18, Berlin*, American Bar Association (2016)

Goldberg, Myrna and Amy H. Shapiro (eds.), *Different Horrors, Same Hell: Gender and the Holocaust*, University of Washington Press (2013)

Gottfried, Claudia, et al., *Glanz und Grauen. Kulturhistorische untersuchungenzur Mode und Bedleidung in der Zeit des Nationalsozialismus*, LVR-Industriemuseum, Textilfabrik Cromford Hg. (2020)

Grabowski, Jan, *Hunt for the Jews: Betrayal and Murder in German-Occupied Poland*, Indiana University Press (2013)

Grant, Linda, *The Thoughtful Dresser*, Virago (2009)

Grosman, Ladislav, *The Shop on Main Street*, trans., Iris Urwin Lewitová, Karolinum Press (2019)

Guenther, Irene, *Nazi Chic? Fashioning Women in the Third Reich*, Berg (2004)

Gutman, Israel, and Michael Berenbaum, *Anatomy of the Auschwitz Death Camp*, Indiana University Press (1998)

Gutterman, Bella and Avner Shalev (eds.), *To Bear Witness: Holocaust Remembrance at Yad Vashem*, Yad Vashem (2014)

Hampton, Janie, *How the Girl Guides Won the War*, Harper Press (2011)

Harding, Thomas, *Hanns and Rudolph: The German Jew and the Hunt for the Commandant of Auschwitz*, William Heinemann (2013)

Harding, Thomas, 'Hiding in N. Virginia, a daughter of Auschwitz', *Washington Post*, 7 September 2013

Hart-Moxon, Kitty, *Return to Auschwitz*, Sidgwick & Jackson Ltd (1981)

Haste, Cate, *Nazi Women*, Channel 4 Books (2001)

Heijmerikx, Anton G.M., 'Hedwig Höss-Hensel de vrouw van de kampcommandant en haar rol in Auschwitz', *Genealogie en Streekgeschiedenis*, 7 August 2016, accessed 5.2.20. https://heijmerikx.nl/2016/08/07/hedwig-hoss-hensel-de-vrouw-van-de-kampcommandant-en-haar-rol-in-auschwitz/

Hellman, Peter, with Lili Meier and Beate Klarsfeld, *The Auschwitz Album*, Random House (1981)

Helm, Sarah, *If This Is a Woman: Inside Ravensbruck: Hitler's Concentration Camp for Women*, Little, Brown (2015)

Helman, Anat, *A Coat of Many Colors: Dress Culture in the Young State of Israel*, Academic Studies Press (2011)

Himmler, Katrin, and Michael Wildt, (eds.), *The Private Heinrich Himmler: Letters of a Mass Murderer*, trans., Thomas S. Hansen and Abby J. Hansen, St Martin's Press (2016)

Hlaváčková, Konstantina, *Czech Fashion: Mirror of the Times 1940–1970*, Olympia Publishing (2000)

Hoffman, Eva, *After Such Knowledge: A Meditation on the Aftermath of the Holocaust*, Vintage (2004)

Holden, Wendy, *Born Survivors*, Sphere (2015)

Höss, Rainer, *Das Erbe des Kommandanten*, Belleville Verlag (2013)

Huebner, Karla, 'Inter-war Czech Women's Magazines: Constructing Gender, Consumer Culture and Identity in Central Europe', in *Women in Magazines: Research, Representation, Production and Consumption*, Rachel Ritchie, Sue Hawkins, Nicola Phillips (eds.), Routledge (2016)

Jalowicz-Simon, Marie, *Gone To Ground*, trans., Anthea Bell, Profile Books Ltd (2014)

Junge, Traudl, with Melissa Müller, *Until the Final Hour*, Phoenix (2005)

Kanter, Trudi, *Some Girls, Some Hats and Hitler*, Virago (2012)

Katz, Leslie, 'Love, business and Holocaust bind unlikely couple in S.F.', *The Jewish News of Northern California*, 12 April 1996

Kirschner, Ann, *Sala's Gift*, Free Press (2006)

Klabunde, Anja, *Magda Goebbels*, Sphere (2007)

Klemann, Hein & Sergei Kudryashov, *Occupied Economies: An Economic History of Nazi-Occupied Europe 1939–1945*, Berg (2012)

Klemperer, Victor, *I Shall Bear Witness: The Diaries of Victor Klemperer 1933–1941*, trans., Martin Chalmers, Phoenix (1999)

Knill, Iby, *The Woman Without a Number*, Scratching Shed Publishing Ltd (2010)

Knowles, Anne Kelly and Tim Cole, Alberto Giordano (eds.) *Geographies of the Holocaust*, Indiana University Press (2014)

Kobylański, Tomasz, 'Życie codzienne w willi Hössa', *Polityka*, January 2013

Koontz, Claudia, *Mothers in the Fatherland: Women, the Family and Nazi Politics*, Methuen (1987)

Kornfeld-Jacobs, Gila, with Varda K. Rosenfeld, *The Rooster Called: Our Father's Life Journey from Hungary to Israel*, PHP (2019)

Kornreich Gelissen, Rena, with Heather Dune Macadam, *Rena's Promise: A Story of Sisters in Auschwitz*, Beacon Press (2015)

Kounio Amariglio, Erika, *From Thessaloniki to Auschwitz and Back*, Valentine Mitchell (2000)

Kramer, Clara, *Clara's War*, Ebury Press (2008)

Kremer, Roberta S. (ed.)., *Broken Threads. The Destruction of the Jewish Fashion Industry in Germany and Austria*, Berg (2007)

Lachendro, Jacek, *Auschwitz After Liberation*, trans., William Brand, Auschwitz-Birkenau State Museum (2015)

Langbein, Hermann, *People in Auschwitz*, trans., Harry Zohn, University of North Carolina Press, USHMM (2004)

Langford, Liesbeth, *Written By Candlelight*, Ergo Press (2009)

Lasker-Wallfisch, Anita, *Inherit the Truth 1939–1945*, Giles de la Mare Publishers (1996)

Lebert, Stephan, *My Father's Keeper: The Children of the Nazi Leaders: An Intimate History of Damage & Denial*, Little, Brown & Company (2001)

Lengyel, Olga, *Five Chimneys: A Woman Survivor's True Story of Auschwitz*, Ziff-Davis Publishing (1947)

Libitzky, Eva, and Fred Rosenbaum, *Out on a Ledge: Enduring the Łódź Ghetto, Auschwitz and Beyond*, Wicker Park Press Ltd (2014)

Lipszyc, Rywka, *Rywka's Diary*, Anita Friedman (ed.), trans., Malgorzata Markoff, HarperCollins (2015)

Loridan-Ivens, Marceline, *But You Did Not Come Back*, trans., Sandra Smith, Faber & Faber (2017)

Lower, Wendy, *Hitler's Furies: German Women in the Nazi Killing Fields*, Chatto & Windus (2013)

Margolius Kovály, Heda, *Under a Cruel Star: A Life in Prague 1941–68*, Granta Books (2012)

Mičev, Stanislav, *My Experiences During a Three-Year Imprisonment in the Auschwitz Concentration Camp: Memoirs of Berta Berkovičová-Kohútová*, Matica Slovenska, January 2019

Meiri-Minerbe, Chaya, *Juden in Kesmark: und Umgebung zur Zeit der Shoah: jüdisches Leben und Leiden in der Slowakei-RäumungAbteilung*, trans., Magali Zibaso, Hartung-Gorre (2002)

Moorehead, Caroline, *A Train in Winter: A Story of Resistance*, Vintage (2012)

Nicosia, Francis, R. & Jonathan Huener (eds.), *Business and Industry in Nazi Germany*, Berghahn Books (2004)

Nomberg-Przytyk, Sara, trans., Roslyn Hirsch, *Auschwitz: True Tales from a Grotesque Land*, The University of North Carolina Press (1985)

Overy, Richard, *Interrogations: The Nazi Elite in Allied Hands, 1945*, Allen Lane (2001)

Owen, James, *Nuremberg: Evil on Trial*, Headline Review (2006)

Owings, Alison, *Frauen: German Women Recall the Third Reich*, Penguin (2001)

Paskuly, Steven (ed.), *Rudolph Höss, Death Dealer: The Memoirs of the SS Kommandant of Auschwitz*, trans., Andrew Pollinger, Prometheus Books (1992)

Rader, Henning, and Vanessa-Maria Voigt (eds.), *Einem Jüdischer Besitz Erwerbungen des München Stadtmuseums im Nationalsozialismus*, Hirmer Verlag (2018)

Rawicz, Jerzy (ed.), *KL Auschwitz Seen by the SS*, Auschwitz State Museum (1970)

Rees, Laurence, *Auschwitz: The Nazis and the Final Solution*, BBC Books (2005)

Rougier-Lecoq, Violette, *Témoignages. 36 Dessins à la Plume de Ravensbrück*, Imprimerie Auclerc (1983)

Sadowski, Tanja, 'Die nationalsozialistische Frauenideologie: Bild und Rolle der Frau in der "NS-Frauenwarte" vor 1939'. https://www.mainz1933-1945.de/fileadmin/Rheinhessenportal/Teilnehmer/mainz1933-1945/Textbeitraege/Sadowski_Frauen-ideologie.pdf. Accessed 28.4.20

Sandes, Philippe, *East West Street: On the Origins of Genocide and Crimes Against Humanity*, Weidenfeld & Nicholson (2016)

Schechter, Hillel, *Jewish Life in Leipzig during the 1930s*, Shoah Resource Centre, Yad Vashem, accessed 23.6.20

Schloss, Eva, *Eva's Story: A Survivor's Tale by the Stepsister of Anne Frank*, William B. Eerdmans Publishing Company (1988/2010)

Schneider, Helga, *The Bonfire of Berlin*, trans., Shaun Whiteside, William Heinemann (2005)

Schneider, Helga, *Let Me Go: My Mother and the SS*, Vintage (2005)

Schwarz, Gudrun, *Eine Frau an seine Seite*, Aufbau Taschenbuch Verlag

Setkiewicz, Piotr (ed.), *The Private Lives of the SS*, trans., William Brand, Auschwitz-Birkenau State Museum (2015)

Shelley, Lore (ed. and trans.), *Secretaries of Death: Accounts by Former Prisoners Who Worked in the Gestapo of Auschwitz*, Shengold Publishers Ltd (1986)

Shelley, Lore (ed. and trans.), *Criminal Experiments on Human Beings in Auschwitz and War Research Laboratories*, Mellen Research University Press (1991)

Shelley, Lore (ed. and trans.), *Auschwitz – The Nazi Civilisation: Twenty-three Women Prisoners' Accounts*, University Press of America (1992)

Shelley, Lore, *The Union Kommando in Auschwitz: The Auschwitz Munition Factory Through the Eyes of Its Former Slave Laborers*, Studies in the Shoah Volume XIII, University Press of America (1996)

Shelley, Lore, *Post-Auschwitz Fragments*, Morris Publishing (1997)

Shik, Dr Na'ama, Online lecture for Yad Vashem, YouTube, 13th July 2020

Shuter, Jane, *The Holocaust: The Camp System*, Heinemann (2002)

Škodová, Júlia, *Tri Roky Bez Mena*, Osveta (1962)

Smith, Lyn, *Forgotten Voices of the Holocaust*, Ebury Press (2005)

Snyder, Louis L., *Encyclopedia of the Third Reich*, Wordsworth Editions Ltd (1998)

Speer, Albert, trans., Clara and Richard Winston, *Inside the Third Reich*, Phoenix (1995)

Stargardt, Nicholas, *The German War: A Nation Under Arms, 1939–45*, Vintage (2016)

Steinbacher, Sybille, *Auschwitz: A History*, trans., Shaun Whiteside, Penguin (2004)

Steiner, Jean-François, *Treblinka*, Meridian (1994)

Stone, Dan, *The Liberation of the Camps*, Yale University Press (2015)

Todorov, Tzvetan, *Facing the Extreme: Moral Life in the Concentration Camps*, Weidenfeld & Nicholson (1999)

Tuchman, Barbara, *Practising History*, Ballantine Books (1982)

Tuvel Bernstein, Sara, *The Seamstress: A Memoir of Survival*, Penguin Putnam Ltd (1999)

Van Pelt, Robert Jan & Debórah Dwork, *Auschwitz 1270 to the Present*, Yale University Press (1996)

Veillon, Dominique, *Fashion Under the Occupation*, Berg (2002)

Vrba, Rudolf, *I Escaped from Auschwitz*, Robson Books (2002)

Vrbová, Gerta, *Trust and Deceit: A Tale of Survival in Slovakia and Hungary, 1939–1945*, Vallentine Mitchell (2006)

Walford, Jonathan, *Forties Fashion: From Siren Suits to the New Look*, Thames & Hudson (2008)

Weissmann Klein, Gerda, *All But My Life*, Hill and Wang (1995)

Westphal, Uwe, trans., Kristine Jennings, *Fashion Metropolis Berlin 1836–1939: The Story of the Rise and Destruction of the Jewish Fashion Industry*, Henschel (2019)

Wiesenthal, Simon, *Justice Not Vengeance*, Weidenfeld and Nicholson (1989)

Willingham II, Robert Allen, 'Jews in Leipzig: Nationality and Community in the 20th Century', PhD thesis, University of Texas at Austin (2005). https://repositories.lib.utexas.edu/bitstream/handle/2152/1799/willinghamr73843.pdf. Accessed June 2020

Wong, Joanna, 'Lincoln teacher recalls parents' Holocaust travails', Abraham Lincoln High School magazine 10 May 2016, accessed April 2020

Zuker-Bujanowska, Liliana, *Liliana's Journal: Warsaw 1939–1945*, Judy Piatkus Publishers (1980)

NOTES ON SOURCES

Introduction

1 *Nazi Chic,* Irene Guenther.

Chapter One: One of the Few Who Survived

1 Olga Kovanová, *née* Kovaczová, (Kovácz) typewritten testimony sent to Dr Lore Shelley. Lore Shelley archives, Tauber Holocaust Library.

2 Author interview with Bracha Kohút, November 2019.

3 Irene Kanka Interview 07138 Visual History Archive, USC Shoah Foundation, translated by her son Pavel Kanka. The Museum of Jewish Culture – part of the Slovak National Museum – is now at number 17 Židovská Street just across from Irene's former home. It holds a permanent exhibition of Judaica with displays memorialising the once vibrant life of the Jewish quarter.

4 Käthe Kohn, *née* Reichenberg, was born 18 July 1917; Frieda, born 18 May 1913, married Zoltan Federweiss; Edith was born 24 May 1924.

5 Renée's mother was Esther, her father Simcha. She was the eldest child, followed by her brother Shmuel and sisters Gita and Yehudit. Renée's Hebrew name was Shoshana.

6 Bracha was born 'Berta', softened to the affectionate Bracha, or Brochču in Čepa Yiddish. This was despite the fact that her maternal grandmother, steeped in Hungarian culture, wished her to be given the Hungarian name Hajnal, which means Dawn.

However, her paternal grandfather decided on the name Berta, since there was a wealthy Jewish family in Čepa with the surname Farkaš, or Wolf. This Farkaš had a daughter named Berta, so grandfather Berkovič declared, 'If such a name is good for them, it will be good for my granddaughter, too.' Bracha's Hebrew name was Chaya Bracha, which means Life Blessing. (Unpublished correspondence.)

7 Bread was made at home; vegetables were grown in the home plot. Autumn saw people dancing barefoot in barrels of cabbage to squeeze the water out and ready it for pickling. Other winter vitamins came from fruit jam, and carrots stored in straw – children would creep into the cellar to nibble on them in secret. Self-sufficiency was essential. It was a hard life.

8 Bracha's grandfather Ignatz's experiences fighting in the Great War left him unstable, angry and sometimes in need of an escape into alcohol. In contrast, her grandmother Rivka, who'd brought up five children while Ignatz was fighting, was a gentle and patient woman. Both were honest and hardworking – qualities that their son Salomon, Bracha's father, inherited.

9 Katka's Hebrew name was 'Tova Tsipora' or *good bird*. In Yiddish Tova is Gitl, so her family called her Gitu, a term of endearment. She was born in 1925.

10 The photograph was a favourite of the middle Höss daughter, Inge-Brigitt. Author Thomas Harding, interviewing her for his book *Hanns and Rudolph*, was permitted a viewing of the photo in situ. In a memoir of his grandfather Rudolf, *Das Erbe des Kommandanten*, Rainer Höss describes a different wedding day photograph, which shows the men in a country costume of knickerbockers and short waistcoats, while the bride and her best friend Ilse von Seckendorff are pretty in plaits, with white embroidered blouses and long dark skirts. In later decades, Hedwig and Ilse would reminisce about the 'splendid wedding' held at the beautiful baroque palace of Meseberg: fantasy or reality?

11 *Death Dealer: The Memoirs of the SS Kommandant of Auschwitz*, Rudolf Höss.

12 Dr Willibald Hentschel founded the Artaman Society in 1923, with the idea of renewing the German race by taking young people disillusioned by modern city life, and resettling them as farmers in the countryside. During the Third Reich, the Artamans were absorbed into the Nazi Party.

13 *Hanns and Rudolph*, Thomas Harding.

14 Female Slovak surnames are often given the suffix -à or -ovà, ie. transforming Fuchs to Fuchsovà. However, familiar usage in the English language is to drop to the suffix, which I've chosen to do for core characters in this history, including Marta Fuchs.

15 Marta was a big reader and a music lover, even taking piano lessons with family friend Eugen Suchoň, from Pezinok, whose haunting 1940s opera *Krútňava* – 'The Whirlpool' – established his reputation as Slovakia's greatest composer.

16 *Das Erbe des Kommandanten*, Rainer Höss. Dr Carl Clauberg performed the caesarean. Clauberg would join Höss at Auschwitz and work in the infamous Block 10, where sadistic 'medical' experiments were inflicted on female prisoners, including forced sterilisations. Block 10 was in the Auschwitz main camp, next to Block 11, where prisoners condemned to death awaited execution. Nurse Maria Stromberger testified at Clauberg's post-war trial. She attended Hedwig's final childbirth on 20 September 1943, when baby Annegret was born. As will be seen, Nurse Maria was also active in the Auschwitz underground, with links to Marta Fuchs.

17 Photographer and filmmaker Roman Vishniac captured poignant images of Jewish people in Central and Eastern Europe before deportations, including a black and white portrait of a group of Jewish girls in Kežmarok. One girl has long braids like Bracha, the others have tousled bobbed hair. They wear an assortment

of coats, strap shoes and wrinkled stockings. Their faces are bright; their names and fates unknown.

18 Hunya's birthplace was Plavnitz, a Polish village in the mountains. Her parents soon moved to Kežmarok.

19 *Konzentrationslager Auschwitz Frauen-Abteilung*, USHMM. Hunya's parents are listed as Hermann Storch and Fanny Birnbaum. (They were also known as Zvi Krieger Storch and Zipora Birnbaum Laundau.) On the registration card her surname is Winkler – reference to a marriage of convenience undertaken to help with visa issues while working in Leipzig. Her actual married name was Volkmann. The card states that on arrival at Auschwitz, Hunya had no infectious diseases or infirmity. That would soon change.

20 Helen (Helka) Grossman, *née* Brody, quoted in *Secretaries of Death*, Lore Shelley. Helka was fifteen and a half when her formal education ended. For a while she was hidden in the town of Bardejov. A non-Jew reported her in 1942. She was deported to Auschwitz, and worked in the card-filing department of the SS administration block there, sharing a dormitory with Hunya and the other dressmakers.

21 Irene Kanka Interview 07138 Visual History Archive, USC Shoah Foundation.

Chapter Two: The One and Only Power

1 *Until the Final Hour*, Traudl Junge.

2 A Podolská gown won first prize at the 1938 International Crafts Exhibition in Berlin. It was the last Czech fashion show in Germany before the country was broken up.

3 *Eva* was first published in December 1928. Despite losing a bit of colour during the Great Depression, the magazine endured until 1943. The most resilient fashion magazines defied wartime paper shortages to continue bringing escapism and thrifty dressmaking tips to their readers.

4 Jesenská was arrested by the Gestapo for her work with the underground resistance after the German occupation of Czechoslovakia. She died of kidney failure in Ravensbrück concentration camp on 17 May 1944, her fine clothes exchanged for a striped prison dress.

5 Conversation with Gila Kornfeld-Jacobs, niece of Hermine Volkman-Hecht, *née* Storch. Hunya was at a stage in her life when she felt very disillusioned with most things, including the dressmaking trade.

6 *Memory Book*, Gila Kornfeld-Jacobs.

7 *Blood and Banquets*, Bella Fromm, 26 June 1933.

8 *Broken Threads,* Roberta S. Kremer (ed.). Frau Magda Goebbels, Joseph's wife, became honorary president. Like many high-ranking Nazi wives, she enjoyed the privilege of being able to commandeer the attention and talents of couturiers in Berlin and beyond. Any thoughts she might have had of indulging in Paris fashions were quashed when the Fashion Institute began to promote solidly German companies. Perhaps Magda was too French-leaning, too modish. She was certainly replaced as president.

9 The ideal professions for German women were housekeeping, nursing, teaching, tailoring, secretary, librarian or assistant to men generally. Tanja Sadowski, 'Die nationalsozialistische Frauenideologie: Bild und Rolle der Frau in der "NS-Frauenwarte" vor 1939'.

10 *Blood and Banquets*, 30 August 1932.

11 *Inside the Third Reich*, Albert Speer. Hitler said of the gifts, 'I know these are not beautiful things, but many of them are presents. I shouldn't like to part with them.'

12 *Glanz und Grauen*, Claudia Gottfried et al.

13 In Czechoslovakia national clothes with their brilliant embroidery and traditional styles were used to make a political statement. Bavarian and Tyrolian styles signified an allegiance with the Nazi

Party; particularly local styles were a sign of resistance to German influence or politics.

14 *Documents on the Holocaust,* Yitzhak Arad et al. (eds.).

15 Frau Marlene Karlsruhen, quoted in *Frauen,* Alison Owings.

16 Erna Lugebiel, quoted in *Mothers in the Fatherland,* Claudia Koontz. Lugebiel sheltered Jewish Germans during the war, such was her anger at the persecution.

17 *Documents on the Holocaust.* There were objections to anti-Jewish boycotts from the Minister of Economics, but only on the grounds that they caused economic disruption to business supply chains.

18 *Broken Threads.*

19 When is a dress not just a dress? When it is part of antisemitic history. In the author's collection – a pretty apple-green crepe tea gown, woven with colourful florals, bearing the ADEFA label. A chilling conjunction.

20 *My Life with Goering,* Emmy Goering.

21 *'Aryanisation' in Leipzig: Driven Out. Robbed. Murdered,* Dr Monika Gibas et al.

22 *Pack of Thieves,* Richard Z. Chesnoff. In 1938, 79 per cent of department stores belonged to Jews and 25 per cent of German retail stores.

23 *Jewish Life in Leipzig,* Hillel Schechter.

24 *Hitler's Furies,* Wendy Lower.

25 *Nuremberg Trial Transcripts,* 20 March 1946. Goering defended the statement at his trial, saying, 'It was the expression of spontaneous excitement caused by the events, and by the destruction of valuables, and by the difficulties which arose.' *Interrogations,* Richard Overy.

26 *Elegante Welt* magazine, August 1938, 'Stimmung am movehorizont: vorwiegend heiter' article.

27 *My Life with Goering.*

28 *Pack of Thieves.*

29 *Magda Goebbels,* Anja Klabunde.

30 Irene Kanka Interview 07138 Visual History Archive, USC Shoah Foundation.

31 Irene Kanka Interview 07138 Visual History Archive, USC Shoah Foundation.

Chapter Three: What Next, How to Continue?

1 Irene Kanka Interview 07138 Visual History Archive, USC Shoah Foundation.

2 Ela Weissberger, living in the Lom u Mostu Jewish community. The family suffered brutal treatment during Kristallnacht violence. https://www.holocaust.cz/en/sources/recollections. Accessed June 2020.

3 *Occupied Economies*, Hein Klemann & Sergei Kudryashov.

4 Speech on 6 August 1942 to the Reich leadership at the Aviation Ministry. Goering promised occupiers would 'extract the maximum so that the German people can live their lives.' Quoted in *Hitler's Beneficiaries*, Götz Aly.

5 *Out on a Ledge*, Eva Libitzky.

6 When American photographer Margaret Bourke-White interviewed a young German Panzer Grenadier in the Nuremberg area in 1945, he lamented the lost prosperity of the war years. Bourke-White asked if he meant food, clothes and treats from Poland, France, Belgium and Holland? The young man was affronted. 'No, from Germany,' he insisted, refusing to believe the goods had been foreign plunder rather than patriotic produce of the Fatherland. *Dear Fatherland, Rest Quietly*, Margaret Bourke-White.

7 *I Shall Bear Witness*, Victor Klemperer.

8 Katka Gruenstein, *née* Feldbauer – born 3 March 1922, western Slovakia. *Nazi Civilisation*, Lore Shelley.

9 *Das Schwarze Korps*, 24 November 1938.

10 Jewish bank accounts were frozen. Jewish assets were converted

into government bonds that could not be redeemed. Potential Jewish emigrants had to pay a tax for the privilege of escaping while leaving most of their wealth behind. Jews were targeted for financial levies and even reparation payments for damage done during Kristallnacht. Jewish employees were also ejected from employment in non-Jewish companies. Sometimes this was done under the euphemism of *Umstellung Unseres Unternehmens* – 'company reshuffling'.

11 *Magda Goebbels.*

12 *The Shop on Main Street*, Ladislav Grosman.

13 *Aryanization in Leipzig.*

14 *Pack of Thieves.*

15 Adolf Eichmann established the *Zentralstelle Fuer Juedische Auswanderung* – Central Office for Jewish Emigration – which was to 'encourage' Jews from the Protectorate to emigrate. In Slovakia, Dieter Wisliceny was part of outlandish Reich plans to deport Jews to Madagascar. Extermination centres were to provide a far more emphatic clearance 'solution'.

16 Irene Kanka Interview 07138 Visual History Archive, USC Shoah Foundation. Irene took sewing lessons between 1939 and 1942.

17 Margita (Grete) Rothova, *née* Duchinsky, born 1902, Pressburg/ Bratislava. Grete survived the Holocaust. After the war, her weaving skill was a vital source of income. *Secretaries of Death*, Lore Shelley.

18 Katka's mother helped neighbours with their sewing to supplement the family income. *Nazi Civilisation.*

19 *Deutsches Moden Zeitung*, Leipzig, summer 1941.

20 Apron illustration from *Deutsches Moden Zeitung*, Leipzig, summer 1941.

21 *Glanz und Grauen.*

22 *Magda Goebbels.*

23 *Mothers in the Fatherland.*

24 Speech at Berlin University on 11 November 1941, to justify Jewish labour. *Documents on the Holocaust.*

25 Only in 2019 was Emil's fate confirmed by family research; caught up in the Slovak hunt for Jewish youths, he was deported to Majdanek camp in the Lublin district of German-occupied Poland, receiving the low prisoner number #319. He and other inmates laboured on building works at the camp. He was murdered in the new CO_2 gas chambers at Majdanek 7 September 1942, the 4941st registered execution.

26 From 1944 Sered' was run by the SS and became a fully-fledged concentration camp for Jews, partisans and participants in the Slovak uprising. Sered' was also used as a transit camp for Jews being deported to Theresienstadt, Ravensbrück, Auschwitz and Sachsenhausen. From May 1942, a small yellow Bakelite badge in the shape of a yellow Star of David, marked with HŽ, was given to any *Hospodárský Žid* – economically vital Jew. (Yad Vashem Artifacts collection.)

27 Gila Kornfeld-Jacobs, *Memory Book.*

28 The school's founder, Rabbi Carlebach, emigrated to Palestine in 1935. When the school was eventually cleared of its temporary occupants, Hunya was moved to a new fourth-floor room in a Jewish orphanage, which she shared with seven other women.

29 *The Girl in the Green Sweater*, Krystyna Chiger.

30 *Out on a Ledge.*

31 *Hope is the Last to Die*, Halina Birenbaum.

32 *The Girl in the Green Sweater.*

33 *Fashion Metropolis Berlin.*

34 In November 1941, one Mr Straub, an employee of the 'Charlotte Röhl' company in Berlin, wrote to express his excitement about the quality of eight dresses recently received from Łódź ghetto. He ended the letter expressing 'the pleasant hope that you will continue working for me and keep making prompt deliveries as promised.' *Fashion Metropolis Berlin*, Uwe Westphal.

35 *Out on a Ledge.*
36 *My Father's Keeper,* Stephan Lebert.
37 Brigitte Frank correspondence, quoted in *East West Street,* Philippe Sandes.
38 *Occupied Economies.*
39 *Hunt for the Jews,* Jan Grabowski.
40 Herta Fuchs, born 1923 to Frieda and Moric Fuchs.
41 Alida Charbonnier was born on 23 July 1907 in Fécamp. On 6 October 1928 she married Robert Delasalle, a baker, who joined her political resistance to the German occupiers. They became members of the French Communist Party in 1936. She was dismissed from her couturier job in November 1938 for triggering a strike, and took up work with a corset maker in Rue Alexandre Legros in Fécamp. Their home at 13 Sautreuil Passage, was searched by police several times before their eventual arrest. Robert Delasalle was executed on 21 September 1942. Alida met him before his death for a brief farewell.
42 Herta Soswinski, *née* Mehl, worked under Maria Mandl in Ravensbrück. She was later transferred to Auschwitz and joined other Slovakian women in the SS admin block. *Nazi Civilisation.*
43 Jeannette (Janka) Nagel, *née* Berger, *Secretaries of Death.*
44 *If This Is a Woman,* Sarah Helm. The output of garments from Ravensbrück was so prodigious that local businesses lost trade. Industry giant TexLed Ltd – Textil-und Lederverwertung GmbH – had factories at both Dachau and Ravensbrück concentration camps.
45 *Business and Industry in Nazi Germany,* R. Francis Nicosia and Jonathan Huener.
46 Renée Ungar family correspondence, Bratislava, 17 August 1945.
47 *Where She Came From,* Helen Epstein.
48 *Architects of Annihilation,* Götz Aly and Susanne Heim.

Chapter Four: The Yellow Star

1 A 1957 letter from Herta Fuchs applying for compensation for 'Damage to Freedom', due to being compelled to wear the *Judenstern* – Jewish Star. Leo Baeck archive. Translated from the German.

2 Irené Reichenberg ID card, from Bratislava. Born 25 February 1915, perished in the Holocaust. Yad Vashem photograph archive https://photos.yadvashem.org/photo-details.html?language=en&item_id=4408243&ind=0

3 Gustav 'Gusti' Kohn actually escaped from Sered' forced labour camp. He picked up the tool box of a visiting contractor and calmly walked out with it. The false ID kept him undercover for the rest of the war. Leo Kohút – originally Leo Kohn – was arrested late in 1944 when a guard recognised his photo on the ID. Deported to Sered' first, he then endured incarceration at Sachsenhausen, Bergen-Belsen and a sub-camp of Dachau. He told Käthe to leave Bratislava in the event of his capture. Afraid and isolated, Käthe turned herself in to the Gestapo. After his liberation by American troops, he returned to Bratislava, where he learned of his wife's fate. Tauber Institute, Shoah Foundation Oral History | Accession Number: 1999.A.0122.708 | RG Number: RG-50.477.0708.

4 Irené Reichenberg, born on 25 February 1915, perished in the Holocaust. Her identity card is part of the collection of the Slovensky Narodny Archiv in Bratislava. Yad Vashem item # 4408243.

5 Nathan Volkmann, born 14 May 1908. Gedenkbuch – Memorial book entry (bundesarchiv.de) https://www.bundesarchiv.de/gedenkbuch/en995526

6 *Secretaries of Death.*

7 https://www.youtube.com/watch?v=62u6IaRHsKw&list=UU-8VxYewh49NnyNsjh7s9Mw&index=5&t=22s.

8 *Secretaries of Death.*

9 Luckily, Irene's youngest sister Grete was ill in hospital with scarlet fever and so avoided the summons. She was later sent to Sered' labour camp with her father and so survived the war.

10 In Auschwitz Bracha became friends with a Belgian woman named Gisela Reinhold. The Reinhold family were diamond merchants. Before her deportation, Gisela hid some diamonds in an old wooden coat hanger, which she then covered with a coat, leaving the coat on a chair. She told Bracha, 'If I survive, I know where we hid our diamonds.' After the war, Gisela returned to her apartment and, sure enough, found her treasures still inside the hanger.

11 Olga was born on 1 December 1907 in Szekesfehervár, Hungary. She trained as a dressmaker at a technical college.

12 Alice Dub, *née* Strauss, born 1922, was arrested at her home in Trstená na Orave in northern Slovakia. Her entire close family died in the Holocaust, except one brother who survived a labour camp and as a partisan. Tauber Holocaust Library, private correspondence between Alice Dub and Lore Shelley, Lore Shelley archive.

13 Helka Grossman *née* Brody, like Bracha, could 'pass' for a Catholic. She was spotted out walking and denounced as Jewish. While waiting at Poprad collection centre, she befriended a professional singer, who sang the girls to sleep after lights out. *Secretaries of Death,*

14 Renée Adler, *née* Ungar, 1945 letter.

15 Edita Maliarová, *Nazi Civilisation.*

16 *Secretaries of Death.* Rivka's note was found by a forced labourer called Leo Cips. Leo delivered the warning to her brother, who promptly went into hiding.

17 *Auschwitz: The Nazis and the Final Solution*, Lawrence Rees.

18 Wisliceny acknowledged complete understanding of Himmler's intentions at his trial: 'I realised that this meant the death warrant for millions of people.' *Interrogations.*

19 *Atlas of the Holocaust*, Martin Gilbert.

20 *Pack of Thieves.*

21 *Hitler's Beneficiaries.*

22 The work of ERR was taken over by *Dienstelle Western* – Western Service.

23 *Nuremberg Trial Transcripts*, 31 August 1946.

24 Hitler signed a memorandum to this effect on 31 December 1941.

25 *Stealing Home*, Shannon L. Fogg.

26 Correspondence with Lore Shelley, Tauber Holocaust Library. Marilou was raised in Paris, in the Nineteenth Arrondisement first, then lived in the suburbs.

27 *Witnessing the Robbing of the Jews*, Sarah Gensburger.

28 Jewish transports from Leipzig began on 21 January 1942.

29 *The German War*, Nicholas Stargardt.

30 Quoted in *Nazi Women*, Cate Haste.

31 The Bata shoe factory near Chełmek, about six miles from Auschwitz, was taken over by Ota-Silesian Shoe Works.

32 The experiences of Jewish women on the first official transport of Slovakian Jews to Auschwitz are detailed in *999 Women*, Heather Dune Macadam.

33 Janka Nagel, *née* Berger. *Secretaries of Death.*

34 Correspondence between Alice Dub Strauss and Lore Shelley. Lore Shelley archive, Tauber Holocaust Library.

35 *Le Convoi du 24 Janvier*, Charlotte Delbo.

36 *Nazi Civilisation*. Hunya was imprisoned under the name Hermine Winkler, referring to her marriage of convenience to obtain a Czech passport. Her concentration camp documents all refer to Winkler.

37 *Memory Book*, Gila Kornfeld-Jacobs. Hunya's companion on the journey was Ruth Sara Ringer (the middle name Sara was a compulsory addition by German law), *née* Kamm, born 1909, so just a year younger than Hunya. Her Auschwitz number was

46349, only two digits behind Hunya's. Her husband Hans Wilhem Ringer was murdered in the Shoah.

38 *Nazi Civilisation*. By January 1944 most of the Leipzig transport were dead.

Chapter Five: The Customary Reception

1 *Nazi Civilisation*.

2 The rail spur connecting the mainline with the separate camp of Birkenau was not complete until 1944, in time for arrivals from Hungary. It speeded up the process of mass murder, as new arrivals no longer had to walk, or be transported by truck, from the old ramp into the camps. They were simply marched in columns either to quarantine or the gas chambers.

3 These workshops – all patronised by the SS, including Hedwig Höss – were razed to make way for twenty new accommodation blocks built as an extension of the main camp. The Auschwitz dressmakers were housed here from 1944. Post-war, the blocks were converted for civilian use. *Private Lives of the SS*, Piotr Setkiewicz.

4 Alice Gruen. *Criminal Experiments*, Lore Shelley.

5 Lilli Kopecky. *Secretaries of Death*.

6 Alice Strauss, private correspondence with Lore Shelley, Tauber Holocaust Library. When the convoy of French political prisoners arrived in Auschwitz on 27 January 1943, the women – including Marilou Colombain and Alida Delasalle – marched past this gate defiantly singing the 'Marseillaise'.

7 In turn, the women in Block 7 would warn the next batch of new arrivals to hide personal possessions . . . and in turn they would appear to be gesticulating mad men. Testimony of Margit Bachner, *née* Grossberg, from Kežmarok. *Nazi Civilisation*.

8 Edita Maliarová came to Auschwitz on a transport from Bratislava, and wanted to reassure her young friends as they

were stripped and shaved. She was given camp number 3535. *Nazi Civilisation.*

9   Helen (Helka) Grossman, *née* Brody, from Kežmarok. *Secretaries of Death.*

10 *Memory Book.*

11 Younger women might wear trousers (usually buttoned/zipped on the hip) or ski pants in winter.

12 Sexual violence in the camps was always a threat despite it being a crime for an Aryan German to have sexual relations with a Jew. There was also the risk of assault from other inmates. Consensual sex was not unusual between prisoners, for the physical pleasure, the human contact, or as a form of barter for food and other essentials. Understandably, many inmates lost all sexual urges. Some contended this was due to bromide powders put in the tea. Starvation, illness and despair also crushed the libido.

13 Katka Grünstein, *née* Feldbauer, a twenty-year-old seamstress from West Slovakia. She became number 2851.

14 Lidia Vargo, *née* Rosenfeld, born 1924 in Transylvania, deported June 1944 from Hungary, processed in Birkenau. *The Union Kommando in Auschwitz*, Lore Shelley.

15 Anita said the shaving of her hair in Auschwitz was the most traumatic experience: 'It made me feel totally naked, utterly vulnerable and reduced to a complete *nobody.*' Anita found her salvation by becoming a member of the camp orchestra. *Inherit the Truth.*

16 Irene Kanka Interview 07138 Visual History Archive, USC Shoah Foundation.

17 Renée Düring sketched several crude scenes from camp life, all the more poignant for their lack of artistic skill. She was good friends with an inmate called Lien, who became a 'pet' seamstress for SS women. *Criminal Experiments.*

18 *Holocaust, the Camp System*, Jane Shuter.

19 Former inmate David Olère sketched diagrams of Auschwitz-Birkenau processes and buildings in 1946, including a cross-section of Crematorium 3, showing hair combers at work above the ovens, and above the SS overseers' office. *Auschwitz. Not Long Ago. Not Far Away.*

20 *Auschwitz: A History*, Sybille Steinbacher. Additional companies that profited from camp hair include Held in Friedland, Alex Zink at Roth near Nuremberg, Dye-Forst Limited at Lausitz and the Alex Zing felt factory at Katscher. When Auschwitz was liberated in January 1945, almost seven tonnes of hair were found in the camp tannery, ready to be freighted out. *KL Auschwitz Seen by the SS; People in Auschwitz.*

21 *Fashion Under the Occupation*, Dominique Veillon.

22 *Interrogations.*

23 This claim was made by Martin Bormann Junior, who claimed Potthast showed him furniture in her attic, crafted from human bones. *My Father's Keeper.*

24 Amazingly, typhus-infected lice were used in deliberate attempts to kill SS in Auschwitz. According to inmate Hermann Langbein, Polish prisoner Teddy Pietrzykowski cleaned for the SS and so had the opportunity to sprinkle infected lice under SS coat collars (*People in Auschwitz*). Inmate Józef Garliński was told that Witold Kosztowny, an early member of the underground, bred infected lice to throw onto hated SS such as Grabner and Palitzsch. Frau Luise Palitzsch did die of typhus on 4 November 1942, but no connection could be proven. Senior Medical Officer Siegried Schwella died from typhus in May 1942, allegedly from a planted louse. Polish informer Stefan Ołpinski was said to have been murdered when he accepted the gift of a lice-infected sweater from members of the Auschwitz underground. He fell ill with typhus after two weeks and was taken to Block 20, dying about two weeks later, in early January 1944. *Fighting Auschwitz.*

25   *Auschwitz 1270 to the Present*, Robert Jan Van Pelt.

26   Emilia found that it was hard to keep textiles white as the water was yellow. Soapy laundry had to be carried to the nearby well to be rinsed in clearer water. Prisoners working in the Fritzsch garden secretly asked for laundry soap, as well as garlic and onions to boost their vitamin intake. Frau Fritzsch made soup for prisoners working in the garden, including Stanilsaw Dubiel, who also laboured at the Höss villa, but her husband banned this generosity. *Private Lives of the SS*.

27   *KL Auschwitz Seen by the SS*, reminiscences of Pery Broad.

28   At his trial Moll defended his actions, stating, 'I was not responsible for the actual physical ending of their lives.' This countered numerous eyewitness testimonies of sadism, venality and thousands of murders at his hands. *Interrogations*.

29   *Nazi Civilisation*.

30   *Death Dealer*.

31   *Memory Book*.

32   *The Tin Ring, or How I Cheated Death*, Zdenka Fantlová. Zdenka was deported to Terezín concentration camp, Auschwitz, then Bergen-Belsen. She survived.

33   Austrian Eva Schloss, deported to Auschwitz with her mother. They both survived. Eva's mother married Otto Frank – father of diarist Anne. *Eva's Story*, Eva Schloss.

34   *Five Chimneys*, Olga Lengyel.

35   Rivka Paskus of Bratislava. *Secretaries of Death*.

36   *The Tin Ring*.

37   Marcelle Itzkowitz's bra from a man's shirt is on display at the exhibition in Buchenwald's former clothing warehouse, on loan from the Musée de la Résistance nationale de Champigny-sur-Marne. She was arrested for her activities in the French resistance and imprisoned near Leipzig.

38   *Facing the Extreme: Moral Life in the Concentration Camps*, Tzvetan Todorov.

39 Alexander Petöfi, freedom fighter, died 1849. Referenced in *The Union Kommando in Auschwitz*.

40 Helen Kuban, *née* Stern, *Nazi Civilisation*.

41 Irene Kanka Interview 07138 Visual History Archive, USC Shoah Foundation.

Chapter Six: You Want to Stay Alive

1 *Memory Book*.

2 Paul Kremer diary entry, 31 August 1942 and 2 September 1942, *KL Auschwitz Seen by the SS*.

3 Interview with the author, 2019.

4 Private family correspondence, 1945.

5 In 1942, the WVHA SS Wirtschaftsverwaltungshauptamt – SS economic & administrative head office – was organised into five groups, which included Amtsgruppe D (Group D) covering concentration camps, and Group W comprising SS enterprises. Historians estimate a staggering total of 30 million RM of pure profit was generated for the Nazi state by selling forced labour to private businesses. *Auschwitz: The Nazis and the Final Solution*.

6 *Post-Auschwitz Fragments*, Lore Shelley.

7 *Interrogations*.

8 *Death Dealer*.

9 Dr Claudette Kennedy, *née* Raphael, widowed Bloch, born 1910 near Paris, became friends with Marta Fuchs. Testimony, *Criminal Experiments on Human Beings*.

10 Recounted by Anna Binder, friend of Marta Fuchs, *Auschwitz – The Nazi Civilisation*. Having underwear was a forbidden luxury for most Jewish prisoners, although this didn't always stop them acquiring contraband bras and knickers.

11 Lore Shelley archives, Tauber Holocaust Library.

12 Rivka Paskus testimony, *Secretaries of Death*.

13 1945 letter, family correspondence.

14 Jeannette (Janka) Nagel, *née* Berger, testimony, *Secretaries of Death*.

15 Marie-Claude Vaillant-Couturier trial testimony, quoted in *People in Auschwitz*.

16 This was in 1944, in time for an unprecedented volume of murders under Höss's direction: the deportation of Jews from Hungary.

17 Lore Shelley archives, Tauber Holocaust Library, testimony of Marie-Louise Rosé, widowed Colombain, *née* Méchain.

18 Lidia Vargo testimony, *The Union Kommando in Auschwitz*.

19 *Born Survivors*.

20 *People in Auschwitz*.

21 Ora Aloni, *née* Borinski, testimony, *Auschwitz – The Nazi Civilisation*.

22 Irma Grese, Lüneberg trial testimony. When asked what kind of whip she carried, she replied that it was made in the weaving factory in the camp out of cellophane.

23 *Memory Book..*

24 *Auschwitz Chronicle*.

25 The Auschwitz Album was discovered by Lili Jacobs as she recuperated in a requisitioned SS building after her concentration camp ordeal. Her own family are featured in the album – murdered for being Jewish. After many decades the album was acquired by Yad Vashem and is now on display there.

26 *Five Chimneys*.

27 *Deutsche Ausrüstungwerke GmbH* – German Armaments Works Ltd.

28 *I Escaped from Auschwitz*, Rudolph Vrba.

29 The first batches of booty were stored at the main camp, in the tannery buildings. From mid-1944, clothes were stored in the camp extension, near SS and prisoner accommodation blocks.

30 *But You Did Not Come Back*, Marceline Loridan-Ivens.

31 Sometime afterwards the kapo caught typhus and died.

32 Vera Friedlander, interviewed for *Mothers in the Fatherland*.

Salamander, established in 1904, became Germany's largest chain of shoe shops, now with 150 stores across Europe. Their 2020 website profile declares, 'Salamander passionately combines fashion, quality and outstanding service and offers good value for money.'

33 *Nazi Looting; Hitler's Beneficiaries.*

34 Höss trial transcripts 1946. A dental technician from Kraków named Marushka had the unenviable task of sorting whole gold teeth and fastening them onto cards. 'Believe me, it is not a pleasant occupation,' she reported, with sublime understatement. *Criminal Experiments on Human Beings.*

35 This order came from the SS administration WVHA on 6 January 1943, with details of the account at the savings bank where all sums of money acquired were to be paid. *The Auschwitz Chronicle*, Danuta Czech.

36 *I Escaped from Auschwitz.*

37 Hannah Lax from Czechoslovakia was a teenager in the Birkenau branch of Kanada. In an unpublished questionnaire about her camp experiences she wrote, 'We sabotaged the valuable things we found and we didn't hand them over to the Germans.' Lore Shelley archives, Tauber Holocaust Library.

38 *Out on a Ledge.*

39 *All But My Life*, Gerda Weissman Klein.

40 Libuša Breder, *née* Reich, testimony, *999: The Extraordinary Young Women of the First Official Jewish Transport to Auschwitz*. As inmate number 1175, Libuša Reich featured in the series of 1944 photos taken by Karl Höcker. She twice testified post-war against sadistic SS of the Kanada complex, including SS Unterscharführer Franz Wunsch, who had been a mere twenty years old when he began service in Auschwitz. Libuša's daughter Dáša Grafil is one of the Board of Directors for Cultural Homestay International in San Francisco, an educational exchange programme established by Bracha Berkovič's eldest son Tom. Bracha was friends with Libuša

until her death. She described her as 'a little mouse, running here and there', and said, with a smile, that she often disrupted roll call in the camp, because she wouldn't stay long in one place. Interview with the author, November 2019.

41 Frieda's husband Zoltan was also murdered in the Holocaust, as was Jolli's husband Bela.

42 Jolan Grotter, *née* Reichenberg's date of death is noted as 27.9.42 in the Auschwitz State Museum 'Death Register', document number 33157/1942. She was born on 14 March 1910.

43 Riva Krieglova testimony, *Criminal Experiments on Human Beings.*

44 Entry on 6 Sept 1942, *KL Auschwitz Seen by the SS.* One of Bracha's friends from school, Motzen, saw her mother selected during this same event and asked to go with her, even though she knew it was for gassing. The two of them were among those Kremer so complacently witnessed.

45 Irene later recounted this episode and said it was not God who saved her life in Auschwitz, but Bracha.

46 Cylka or Cyla is referenced in *People in Auschwitz* and *True Tales from a Grotesque Land* by Sara Nomberg-Przytyk. Although they are understanding of Cylka's youth and survival instincts, both sources assert that however much she hated being complicit in her mother's departure for the gas chamber, she otherwise relished her role as perpetrator. Her story has been romanticised by novelist Heather Morris in *Cilka's Journey.*

Chapter Seven: I Want to Live Here Till I Die

1 From the post-war testimony of Stanisław Dubiel. APMA-B, Höss trial collection, vol. 4, quoted in *Private Lives of the SS.*

2 Agniela Bednarska, APMA-B, Statements Collection, vol. 34, quoted in *Private Lives of the SS.*

3 This claim made by Leo Heger, Rudolf's chauffeur, recounted to Rainer Höss, Rudolf's grandson.

4   Zofia Abramowiczowa testimony, *Criminal Experiments on Human Beings*.

5   Lotte Frankl testimony, *Auschwitz – The Nazi Civilisation*; Lidia Vargo testimony, *Criminal Experiments on Human Beings*.

6   *Auschwitz and After*, Charlotte Delbo.

7   Tomasz Kobylanski, 'Życie codzienne w willi Hössa'.

8   Immediately post-war Danimann, along with former inmate Kurt Hacker, began to spread the word about Auschwitz atrocities. Danimann was also involved in helping bring Nazi criminals to justice, including sadistic Maximilian Grabner. He gave up gardening to practise law.

9   *Fighting Auschwitz*.

10 APMA-B, Höss trial collection, vol. 4, quoted in *Private Lives of the SS*.

11 *Death Dealer*.

12 Tova Landsman video testimony VT 10281 Yad Vashem.

13 'Hiding in N. Virginia, a daughter of Auschwitz', Thomas Harding, *Washington Post*.

14 From 3 June 1943, SS garrison families were to pay 25 RM to the camp administration for the use of female prisoner labour in their homes. There are no surviving records of transactions. Certainly none of these 'wages' ever reached the prisoners themselves.

15 In 1974 Maria Jędrysik, working in the Oświęcim State Museum, interviewed women assigned to work in the homes of SS officers and NCOs from the Auschwitz garrison. The witnesses gave unique insights into the domestic life of the SS, showing them as complex, immensely flawed human beings, rather than mythical demons in human form. Danuta Rzempeil testified that Höss was very affectionate to his children at home: 'He never said a word to me. Frau Höss arranged everything. A good thing, because I was very afraid of him.' *Private Lives of the SS*.

16 Rudolf was clearly devoted to his children. In his final letter to

Hedwig, he asked her 'to educate our children in a true humanitarianism'. Unconscious irony from a confessed mass murderer and racist, or a desire that they would not repeat his mistakes? *Death Dealer.*

17 Dubiel testimony.

18 Kmak was shot on 4 September 1943 to cover up SS involvement with black-market trading at the Auschwitz slaughter house: as a witness to corruption he had to be silenced.

19 Grönke was manager of the *Bekleidungswerk Stätten-Lederfabrik* – the clothing workshop in a former tannery.

20 These signed documents are in the archives of the USHMM.

21 Story from Rainer Höss, via Robert Van der Pelt, *Auschwitz. Not Long Ago. Not Far Away.* exhibition talk, accessed 10.2.20. The Buttons in the 'Auschwitz. Not long ago. Not far away.' exhibition – YouTube.

22 Janina Szczurek testimony, APMA-B Statements Collection, vol. 34.

23 *Auschwitz Chronicle.*

24 Correspondence with Dr Lore Shelley, Tauber Holocaust Library; *Criminal Experiments on Human Beings.*

25 Flora Neumann testimony, *The Union Kommando in Auschwitz.*

26 Ora Aloni, *née* Borinski, testimony, *Auschwitz – The Nazi Civilisation.* Ora stated that it was the 'death angel' who requested this special doll, a term often used of notorious guard Irma Grese.

27 *Five Chimneys.*

28 *People in Auschwitz.*

29 *KL Auschwitz Seen by the SS.*

30 Höss trial, vol. 12, card 178, quoted in *KL Auschwitz Seen by the SS.*

31 Maria Stromberger, Höss trial testimony.

32 Heinrich Himmler speech to the SS at Poznan on 4 October 1943, *Documents on the Holocaust.*

33 Testimony of Sonja Fritz, *Criminal Experiments on Human Beings.*

34   *The Times*, February 2019, 'East Germany "turned a blind eye to Auschwitz war criminals"', Oliver Moody, accessed February 2019. https://www.thetimes.co.uk/article/east-germany-turned-a-blind-eye-to-auschwitz-war-criminals-s9lg7tl8j.

35   Quoted in *Auschwitz. Not Long Ago. Not Far Away.*

36   Interviewed by journalist Uwe Westphal May 1985, *Fashion Metropolis Berlin*.

37   SS technical sergeant Robert Sierek, testifying before Robert Mulka.

38   Dr Kremer was a guest at this dinner and recorded the menu in his diary entry for 23 September 1942. *KL Auschwitz Seen by the SS*.

39   Unpublished manuscript, 'Memories of Auschwitz and my brother-in-law Rudolf Höss', quoted by Rainer Höss, *Das Erbe des Kommandanten*.

40   *Das Erbe des Kommandanten*.

41   *People in Auschwitz*.

42   *Gästbuch der familie Höß 1940 Auschwitz – 1945 Ravensbrück*, Yad Vashem 051/41, 5521.

43   Solahütte details: as shown in the extraordinary album of photographs collected by adjutant Karl Höcker, now in the USHMM. Bizarrely, ex-Auschwitz inmate Dr Lore Shelley, who was responsible for collating and publishing many survivor testimonies, including those from the *Obere Nähstube*, had some of her family possessions returned to her after the war thanks to Höcker's intercession with those who had hidden the belongings. He became a respected post-war citizen of Shelley's home town Lübbecke. *Post-Auschwitz Fragments*.

44   Herta Fuchs testimony, *The Union Kommando in Auschwitz*; Langbein, *People in Auschwitz*.

45   Letter from Helena Kennedy, *née* Hochfelder, to orchestra member Lili Mathe, Holocaust Education and Learning Centre, University of Huddersfield.

46 *Memory Book.*

47 *Death Dealer.*

48 Stromberger, 1947 Höss trial testimony.

49 This version of the story was told by Hedwig's grandson Rainer Höss, *Das Erbe des Kommandanten.*

50 Correspondence between Rudolf Höss and psychiatrist G.M. Gilbert, *Death Dealer.*

51 Police statement, quoted in *Eine Frau an seine Seite.*

52 Dr Hans Münch, correspondence with Lore Shelley, *Criminal Experiments on Human Beings.* According to an account in *The Nazi Doctors* by Robert Jay Lifton, he composed himself well enough to complete a dissertation on typhoid fever, to carry out typhus experiments on prisoners, and to assist at selections for the gas.

53 A German edition of Hermann Langbein's *People in Auschwitz* owned by Hedwig Höss.

54 Poznan speech on 4 October 1943, *Documents on the Holocaust.*

55 *The Private Heinrich Himmler*, Katrin Himmler and Michael Wildt (eds.).

56 Höss trial transcripts, 1946.

57 *People in Auschwitz.*

58 *Eine Frau an seine Seite.*

59 *People in Auschwitz.*

60 Testimony of fourteen-year-old Aleksandra Stawarczyk, *Private Lives of the SS.*

61 *People in Auschwitz.*

62 Testimony of fourteen-year-old Władysława Jastrzębska, *Private Lives of the SS.*

63 *People in Auschwitz.*

64 Email correspondence with the author.

65 *Private Lives of the SS.*

66 This second seamstress is most likely Berta Weiss, aunt of Rahel 'Rózsika' Weiss, the teenager protected by Marta in the *Obere*

Naehstube. Berta helped establish the original fashion salon but died in Auschwitz.

67 Kobylanski.

Chapter Eight: Out of Ten Thousand Women

1 *Death Dealer.*

2 *Death Dealer.*

3 'Record-Keeping for the Nazis and Saving Lives, a conversation with Katya Singer', by Susan Cernyak-Spatz & Joel Shatzky. https://jewishcurrents.org/record-keeping-for-the-nazis-and-saving-lives/. Accessed 29.9.19.

4 *I Escaped from Auschwitz.*

5 Irene Kanka Interview 07138 Visual History Archive, USC Shoah Foundation.

6 Hunya was threatened with a permanent residence on the medical experimentation block. *Memory Book.*

7 Marishka was a cousin of Hunya's brother-in-law. She survived the camps and emigrated to the USA not long after the war ended, living in the New York area with her adopted daughter Margery.

8 Tova Landsman video testimony VT 10281 Yad Vashem.

9 Maria Maul was well liked by those she supervised. She testified before the District Court of Pirna, 21.5.1963.

10 Erika Kounio, deported with her mother from Thessalonika in Greece, was set to work in the *Todesabteilung*, the Death Department, where prisoner mortality was registered with a chilling lack of accuracy: none were noted as 'murdered', all were to be listed as dying of natural causes. Eventually, even the most efficient staff could not keep up with the tens of thousands of fatalities and they were told not to register Jewish deaths at all. *Secretaries of Death.*

11 *Memory Book.* The basement rooms of the Stabsgebäude where

the first Polish prisoners sent to Auschwitz were inducted into camp life. Here they were beaten, stripped, shaved and numbered.

12 *Auschwitz – The Nazi Civilisation*, testimony of Sophie Sohlberg, *née* Löwenstein, born 1923, Germany.

13 Postcard in German, dated 7.VI.43 Birkenau. Ghetto Fighter's House archive.

14 Family correspondence, private collection, postcard dated 3. IV. 44.

15 *Secretaries of Death.*

16 *Death Dealer.*

17 Irene Kanka Interview 07138 Visual History Archive, USC Shoah Foundation.

18 *Death Dealer.*

19 There is, to date, some confusion over Šari. Hunya's niece Gila remembers a Šari Grünwald, most likely an inmate who worked in the Politische Abteilung in Auschwitz, but it is more likely that the Šari of the sewing room was Šari Grünberg. Marta's oldest son recalls a Šari Maltz née Grünberg who survived the camps and emigrated to Israel after the war, starting a family there. She joined the informal reunions of other survivors, also taking Juraj to visit Hunya in her Tel Aviv apartment, and telling him how grateful she was that Marta had organised her transfer from construction labour to the sanctuary of the dressmaking salon.

20 *Auschwitz – The Nazi Civilisation.*

21 Dina Gold, *Stolen Legacy;* Uwe Westphal, *Fashion Metropolis Berlin.*

22 Testimony from Rezina Apfelbaum and Professor Avri Ben Ze'ev via correspondence with the author. Rezina, who was called *schneider'ke* by her family – 'young dressmaker' in Yiddish – survived the camps. The word 'impossible' was not in her vocabulary and she became legendary in her family after her emigration to Israel. The beautiful Lilly was shot by her SS lover just before the evacuation of Auschwitz.

23 *Memory Book.*

24 *Auschwitz – The Nazi Civilisation.*

25 Tova Landsman video testimony VT 10281 Yad Vashem.

26 *Auschwitz – The Nazi Civilisation,* Hunya Hecht testimony.

27 *Auschwitz – The Nazi Civilisation,* Hunya Hecht testimony.

28 *Auschwitz – The Nazi Civilisation,* Hunya Hecht testimony; also, handwritten note, Lore Shelley archives, Tauber Holocaust library.

Chapter Nine: Solidarity and Support

1 Alida Vasselin correspondence, Lore Shelley archives, Tauber Holocaust Library: 'Notre vie quotidienne était axée sur la Solidarité et le soutien à ceux qui souffraient plus que nous.'

2 This story was reported by Sara Nomberg-Przytyk in *Auschwitz: True Tales from a Grotesque Land,* and the anecdote was acknowledged by Hermann Langbein in *People in Auschwitz,* although not confirmed. Josef Garlinksi in *Fighting Auschwitz* gives an alternative – and more widely accepted – version of the story in which it was a Polish dancer named Franciszka Mann, who fatally wounded SS officer Josef Schillinger on 23 October 1943, at Crematorium II. Manci Schwalbová completed her medical training after the war and worked as a doctor in Bratislava's children's hospital. Her book, *Vyhasnute oči* ('Extinguished Eyes') was one of the first accounts of Auschwitz to appear in the Slovak language. Before her death in the Jewish Old People's Home, she was visited by survivors of the Stabsgebäude.

3 Interview with the author, November 2019.

4 Interview with the author, November 2019. The unnamed woman was friends with Tomáš Masaryk's wife Charlotte Garrigue.

5 The woman was named Sabina. She survived in the Political section of the Stabsgebäude. *Memory Book.*

6 Anna Binder testimony, *Auschwitz – The Nazi Civilisation.*

7 Alida Vasselin correspondence, Lore Shelley archives, Tauber

Holocaust Library: 'Dans notre Commando de couture nous avons chapardé tout ce que nous avons put pour le transmettre a ceux qui en avait le plus besoin.'

8 Conversation with Paul Kanka, January 2020.

9 *Memory Book*. Lina is possibly Helene Wilder, *née* Stark.

10 Maria Bobrzecka – codename 'Marta' – sent covert supplies from her chemist's shop in nearby Brzeszcze. Locals Maria Hulewiszowa and Justyna Hałupka were 'mules' for thousands of ampules of life-saving medicine. Galinski, *Fighting Auschwitz*.

11 https://www.mp.pl/auschwitz/journal/english/206350,dr-janina-kosciuszkowa. Dr Kosciuszkowa treated survivors of the Warsaw Uprising while in Birkenau.

12 Maria Stromberger testimony, Höss trial in Kraków, 25 March 1947.

13 *People in Auschwitz*.

14 Herta Soswinkski, *née* Mehl, testimony, *Auschwitz – The Nazi Civilisation*. Herta was an active member of a communist resistance cell.

15 Handwritten postcard, family correspondence, private collection: 'Lieber Ernö, mit unendlich viel Freude erhielt ich deine Karte von 28.4. in der Du uns so ausführlich über alle meine Lieben berichtest. Für meine Dankbarkeit Dir und Euch gegenüber find ich keine Worte (. . .) Ich küsse Euch tausendmal und bin im Gedanken immer mit Euch.'

16 Ghetto Fighter's House Museum archive, addressed to E. Reif, Bratislava Törökova 11, signed 'Berta'. Sadly Ernst Reif had to leave his hiding place and was shot by the Nazis. The woman who had hidden him, classmate Margita Cíglerová, was saved from deportation at the very last moment and survived the war, as did Ernst's sister.

17 Katarina Prinz, in the *Unterkunst* – the Accommodation kommando. Her helper was Eugen Nagel from Bratislava. She married him post-war and emigrated to Australia. Correspondence with Lore Shelley, Tauber Holocaust Library.

18 Rudasch was arrested post-war but charges were dropped when a former inmate testified on his behalf. Testimony of Lilly Kopecky, *Secretaries of Death*.

19 Ghetto Fighter's House Museum archive. From Margit Birnbaum, Stabsgebaude, Birkenau, June 1943. 'Du kannst Dir garmicht verstellen was für unsagbar grosse Freude wir haben, wenn so Pestausteilung gibt und wir wenigstens von Euch Post bekommen.'

20 Handwritten postcard, family correspondence, private collection, 1 January 1943: '*Ladet Euch Frau Vigyáz ein soll sie immer bei Euch sein sie ist sehr nützlich im Haushalt.*' Marta's mother Rósa survived the war in hiding, in Hungary. Her father Dezsö died of cancer while in hiding, in 1944.

21 *The Rooster Calls*, Gila Kornfeld-Jacobs.

22 Inmate in the Central Construction Office. *Auschwitz – The Nazi Civilisation*.

23 This was in mid-1944. The three women involved in the copying were Krystyna Horczak, Valeria Valová and Věra Foltýnová.

24 The volumes are now in the care of the Auschwitz-Birkenau State Museum.

25 Łasocka's codename was Tell. She worked for *Pomoc Więźniom Obozó Kocentracyjnych* – Assistance for Concentration Camp Prisoners. Photographer Pelagia Bednarska was a soldier in the Polish Home Army, *Armia Krajowa*. The negatives she processed were smuggled out of Auschwitz in September 1944, intended to show the world proof of death camp atrocities. They were used as evidence in the trial of Rudolf Höss. In her post-war testimony, Maria Stromberger stated that the books of records (prisoner lists) were given to underground courier Natalia Spak on 29 December 1944. Stromberger had salvaged the two volumes from the rubble of a building bombed by the Allies on 26 December 1944, with the help of a Yugoslavian prisoner named Mira, who was only fourteen years old when she was

first deported to Auschwitz. Stromberger left Auschwitz on 7 January 1945, to be transferred to a neurological clinic in Prague.

26 *Fighting Auschwitz.*

27 Świerczyna plotted his own escape attempt in November. Aided and abetted by two SS men, he and four other men hid in a lorry of dirty linen leaving the camp on 27 October 1944. They were betrayed, interrogated and hanged outside the main camp kitchen, shouting defiance to the end. *Fighting Auschwitz.*

28 Figures regarding escapes are understandably difficult to confirm. Höss's own estimates are unreliable. 802 people are believed to have escaped – 757 men and 45 women – of whom 327 were definitely recaptured and 144 got away. It cannot be assumed that the rest evaded detection elsewhere, or that they survived the war. *Auschwitz: A History.*

Half the escapees were Polish, taking advantage of being on the run in their own country. We can only speculate as to why there are relatively few female escapees: they were not key members of underground movements comprising military men; they had fewer opportunities for contacts with civilian contractors outside the camp; their conditions in Birkenau were often too debilitating to support the energy required for a breakout; culturally they were brought up to be more risk averse; they were committed to caring roles for other inmates; and they faced the additional danger of sexual violence while on the run. Many of the female escapees were from the Penal Kommando at Budy, one of the satellite camps.

29 *Memory Book.*

30 The escape was successful and they both survived the war but were separated, and only reunited decades later. http://www.jerzybielecki.com/cyla-cybulska.html.

31 *I Escaped from Auschwitz.*

32 In May, Czeslaw Mordowics and Arnošt Rosin also made a

successful escape, giving their own testimonies and eventually liaising with Vrba and Wetzler. *I Escaped from Auschwitz.*

33 Letter to British Foreign Secretary Anthony Eden, 11 July 1944. Eden spoke in the House of Commons, using information taken from the Vrba–Wetzler report. *I Escaped from Auschwitz.*

34 Tova Landsman video testimony VT 10281 Yad Vashem.

35 Renée Adler, *née* Ungar, letter, 1945, family correspondence, private collection.

36 Herta Soswinski, *née* Mehl, from southern Moravia: member of the communist underground in Auschwitz with Dr Anna Binder, liaising with Ernst Burger, and worker in the Stabsgebäude Central Construction Office. *Auschwitz – The Nazi Civilisation.*

37 Raya Kagan, *née* Rapaport – also known as Raissa and Raïa – was born in 1910 in Tsarist Russia. She was deported from Drancy in France on 22 June 1942, and eventually worked as an interpreter for interrogations in the Politische Abteilung. She wrote a full account of Mala and Edek's escape in her 1947 book *Nashim b'lishkat HaGehinom*: 'Hell's Office Women – a Chronicle of Oświęcim.' She was friends with Hunya Volkman-Hecht, and Dr Lore Shelley, who collected testimonies from Stabsgebäude inmates. She also gave evidence at the 1961 trial of Adolf Eichmann in Israel. In trial footage, Kagan is clear and concise in her statements; Eichmann looks bored. She was eventually institutionalised with a mental illness and died in 1997 in Israel, aged 87. Mala Zimetbaum's history is also described by Jenny Spritzer in *Secretaries of Death.*

38 Interview with the author, November 2019.

39 Interview with the author, November 2019.

40 *Al HaMishmar*, 29 December 1964.

41 *Memory Book.*

42 Dr Na'ma Shik, 'Women Heroism in the Camp' – Yad Vashem online lecture, accessed 30.5.20. https://www.youtube.com/watch?v

=eVpO3IvhVmA&feature=youtu.be&utm_source=newsletter&utm
_medium=email&utm.

43 Lore Shelley, *The Union Kommando in Auschwitz*.

44 Israel Gutman testimony, *The Union Kommando in Auschwitz*.
Gutman believed that a prisoner named Eugen Koch was
responsible for the women's arrests. Koch allegedly seduced
Ala Gartner.

45 Tova Landsman video testimony VT 10281 Yad Vashem. There
is a memorial plaque for the four young women who were
executed for their part in the Sonderkommando uprising, in
Forendenberg, Germany – location of the Weischellmetal Union
Werke HQ; another plaque is in Jerusalem.

46 Note from Hunya Hecht (Volkmann) in the Lore Shelley archives,
Tauber Holocaust Library.

Chapter Ten: The Air Smells Like Burning Paper

1 *Rena's Promise: A Story of Sisters in Auschwitz*, Rena Kornreich
Gelissen and Heather Dune Macadam.

2 *Auschwitz Chronicle*.

3 *Auschwitz Chronicle*.

4 The last recorded mention of Jehovah's Witness prisoners being
employed in the Höss household is 6 November 1944, suggesting
the departure was around this time. *Auschwitz Chronicle*.

5 *Memory Book*.

6 Interview with the author, November 2019.

7 Irene Kanka Interview 07138 Visual History Archive, USC Shoah
Foundation.

8 Correspondence with Rezina Apfelbaum and Avri Ben Ze'ev.
There were approximately 4,000 sick females left in Auschwitz.
After liberation Rezina, endlessly resilient, said, 'We can't wait,
we have to take things into our own hands,' so she co-opted a
German to escort them from the camp as well as a horse and

cart to get them as far as the nearest train station. She weighed only 29kg by the time she made it to Budapest.

9   It is estimated that between 9,000 and 15,000 people died on the final on-foot evacuations from Auschwitz. Post-war initiatives have attempted to put names to the anonymous deaths, and to mark their grave sites.

10 Interview with the author, November 2019.

11 Lily Hönig, *née* Reiner, testimony, *Secretaries of Death*.

12 *Memory Book.*

13 Lidia Vargo testimony, *The Union Kommando in Auschwitz.*

14 Interview with the author, November 2019.

15 *Memory Book.*

16 Alida and Marilou were liberated by the Russians at Mauthausen on 22 April 1945. At this time Marilou learned that her husband had died in one of Mauthausen's sub-camps.

17 *Memory Book.*

18 *Memory Book.*

19 Interview with the author, November 2019.

20 After liberation, Ilona's talents were noted by the British medical staff, and the wives of British officers stationed at/near Belsen. She sewed for them until she'd saved enough cigarettes to barter for a ride on a coal train back to Budapest. Her home was occupied by a bus driver. His wife was wearing one of Ilona's own dresses, taken from her wardrobe. 'Why did you come back at all?' the wife asked. Ilona started sewing for former customers again, once they discovered she was still alive. Inflation made fabric purchases impossible and there were still antisemites who talked of sending Jews back to Auschwitz, so she escaped to Vienna with her husband Lazlo Kenedi in the 1950s (her first husband had been killed in Russia) and from there to England. As Helena Kennedy she opened a prestigious dressmaking salon in Leeds, specialising in wedding gowns and occasion wear for elite local families – Helena Kennedy Obituary, *Jewish Chronicle*, 27 October 2006; Hilary Brosh, *Threads of Life*.

21 Interview with the author, November 2019.

22 *Memory Book.*

23 *Memory Book.*

24 Erika Kounio, *From Thessaloniki to Auschwitz and Back.*

25 *Memory Book.*

26 *Das Erbe des Kommandanten.*

27 *Glanz und Grauen.*

28 'SS bunker, Dachau SS compound' – catalog.archives.gov. Department of Defense. Department of the Army (US). 14 May 1946. Retrieved 15 December 2019.

29 Vgl Rgensburg-Zweigstelle Straubing I Js 1674/53 (früher München II Da 12 Js 1660/48), StA Nürnberg, GstA beim OLG Nürnberg 244.

30 Among the clothes was a smart Bavarian waistcoat – grey wool with green edging and five metal buttons – plundered from Kanada in Auschwitz and worn by the youngest Höss boy Hans-Jürgen, and eventually by his youngest son Rainer.

31 *Death Dealer.*

32 *Das Erbe des Komandanten.*

33 Hedwig Höss interrogation Stg of the 92 Field Security Section (Southern Sub-Area) Yad Vashem Archives file 051/41, 5524 Hoess, quoted in *Eine Frau an seine Seite*, Gertrud Schwartz.

34 *Hanns and Rudolph.* In the early 1950s, Hedwig's former seamstress friend Mia Weiseborn found her an apartment in the town of Ludwigsburg.

35 *Dear Fatherland*, Margaret Bourke-White. American journalist Bourke-White toured Bohemia, Moravia and Slovakia after the 1938 Anschluss. She also witnessed first-hand looting by Americans of German belongings. A one-time friend she found in Berlin after the war showed her undiluted antisemitism when she scoffed at the so-called privilege of concentration camp survivors who went into German shops asking to be served first, taking shirts, stockings and underwear.

36   Irene Kanka Interview 07138 Visual History Archive, USC Shoah Foundation.

37   Aranka Pollock, *née* Klein, testimony, *Secretaries of Death*.

38   Interview with the author, November 2019.

39   Rezina continued sewing for her children and grandchildren after her marriage and emigration to Israel, both everyday clothes and high-quality fashions.

40   When she got home to Fécamp she was met at the station by Max Vasselin, another prisoner of war. They lived together in mutual support for thirty-two years before getting married. *Auschwitz – The Nazi Civilisation.*

41   Correspondence with Lore Shelley, Tauber Holocaust Library.

42   Diary notes made by Marta Fuchs after liberation, private family papers.

43   Marta jotted down notes about her escape and subsequent travels, using stationery presumably organised from Stabsgebäude offices. In Russian-occupied Poland she was interrogated by Stanisław Kowalsky of the NKVD – Russian political police – and gave the names of communist comrades who could vouch for her: Dr Anna Koppich, Cica Shapira, Gabor Ditta, Franz Danimann, Hans Goldberger, Erich Kosak, Kurt Hacker and Emil Gumeiner.

44   Conversation with the author, May 2020.

45   Dr Leo Kohút Oral History testimony, Tauber Holocaust Library. Accession Number: 1999.A.0122.708 | RG Number: RG-50.477.0708.

46   Rózsika, or Tschibi – the Little Hen – also known as Rahel Weiss, eventually found a surviving aunt to live with. She emigrated to Israel, married and had children there. Bracha visited her in Israel.

47   The marriage lasted 67 years.

48   The salon was owned by Helena Baumgartnerová, address Praha 1, Kříževníká 3. In April 1947, her work card notes employment

as seamstress for Ondřej Meisel, výroba konfekce, Praha 1, Templova 6.

49 Marta's three children were Juraj, Peter and Katarina (twins), born 1949 and 1950, in Prague.

50 The Katz family changed their name to Kanka in 1963, to avoid antisemitism, as Katz was a noticeably Jewish name. Similarly the Reichenbergs changed their name to Liberec, which was the Czech version of the town of Reichenberg.

51 Conversation with Yael Aharoni, Tel Aviv, January 2020.

52 Interview with Avri Ben Ze'ev, Tel Aviv, January 2020.

Chapter Eleven: They Want Us to Be Normal?

1 Conversation with Yael Aharoni, Tel Aviv, January 2019.

2 When she heard nothing from her daughters after their deportation, Karolína Berkovič knew that a tragic outcome was likely for all the family. She gave papers and photograph albums to one of Bracha's Catholic friends, Vlado Kinčik, who had already refused to join the Hlinka guard in Slovakia, calling them 'rabble'. He looked after these precious items and restored them to Bracha and Katka after the war.

3 In the 1960s, Renée passed her oldest son Rafi a booklet in Hebrew entitled 'Marta's Sewing Workshop' – an account of the Upper Tailoring Salon in the Auschwitz Stabsgebäude. He knew it must be significant, but cannot now remember the contents. To date, no copies have been located.

4 Erika Amariglio Kounio, *From Thessaloniki to Auschwitz and Back*.

5 Irene's son Pavel transcribed her video testimony from German to English, to help with the writing of this book. He had never before been able to watch the recording and found it a harrowing yet cathartic process. It takes great courage fully to acknowledge the trauma experienced by a loved one.

6 Marta Fuchs's cousin Herta successfully emigrated to the USA and married there, but her personal documents show a long battle to get recognition for the profound after-effects of incarceration, both physically and psychologically.

7 Over the last forty years more than 1 million Americans, 400,000 overseas students and millions of overseas parents and relatives of these students have been involved with CHI projects to build bridges of friendship around the world. A worthy antidote to bigotry, division, intolerance and racial hatred.

8 Tova Landsman Shoah foundation video testimony.

9 Email correspondence with the Minárik family, 2019–20.

10 Conversation with Yael Aharoni, Tel Aviv, January 2019.

11 Gila's high school project was shared among the immediate family, then overlooked for many years. Her cousin Yael found a typewritten copy. Through a network of connections, I had the privilege of getting in touch with Gila. She generously took the time to translate the *Memory Book*, as it was titled, from Hebrew to English, and so Hunya's story can now be shared with a far wider audience, as it deserves.

12 Fritz Institut, Frankfurt-am-Main.

13 Interview with Eldad Beck in 'The Criminal Grandson of the Commander of Auschwitz', *Israel Hayom*, 28.7.20.

14 *Das Erbe des Kommandanten.*

15 Historian Tom Segev interviewed several prominent SS wives. *Eine Frau an seine Seite.*

16 Letter from Lore Shelley to Ann West, 26 April 1987. Lore Shelley archives, Tauber Holocaust Library

17 Dr Lore Shelley, *Post-Auschwitz Fragments.*

18 Hunya's final marriage was to Otto Hecht in Israel.

19 'Jewish Holocaust Survivors' Attitudes Toward Contemporary Beliefs About Themselves', Shelley, Lore PhD, The Fielding Institute 1982, reprinted from *Dissertation Abstracts International*, vol. 44, No. 6, 1983.

20 Correspondence between Hunya Hecht and Lore Shelley, Tauber Holocaust library.

21 30 November 1987 letter to Menachem Rafalowitz, Lore Shelley archive, Tauber Holocaust Library.

22 Hermann Langbein describes the 1968 reunion in Ramla, Israel, of a group of former Stabsgebäude workers, most probably hosted by Regina Steinberg, SS Rottenführer Pery Broad's secretary. Broad had adored the music of the Birkenau gypsy orchestra. He also helped manage the gassing of the entire gypsy camp in Birkenau. The twenty women at the reunion were almost all from the first set of Slovakian transports. Langbein had hoped to collect information for his book; instead he could only watch in wonderment as the women all talked at once, reminding each other of funny episodes. *People in Auschwitz*.

23 Alida Vasselin testimony, *Auschwitz – The Nazi Civilisation*.

24 Eva was the daughter of Marta's sister Turulka and Irene's brother Laci Reichenberg.

25 In conversation with Thalia Reichenberg Soffair, daughter of Irene's brother Armin Reichenberg.

26 Bracha also made a rare trip out of the socialist Czechoslovakian regime into the 'West'. She visited Mauthausen camp in Austria then had a day in Vienna, where she drank her first Coca-Cola. Irene Reichenberg did not return to Auschwitz. It was devastating enough for her to visit Bratislava and see that much of Židovská Street – including her house at number 18 – had been demolished to make way for a modern road.

27 The Soj family lived in the house until 1972, when it was sold to the Jurczak family, who were resident at the villa when Rainer Höss, grandson to Hedwig and Rudolf, made a visit during the filming of a documentary. Kobylański, Tomasz, 'Życie codzienne w willi Hössa', *Polityka*, January 2013.

28 Auschwitz State Museum has a well-equipped conservation team who work to stabilise vulnerable textiles such as Jewish prayer

shawls and other key items from the vast collection of clothing. Inevitably organic items deteriorate . . . at what point will the remnants of mass murder be permitted to decay? Or should they be conserved beyond their natural existence, to continue to act as evidence?

29 Correspondence with the author.

30 Alida Vasselin testimony, *Auschwitz – The Nazi Civilisation*. On the subject of human behaviour, Hunya used the expression *Der Liebe Gott hat ein grosser Tiergarten* – God has a large zoo – or, the world is full of all sorts of people. Hunya's niece Gila commented, 'My aunt Hunja used this expression, and she, as a survivor of Auschwitz, surely knew the depth of this zoo.' Correspondence with the author.

31 Conversation with Pavel Kanka, January 2020.

INDEX